The Soviet Union in the 1980s

The Soviet Union in the 1980s

Proceedings of
The Academy of
Political Science

Volume 35
Number 3

ISSN 0065-0684

Edited by Erik P. Hoffmann

New York, 1984

Contents

Preface

Americans — and indeed people all over the world — are influenced by the Soviet Union. We are affected in countless ways, profoundly so, by our government's responses to the beliefs articulated by generations of communist leaders and to the Soviet Union's policies and actions.

Not much imagination is required to picture a dramatically different future — for better or worse — that could result from the changes taking place in the Soviet Union today. Obviously, all persons of good will must hope for changes for the better, but we must also be prepared for the worst. We therefore need the most reliable and the most authoritative analyses that we can obtain.

When Professor Erik P. Hoffmann accepted the responsibility for planning this volume, he was urged to seek out the most distinguished experts in the field. This collection of essays attests to his success. Although the contributors are experts, they have written for nonexperts. The reader will, I believe, find all of the essays highly informative.

The views expressed are those of the authors and not necessarily those of any organizations with which they are associated. The Academy of Political Science serves as a forum for the development and dissemination of opinion on public-policy questions, but it does not make recommendations on political and social issues.

Finally, the Academy is indebted to William Farr and David Ordan for skillfully editing the manuscripts.

C. Lowell Harriss
Executive Director

Editor's Note

The essays in this volume focus on Soviet domestic politics and foreign policy in the 1980s. They analyze (1) the *nature* and *extent* of the Soviet Union's present-day problems and opportunities in specific fields; (2) the *options* open to the Communist party leadership; and (3) the *course of action* it is taking and will probably take in response to emerging conditions at home and abroad. The contributors elucidate Soviet perspectives on internal and international trends, identify Soviet priorities and policy-making procedures, and explain Soviet replies to civilian and military challenges. Political-administrative, socioeconomic, and scientific-technological developments and their interrelationships are assessed. It is to be hoped that the authors' insights and information will further Western understanding of the Soviet Union's aims, capabilities, and achievements as well as shortcomings of the Soviet Union at a significant juncture in its history. The editor's introduction traces the evolution of the Soviet political system, and his conclusion examines its impact on current and future Soviet choices and policies.

Readers who wish to deepen their understanding of such questions by traveling to the Soviet Union are invited to contact the Citizen Exchange Council, 18 East 41st Street, New York, New York 10017. This nonprofit and nonpartisan organization arranges programs for students, educators, and professional and avocational groups enabling Americans of all ages to meet their Soviet counterparts.

Erik P. Hoffmann

Contributors

JOSEPH S. BERLINER is Professor of Economics, Brandeis University, and Associate, Russian Research Center, Harvard University. He is the author of *The Innovation Decision in Soviet Industry*.

SEWERYN BIALER is Director, Research Institute on International Change, and Ruggles Professor of Political Science, Columbia University. He is the author of *Stalin's Successors: Leadership, Stability and Change in the Soviet Union*.

ZBIGNIEW BRZEZINSKI is Herbert Lehman Professor of Government, Columbia University. He served as Assistant to the President for National Security Affairs under Jimmy Carter. Professor Brzezinski is the author of *Power and Principle: Memoirs of the National Security Advisor, 1977–81* and *The Soviet Bloc: Unity and Conflict*.

TIMOTHY J. COLTON is Professor of Political Science, University of Toronto. The author of *Commissars, Commanders, and Civilian Authority*, he is presently writing a book on the management and politics of the city of Moscow.

MURRAY FESHBACH is Senior Research Scholar, Kennedy Institute of Ethics, Center for Population Research, Georgetown University. He is the author of *The Soviet Statistical System*.

CHARLES GATI is Professor of Political Science, Union College, and Visiting Professor of Political Science, Columbia University. His books include *The Debate Over Détente*.

LOREN R. GRAHAM, Professor of the History of Science, Massachusetts Institute of Technology, is the author of *Between Science and Values*.

C. LOWELL HARRISS is Professor Emeritus of Economics, Columbia University; Executive Director, the Academy of Political Science; Economic Consultant, Tax Foundation, Inc.; and Associate, Lincoln Institute of Land Policy.

JOHN N. HAZARD is Nash Professor Emeritus of Law, Columbia University. He is the author of *The Soviet System of Government* and *Managing Change in the USSR*.

DALE R. HERSPRING is Deputy Director for Northern Tier Countries, Office of Eastern Europe and Yugoslav Affairs, U.S. Department of State, and Adjunct Professor, Georgetown University. He is coauthor, with Robbin F. Laird, of *The Soviet Union and Strategic Arms*.

ERIK P. HOFFMANN is Associate Professor of Political Science, The Nelson A. Rockefeller College of Public Affairs and Policy, State University of New York at Albany, and Senior Associate, Research Institute on International Change, Columbia University. He is coauthor, with Robbin F. Laird, of *The Politics of Economic Modernization in the Soviet Union* and *"The Scientific-Technological Revolution" and Soviet Foreign Policy*.

ROBBIN F. LAIRD is Senior Researcher and European Study Director, Political-Military Affairs, Center for Naval Analyses, Alexandria, Virginia. He is coauthor, with Erik P. Hoffmann, of *The Politics of Economic Modernization in the Soviet Union*, *"The Scientific-Technological Revolution" and Soviet Foreign Policy*, and, with Dale R. Herspring, *The Soviet Union and Strategic Arms*.

GAIL W. LAPIDUS is Associate Professor of Political Science and Chair of the Center for Slavic and East European Studies, University of California at Berkeley. She is the author of *Women in Soviet Society: Equality, Development, and Social Change*, and editor of *Women, Work, and Family in the USSR*.

ELLEN MICKIEWICZ, Dean of the Graduate School of Arts and Sciences and Professor of Political Science, Emory University, is the author of *Media and the Russian Public*.

HENRY W. MORTON, Professor of Political Science, Queens College, City University of New York, is the author of *Soviet Sport* and coeditor, with Robert C. Stuart, of *The Contemporary Soviet City*.

HENRY S. ROWEN, formerly Chairman, National Intelligence Council, Central Intelligence Agency, is Professor of Public Management, Stanford University. He is coauthor, with Ryukichi Imai, of *Nuclear Energy and Nuclear Proliferation: Japanese and American Views*.

ROBERT SHARLET, Professor of Political Science, Union College, and formerly Visiting Professor of Political Science, Columbia University, is the author of *The New Soviet Constitution of 1977*.

MARSHALL D. SHULMAN is Adlai E. Stevenson Professor of International Relations and Director of the W. Averell Harriman Institute for Advanced Study of the Soviet Union, Columbia University. He served as Special Adviser to Secretaries of State Cyrus Vance and Edmund Muskie. Professor Shulman is the author of *Beyond the Cold War* and *Stalin's Foreign Policy: A Reappraisal*.

The Evolution of the Soviet Political System

ERIK P. HOFFMANN

Important changes took place in the Soviet polity under the successive leaderships of V. I. Lenin, J. V. Stalin, N. S. Khrushchev, and L. I. Brezhnev. These changes occurred in the relations among the highest Soviet leaders, between the Communist party and other major bureaucracies, and between the bureaucratic elites and Soviet citizenry. In turn, Soviet perspectives on leadership and administration varied from one historical period to the next. There were elements of continuity as well, including similarities between the tsarist and Soviet political systems.[1]

Lenin

Lenin (not Karl Marx or Friedrich Engels) was the chief source of ideas about the structure and functioning of a one-party polity, and Lenin was the dominant (some would say dictatorial) leader of the Bolshevik party that seized power in Russia a year before the end of World War I. Lenin's seminal idea was that a "conscious" political elite, informed and motivated by a Marxist worldview, must use this knowledge to reduce the "spontaneity" of the exploited and alienated laboring classes. According to Lenin, only a "vanguard of the proletariat" could enlighten the oppressed, uneducated, and fragmented Russian workers and peasants and could energize and organize them to play a pivotal role in the global transition from capitalism to socialism. Lenin's party, before and after the October 1917 revolution, attempted to influence the masses through links with governmental, economic, military, and educational organizations and through continuous pedagogical efforts in all communications media.

Part of this essay has been adapted from Erik P. Hoffmann, "Soviet Perspectives on Leadership and Administration," in *The Soviet Union since Stalin*, ed. Stephen F. Cohen, Alexander Rabinowitch, and Robert Sharlet (Bloomington, Indiana: Indiana University Press, 1980), 71–92.

Leadership, in Lenin's view, required an understanding of the class antag-onisms and power relationships within and among nations, as well as a passion-ate but pragmatic commitment to create a more harmonious and just social order in Russia and eventually throughout the world. Lenin sought to transform the Russian Marxist movement into a small, secretive, and hierarchically struc-tured political party of full-time revolutionaries, with close ties to the workers and other dissatisfied elements of Russian society and eventually to the laboring classes of all nations. After a "bourgeois" revolution had ended Russia's feudal stage of development and a "socialist" revolution had ended its capitalist stage, a single party was to construct a socialist state and society in Russia and help to establish a world socialist system. Without effective organization and propa-ganda, Lenin argued, the discontent of the masses would be dissipated in sporad-ic acts of violence or in a "trade union" mentality that strove only for incremental economic gains, rather than for the overthrow of the capitalist order.

The Mensheviks and the Bolsheviks developed two moderately different views on the nature and operations of the Russian Social Democratic Labor Party founded in 1898. The Mensheviks favored a less centralized, less selective, and less militant working-class party than the Bolshevik prototype. But personal and tactical differences divided the Bolsheviks and Mensheviks more than ideologi-cal differences. They could not agree on the composition and size of the editorial board of the newspaper that was to serve as the nucleus of the emerging revolu-tionary organization. Nor could they agree on whether to boycott the consulta-tive parliament established by the tsar in the wake of the nationwide strikes and uprisings of 1905. After the initial Bolshevik-Menshevik split of 1903 and the establishment of separate political parties in 1912, the political orientations of many Russian Marxists, especially the Bolsheviks, became increasingly author-itarian.

L. D. Trotsky, G. V. Plekhanov, and Lenin formulated competing theories of revolution. Lenin accepted Plekhanov's view that Russia's industrial workers were insufficiently class-conscious and that the economy and society were not ready for a socialist order. But Lenin agreed with Trotsky that the proletariat and peasantry, with strong leadership from the vanguard of the proletariat, could play a major role in the coming bourgeois revolution. Unlike Plekhanov and Trotsky, Lenin called for the concentration of power at the highest levels of a disciplined party *and* for the establishment of a radical coalition government. Although the party was to consist primarily of professional revolutionaries, the coalition government was to include representatives of various Marxist and non-Marxist "progressive" political parties and was to seek broad public support.

Plekhanov's and Trotsky's perspectives on revolution changed little between the upheavals of 1905 and February 1917. But Lenin eventually discarded Plek-hanov's idea that a lengthy period of parliamentary rule was necessary and embraced Trotsky's idea that the initial bourgeois revolution could be "tele-scoped" into a socialist revolution in a few months or in a year at most. As the events from February to October 1917 confirmed Trotsky's prescience, Lenin emphatically appealed for the overthrow of the Provisional Government and for the immediate establishment of a government that would serve the interests of the toiling masses. Trotsky, in turn, accepted Lenin's conception of an elitist party. Both Lenin and Trotsky, after considerable vacillation on Lenin's part, rejected the idea of sharing Bolshevik power with the Petrograd Soviet and the nearly 1,000 other soviets that proliferated in 1917. These councils of workers' and peasants' deputies were created by local initiative and were potentially a coalition government of loosely knit radical parties with nationwide authority.

The coercive elements of Leninism were heightened by the Civil War and foreign intervention (1917–20), during which survival was the overriding goal of the new socialist regime and nearly as many Russians lost their lives as in World War I. Old political and social institutions were destroyed, and only the most militaristic attitudes, activities, and relationships took root in this highly unstable environment. Immediately after the Civil War, authoritarianism was further enhanced by the Red Army's unprecedented suppression of the proletarian and peasant sailors at Kronstadt. These and other "left" oppositionists demanded greater democracy within the Bolshevik party and greater party responsiveness to the aspirations, interests, and organizations of the laboring classes.

Lenin's New Economic Policy of 1921, launched after seven years of war and during a devastating famine, legitimized a mixed capitalist and socialist economy and a society that was relatively tolerant of intellectual, artistic, and cultural diversity. In the early 1920s, a one-party system was consolidated, and measures were taken to concentrate power in the highest party bodies, especially the Central Committee and its key subcommittee, the Politburo. Lenin's resolution "On Party Unity" was a temporary measure, but it had a lasting effect. It curtailed factionalism in the party and interest-group activity in the polity, and it helped Stalin in the ruthless succession struggle before and after Lenin's death in 1924.

Democracy and centralism were to be in "dialectical unity," according to Lenin. But the centralist elements of "democratic centralism" have had a much greater impact on Soviet politics than have the democratic elements. This occurred in large part because of the authoritarianism of the tsars, of the non-Marxist revolutionaries, and of the Bolsheviks and was exacerbated by the turbulence in Russia during the formative years of the Bolshevik party and the Soviet state. The crucial components of Lenin's legacy are the concepts of consciousness and spontaneity. Emblazoned on the cards of present-day communists is probably the most important Leninist maxim of all: "The party is the mind, honor, and conscience of our era."

Stalin

Stalin's view of the ideal political organization of society has been characterized as "monolithic" in the Soviet Union and as "totalitarian" in the West. Western analysts stress that its essential features were the assumption of an extraordinary range of responsibilities by the national government and the extension of state power into virtually all areas of human life. Soviet commentators emphasize that Stalin's basic aim was to unify the civic values, attitudes, and beliefs of the entire population and to mobilize all material resources and human energies for the task of rapidly creating a "socialist" society and eventually transforming it into a "communist" one. The impressive buildup of heavy industry, the brutal but thorough collectivization of agriculture, and the waves of mass terror against the Soviet people are the best known of Stalin's policies in the 1930s. Also important were his efforts to enhance the national defense capabilities of the USSR throughout the decade and to consolidate the mature Stalinist system of the late 1930s by strengthening Soviet law and the Soviet family, by promoting scientific-technical and vocational education, and by recentralizing and expanding the political indoctrination programs.

The political order Stalin created to accomplish these goals was itself a vital product of "the third revolution" that swept away the economic, social, and political systems Lenin had launched in 1917. By 1937 Stalin had replaced the previous oligarchic dictatorship of the party with a personal dictatorship. The party was in no sense a ruling or sovereign body. Its highest organs met with increasing infrequency in the years 1934 to 1953, and over a million of its members (almost half of them) were arrested or perished in the mid and late 1930s.[2]

In the fully developed Stalinist system that emerged after the Great Purges, the party was reduced to more or less equal status with the other major bureaucracies—the secret police, army, and state apparatus (councils of ministers and soviets). Stalin, through loyal agencies, dominated all of these institutions, using them as instruments of his policy and personnel preferences and inner needs for power and adulation. Stalin deliberately pitted officials of these institutions against one another and established overlapping and imprecise spheres of bureaucratic jurisdiction. He did so to ensure that major (and many minor) political decisions and disputes would be resolved by him personally and to increase the likelihood of obtaining accurate information from various organizational sources and speedy compliance with his commands. To ensure further that his dictates would be followed—and that lower-level officials would pursue national goals in the absence of precise and consistent directives and adequate resources—Stalin created an elaborate system of rewards and sanctions, which included extraordinary opportunities for career advancement as well as life-and-death power over all officials and citizens.

Stalin's most important goals were few and clear-cut, and the polity he molded emphasized the unquestioning support of the leader and the effective fulfillment of policies and targets, not the efficient use of resources or cooperation among organizations and groups. Planning was focused on ends, not on means, and generous bonuses were given only for the complete fulfillment of assigned tasks and for immediate, rather than long-term, benefits. The political-administrative system allowed institutions and officials considerable flexibility in choosing the methods of achieving centrally prescribed aims and in competing with one another for political power and material and human resources to do so. As Merle Fainsod has pointed out: "The bureaucratic hierarchies . . . operated as centers of influence in their own right. . . . Behind the monolithic facade of Stalinist totalitarianism, the plural pressures of professional bureaucratic interests found expression."[3] But the participation of bureaucratic elites in the formulation of public policies was not a part of the theory or practice of Stalinism. The power to determine and choose among policy alternatives was highly concentrated in Stalin's personal secretariat (not in the party Politburo) and, above all, in the hands of Stalin himself.

During World War II, Stalin was compelled to enter into a political, economic, and military alliance with the major Western democracies and to allow greater institutional and ideological diversity within the USSR. Collaboration with the United States, "different roads to socialism" in the world communist movement, and relaxation of controls at home—all were paths that former Soviet leaders had advocated unsuccessfully in the 1920s but that had to be explored in a time of crisis.

After World War II, however, Stalin reestablished the Soviet political system of the late 1930s. In a time of peace or "cold war," Stalin reaffirmed his commitment to the prewar resource-allocation priorities and institutional relationships. Despite the leader's caution and possible willingness to consider alternative policies, despite the intensified jockeying for power among the major bureaucracies, and despite considerable public yearning for a less coercive polity, Stalinism was reimposed and the industrial output of the USSR was revived with remarkable rapidity in the time-tested ways (e.g., autarkic economic development, forced labor, and tight supervision over the scientific and cultural intelligentsia). Stalin's chief effort abroad—the forging of a totalitarian interstate system that included Eastern Europe and eventually China—was primarily intended to meet internal economic and national security needs; and, at least in the short run, this effort was successful.

The shortcomings of Stalin's policies and policy-making procedures became increasingly evident to Soviet officials and foreign observers in the new domestic and international conditions of the postwar period. Stalin did not have to persuade anyone to comply with his directives. But the dictatorship he had created could not provide its leader with the information he needed to make large numbers of feasible, timely, and integrated policies in increasingly complex political-administrative, socioeconomic, and scientific-technological environments. Nor did Stalin have the capability, or in some cases the will, to utilize the policy-relevant information he received. The Stalinist political order repressed creativity and initiative in most fields, and it lacked the flexibility to adjust plans and decisions to rapidly changing domestic and international conditions and to unanticipated opportunities and problems. Robert C. Tucker observed that when Stalin died, the question was not "Who shall replace him?" but "What shall take the place of Stalinism as a mode of rule and pattern of policy and ideas."[4]

Khrushchev

Stalin's successors revitalized the Communist party and reasserted its predominant role in Soviet society. The party's power vis-à-vis the other major bureaucracies increased, its involvement in industrial management and operations in the countryside expanded, and its membership grew. Less recognized is that Khrushchev, like Stalin, conceived of the party as primarily an administrative organ for implementing policies formulated by the top leader. By the late 1950s Khrushchev had gradually put together a "grand design"—a coordinated set of new domestic and international goals and policies that included peaceful coexistence with the West; serious efforts to upgrade agriculture, light industry, and consumer goods; systematic application of scientific discoveries and technological innovations to production problems and national defense; and social and economic egalitarianism. He then tried to develop various reform programs to implement these basic ideas. Such programs included the decentralization of economic decision making; major changes in Soviet law; a campaign to improve mass and elite political indoctrination; and a proposed substantial reduction of Soviet ground troops.

Khrushchev did not attain many of his objectives. His lack of accomplishment was in part the result of poor planning, formidable bureaucratic resistance and inertia, unfavorable external developments, and the intractability of human nature. The first secretary's inability to mobilize institutional support for his policies was especially frustrating, and it prompted his increasingly persistent, even frenzied, search for public acclaim and new administrative campaigns to fulfill his cherished and often unchanging aims. Khrushchev, by almost any measure, was less successful in achieving his major goals than Stalin was in achieving his. Unlike Stalin's power and prestige, Khrushchev's depended very much on the success of his policies.[5] Whereas Stalin could govern either through or over the party,[6] Khrushchev found it more and more difficult to do either.

The difficulties of being Stalin's successor may well have been enhanced by residual elements of Stalinism in Khrushchev's conceptions of authority. Khrushchev apparently believed that all party and state officials should actively help to administer national policies that they had little or no part in shaping, and that they could be made to carry out their responsibilities by means of job insecurity and a peculiar mix of performance and moral incentives. The first secretary most assuredly did not conceive of himself as an arbiter of competing "interests" or claims from the major institutions and social strata, or from scientists, technical specialists, or economic executives, to whom power to shape national policy was devolving or should devolve.

Increased elite and popular participation in administration do not necessarily lead to greater democratization of the policy-making process, and Khrushchev almost surely did not intend them to do so. He vigorously tried to use the expertise of the elites and the experience of the masses to implement *his* vision of the national interest and to refine operational, not strategic, decisions.

The grand design advocated by Khrushchev consisted primarily of substantive goals; he was less clear about the means by which these goals were to be achieved. Khrushchev apparently gave no extensive thought to the interrelationships between ends and means, or perhaps he lacked the political-administrative skills to link them. To be sure, Khrushchev made an enormous contribution to Soviet politics by forswearing terror as a means of resolving political disputes. But this decision greatly reduced competition among bureaucratic units to fulfill his objectives. Khrushchev mistakenly assumed that the elimination of physical coercion against party and state officials would increase support for national, rather than departmental and local, goals. He apparently failed to recognize that new decision-making procedures and institutional reorganizations are unlikely to be effective if important groups of bureaucrats perceive them to be illegitimate or threatening. For example, the first secretary insisted on disbanding the economic ministries in 1957 and on bifurcating the regional party apparatus in 1962 — administrative changes that were quite unpopular with state and party officials, respectively.

Khrushchev was unable to accomplish his central aims in the face of bureaucratic obstructionism at home and a frequently unresponsive, even hostile, political environment abroad. Khrushchev possessed a distinctive vision of the national interest and found it very difficult to compromise with his domestic political opponents, except in response to overwhelming opposition or the obvious failure of his policies. Somehow, he never lost the power to initiate programs, such as the expansion of the chemical rather than the steel industry in 1958, the reduction of ground troops in 1960, and the development of chemical fertilizers for agriculture and the rapprochement with the West in 1963. But when accomplishments fell short of his clearly stated goals, responsibility rested squarely with the first secretary. And when entrenched bureaucratic interests undermined the implementation of Khrushchev's dramatic proposals, the credibility and bargaining power of the party's top leader were diminished. Indeed, some Soviet officials may have formally supported Khrushchev's decisions in the expectation that they would fail and thereby reduce his influence.

Khrushchev strove to augment the power of the top leader and to undermine officials, organizations, and social groups that questioned his aims and the desirability or feasibility of his priorities. He frequently refused to accede to his Presidium colleagues when his policies and programs faltered. When Khrushchev was increasingly forced to do so, he attempted to break away from the bonds of oligarchic party rule by appealing to public opinion and by mobilizing "his" regional officials and scientific-technical experts. Khrushchev thereby alienated the leaders and many of the lesser officials of all the major Soviet bureaucracies, including the party.

Khrushchev's ouster in 1964 stemmed mainly from his autocratic ideas about the power of the party's first secretary vis-à-vis the highest party bodies; his cavalier treatment of party and state bureaucrats; his penchant for grandiose but insufficiently planned projects; and his demanding, unpredictable, disruptive, and impatient political style. Important but probably secondary factors were his often farsighted and idealistic goals and priorities. Khrushchev's colleagues objected in varying degrees to the content of his grand design and especially to his methods of advocating and implementing it.

Brezhnev

Khrushchev's policy-making procedures had a major impact on his successors' conceptions of power and authority. The Brezhnev administration, primarily between 1964 and 1969, devoted considerable effort to establishing stable and clearly defined institutional relationships. Notable were the immediate decisions to recentralize the ministerial system and to reunite the regional party committees. Moreover, the new collective leadership gradually worked out methods to promote cooperative problem solving and institutional checks and balances to ensure the "mutual control" of top officials. For example, Brezhnev became general secretary of the party and A. N. Kosygin became chairman of the Council of Ministers — positions that Khrushchev had simultaneously held.

A few key substantive policies were formulated and programs initiated in the first five years of the Brezhnev-Kosygin leadership. The economic reforms of 1965, the repression of dissidents in 1966, and the conventional arms buildup are examples. The most portentous and difficult decision — the military intervention by the USSR and other Warsaw Pact nations in Czechoslovakia in 1968 — was a reaction to the possibility of disintegrating party control or of radical political, economic, and cultural demands, fanned by anti-Sovietism, throughout Eastern Europe. The harsh Soviet response in Czechoslovakia energized the collective leadership, and it expeditiously agreed on the comprehensive and integrated domestic and foreign policies elaborated at the Twenty-fourth Party Congress in 1971.

The content of Brezhnev's grand design was similar to Khrushchev's: it included détente with the United States; the rapid enhancement of strategic defense capabilities; the use of advanced Western technology to spur Soviet economic development; a strong commitment to improve agricultural production; and wage increases for the lowest paid workers. Whereas Khrushchev's grand design had consisted largely of substantive policies, Brezhnev's incorporated significant policy-making practices in addition to internal and international goals. Brezhnev's program was not imposed from above; it was the product of extensive consultation, controlled debate, and bargaining among the top leaders, the major bureaucracies, the scientific, technical, managerial, and educational elites, and, to a much lesser extent, the rank-and-file communists.

Key elements of the emerging policies on how to make policy were broader and deeper participation by specialists at different stages and levels of decision making; group decision making in party committees and departments; major compromises before innovative programs were launched; prior consolidation of bureaucratic support for policy implementation; the presumption that managers are trustworthy, competent, and diligent; clearer and more stable spheres of responsibility; a strong preference for incremental change; and expanded opportunities for party and state executives to assess the consequences of decisions before and after they were made. Also, political-administrative, socioeconomic, and scientific-technological information were to be actively solicited throughout the party hierarchy and more fully utilized at all stages and levels of decision making and implementation.

Brezhnev, much more pragmatic than Khrushchev, recognized the significance of uncontested and regularized methods of governing. He saw numerous benefits in creating durable institutional relationships and more consensual, responsive, and routinized policy-making and administrative practices. Brezhnev hoped that procedural adjustments would generate political and technical support from the officials and specialists whose contributions were essential in formulating, as well as in implementing, realistic and farsighted national programs. Brezhnev believed that the processes by which policies are made and carried out influence greatly their effectiveness and legitimacy. In contrast to Khrushchev's authority, Brezhnev's was not highly dependent on policy successes. The power to set priorities and assess results was exercised by a collective leadership composed of representatives of all the key party and state bodies. Initiative and responsibility were diffused among many individuals and organizations.

The political system under Brezhnev enjoyed a considerable degree of legitimacy among the bureaucratic elites. Administrators liked the prevailing decision-making and recruitment practices, which assigned responsibility for specific segments or phases of a task, did not impose inordinate pressures to learn new skills, and provided professional and financial security in exchange for loyalty and effort as well as performance. Even when an administrative unit or coalition did not get much of what it sought, it had very likely had an opportunity to make its view heard, and it could modify or circumvent the incremental policy changes agreed upon at the center. The highest Soviet officials benefited most of all, because they securely held the positions to which many capable but increasingly restless middle- and lower-level officials aspired.

Brezhnev increasingly questioned his belief that legitimate policy-making practices are necessary and sufficient to produce effective policies. The Soviet elites' intensifying support of the political system was not accompanied by a rise in bureaucratic responsiveness to Politburo initiatives. As more technical and administrative expertise was forthcoming to shape the top leadership's policies, departmental and local interests became ever more powerful. The centralized job assignment procedures notwithstanding, special interests were entrenched in the myriad party and state bodies in Moscow and in the republics, provinces, and urban and rural districts. Politburo officials themselves held different views and continuously debated the merits of current objectives, priorities, and programs. A national perspective, together with a widely supported set of comprehensive and feasible domestic and foreign policies, was the officially stated and probably the operative goals of the highest party leaders. But the Politburo was the only organ in the Soviet polity committed to ascertaining the common good and making it prevail over parochial pursuits. And the Politburo's will and capability to override the interests of the major bureaucracies and localities, as well as to guide the implementation of national policies, declined markedly with the deterioration of Brezhnev's health in the late 1970s to his death in 1982. Such developments were manifestations of immobilization and possibly of socialist though surely not pluralist democratization.

Continuity and Change

Did Khrushchev and Brezhnev alter the essence of Stalinism or merely adapt fundamental characteristics of the Stalinist system to new conditions? One's answer depends largely on one's view of the basic features of Stalinism and of the importance of post-Stalin changes in policy making and administration.[7]

On the one hand, it is difficult to conceive of Stalin's agreeing with the contemporary Soviet officials who acknowledge "the impossibility of decision making from the center on many, let alone all, questions,"[8] or who assert that "one of the basic criteria of the democratic nature of any political organization is its capacity for critical analysis of its own activity, in order to bring to light its own mistakes and take effective measures to prevent them from recurring in the future."[9] On the other hand, one must give considerable weight to the elements of secrecy, arbitrariness, coercion, insularity, inefficiency, mendacity, corruption, careerism, status consciousness, and lack of initiative from below — in short, the Stalinist legacy — in present-day Soviet politics. To be sure, Brezhnev encouraged the bureaucratic, scientific-technical, and educational elites to contribute their expertise on policy-relevant questions, and both conservative and reformist leaders supported the introduction of modern managerial techniques and information technology. But the collective leadership suppressed criticism of Stalinism and its consequences, which greatly reduced the effectiveness of its renewed emphasis on political and administrative rationality and on the democratic elements of democratic centralism in party and state activities. Traditional, though not necessarily Stalinist, bureaucratic patterns (such as resistance to pressures from the center) and communication pathologies (such as reluctance to transmit accurate information about shortcomings to one's superiors) persisted.

The glorification of the top leader has been an element of continuity in the style of Soviet politics since Lenin. But the content and functions of the Stalin, Khrushchev, and Brezhnev "cults of personality" differ in important respects. Stalin sought to create the impression that he was an omniscient and omnipotent leader who possessed a deep understanding of the laws of historical development and of the contemporary relevance of the authoritarian political-religious relationship between the tsars and the masses. Khrushchev portrayed himself as a man of the people who was eager to support practical initiatives and to meet individual citizens' material and psychological needs, rather than to promote conservative bureaucratic interests. Brezhnev cultivated the image of an effective, responsible, businesslike executive who knew how to manage complex organizations and dynamic forces, domestic and foreign.

Correspondingly, Stalin's cult served as a means of strengthening his personal dictatorship and of mobilizing institutional and public support for the radical transformation of society "from above." Khrushchev's efforts to enhance his popularity among the masses were an attempt to weaken collective leadership in the Presidium and to pressure party and state bureaucrats who opposed his reformist policies and his unsettling policy-making and administrative practices. The growing official adulation of Brezhnev was a method of increasing the power of the Politburo vis-à-vis the major bureaucracies, of improving the effectiveness of group decision making by establishing the general secretary as "first among equals," and of producing a prestigious chief-of-state to further Soviet interests in contemporary international relations. The Brezhnev cult may have been a partisan effort to strengthen the hand of one faction within the leadership. But the chief effect of the public praise of Brezhnev was to slow the decline of the Politburo's capability to manage socioeconomic and scientific-technological forces "from below" and from abroad. Hence, Stalin, Khrushchev, and Brezhnev all developed distinctive cults and used them to pursue different priorities, each deliberately perpetuating the cult of Lenin and seeking to identify current aims and methods with Lenin's.

Lenin, Stalin, and Khrushchev had a much greater distrust of party and state bureaucrats than did Brezhnev. Stalin developed powerful rewards and sanctions to motivate officials, whereas Lenin and Khrushchev, by choice and circumstances, placed considerably more reliance on public supervision over cadres' activities. Stalin, hoping to improve administrative performance, engendered in executives the fear of losing their lives and jobs; Lenin and Khrushchev proscribed terror against executives but tried to manipulate their fear of losing their positions and perquisites; Brezhnev, until 1969, did neither. Brezhnev's initial approach to administrative productivity and motivation was reminiscent of the manager who assures his subordinates of career security and ample material and psychological rewards and then tells them "Now get to work!" In contrast to Lenin's and Khrushchev's personnel policies, Brezhnev's were characterized by a low turnover of officials and reduced shifting of officials from one assignment to another. Brezhnev assumed that greater organizational stability and clearer delineation of rights and responsibilities would improve the quality of work in most fields. Only in the early 1970s did Brezhnev begin to lose patience with the concept of "trust in cadres" and periodically link job performance with job security in his public pronouncements.

The top Soviet leaders' perspectives on policy making have undergone greater changes since Stalin than the styles of leadership and administration. Khrushchev and Brezhnev, using quite different methods, were both frustrated by their inability to alter Stalinist attitudes and behavior in the major bureaucracies and economic production units. For example, Soviet factory managers strongly opposed the economic reforms of 1965 and succeeded in obstructing them. This is but one illustration of the persistent tension between national and local interests and between national and departmental interests in the post-Stalin polity. Such tension also suggests that future Politburos must seriously consider basic changes in institutional relationships and bureaucratic incentives and must maintain unified positions on public policies.

The Brezhnev collective leadership recognized that the dramatic scientific-technological and socioeconomic developments since World War II were increasing the volume and interconnections of political-administrative decisions at a rate faster than Leninist, Stalinist, or Khrushchevian methods could handle. Top party officials acknowledged that the extraordinary complexity of modern production had enhanced the interdependence of Soviet institutions and society with one another and with those of other nations and had made the Soviet polity more permeable to powerful domestic and international forces. Party leaders perceived the need to be responsive to, but not to be dominated by, the interrelated scientific and technological advances and social and economic trends whose political and administrative consequences are difficult to anticipate and control.

Although Brezhnev worked diligently to establish stable and effective policy-making procedures, an even more important part of his legacy may be his legitimation of freer public discussion about the priorities of an industrialized socialist society under conditions of rapid change, complex interdependence, mounting scarcities, and hard choices. The Politburo under Brezhnev encouraged certain kinds of creativity, experimentation, and feedback among the major bureaucracies and specialist elites, while simultaneously repressing the most influential spokespersons of all major dissident groups and viewpoints. Whether Soviet leaders after Brezhnev will expand the opportunities for judicious and informed criticism of public policies from various sources, whether they will adopt much more conservative or reformist policies, and whether they can do so without seriously undermining existing institutional relationships and social stability, are among the significant questions addressed in the essays that follow.

Notes

1. See Erik P. Hoffmann and Robbin F. Laird, eds., *The Soviet Polity in the Modern Era* (Hawthorne, N.Y.: Aldine Publishing Co., 1984), and Erik P. Hoffmann and Frederic J. Fleron, Jr., eds., *The Conduct of Soviet Foreign Policy*, 2d ed. (Hawthorne, N.Y.: Aldine Publishing Co., 1980).

2. Andrei Sakharov, *Progress, Coexistence, and Intellectual Freedom* (New York: W. W. Norton & Co., 1968), 55.

3. Merle Fainsod, *How Russia Is Ruled*, 2d ed. (Cambridge, Mass.: Harvard University Press, 1963), 579.

4. Robert C. Tucker, *The Soviet Political Mind: Stalinism and Post-Stalin Change* (New York: W. W. Norton & Co., 1971), 173 (emphasis in original).

5. Carl Linden, *Khrushchev and the Soviet Leadership, 1957–1964* (Baltimore: Johns Hopkins University Press), 15 ff. Cf. George Breslauer, *Khrushchev and Brezhnev as Leaders: Building Authority in Soviet Politics* (London: Allen & Unwin, 1982).

6. Leonard Schapiro, *The Communist Party of the Soviet Union*, 2d ed. (New York: Random House, Vintage Books, 1971), 556 ff.

7. On the essential or fundamental elements of the Soviet system, see John N. Hazard, *The Soviet System of Government*, 5th ed. (Chicago: University of Chicago Press, 1980), 228–43.

8. V. G. Afanas'ev, *Pravda*, 2 May 1976, p. 2.

9. G. Kh. Shakhnazarov, *Sotsialisticheskaia demokratiia*, 2d ed. (Moscow: Politizdat, 1974), 72–73; trans., *Socialist Democracy* (Moscow: Progress, 1974), 47.

What Ails the Soviet System?

TIMOTHY J. COLTON

As the post-Leonid Brezhnev era takes shape, the survival of the Soviet system is not in question, but the utility of many of its policies is. The accumulation of internal problems confronts the regime with choices more vexing than any faced in decades. One hallmark of the changing leadership is its sober realism about the extent of these troubles. Although Brezhnev's ideologists characterized the Soviet Union as a "developed socialist society" in 1967, Yuri Andropov and Konstantin Chernenko have emphasized that developed socialism is still being "perfected." The full attainment of socialist ideals, in Andropov's words, "will be a most complicated process, inevitably connected with the overcoming of contradictions and difficulties," certain of which are more intractable than others. "In some areas we will be able to move more quickly, in others more slowly. This is what the real map of social progress is like. It cannot be smoothed out into a straight line."[1]

Some of these "contradictions and difficulties" do not lend themselves to exact measurement. Individual conduct and attitudes at odds with the party's preferences make up one such problem area. The deviations singled out for recent attack by the regime and said to be on the rise in the Soviet Union include abuse of alcohol, crass materialism, corruption, and signs of anomie among the young. Tensions between the Russian majority and the dozens of smaller Soviet nationalities are also difficult to determine precisely. Andropov, however, found it necessary shortly after being appointed leader to decry "national conceit . . . the tendency toward isolation . . . the disrespectful attitude toward other nations and peoples" finding increasing currency among Soviet ethnic groups.[2]

Other negative trends are more easily pinpointed. Soviet population growth, for example, declined 50 percent between 1960 and 1980, to 0.8 percent a year. This disturbs a regime inclined to identify national power with population size. It also limits the growth of the work force, which will expand by only 0.4 per-

Reprinted with permission from *The Dilemma of Reform in the Soviet Union*, by Timothy J. Colton ($6.95), published by Council on Foreign Relations, 58 East 68th Street, New York, New York 10021.

cent a year in the 1980s, less than a third of the 1970s rate and a sixth of the 1960s figure. And it increases the proportion of retired persons who must be supported by the working population (such people now make up about 16 percent of the total and will be at 20 percent by the year 2000). Perhaps the most unsettling demographic trend is the climb in mortality rates. The Soviet crude death rate, which bottomed out at 6.9 per 1,000 in 1964, jumped by 50 percent to 10.3 in 1980—a turn of events said by a leading United States expert to be "unique in the history of developed countries."[3] The increases posted for infants and men of prime working age were particularly steep.

Easiest to grasp in numerical terms, and of the greatest relevance to politics, are the Soviet Union's economic problems. There is no quibbling over one essential fact: the Soviet economy is in a protracted growth slump, and the population is smarting from the effects. The annual rate of expansion of the Soviet GNP, which topped 5 percent in the early Brezhnev years, dipped to approximately 3 percent in the late 1970s and 2 percent in the early 1980s. Growth in 1983 rebounded to more than 3 percent—helped by good weather and Andropov's first economic decisions—but so far most Western specialists are sticking to their overall predictions for the 1980s. It is generally believed that, year-to-year fluctuations aside, the USSR will be fortunate to maintain 2 percent growth for the remainder of the decade.

Economic consumption, measuring the goods and services the Soviet household gets from the economy, is under similar pressure. Growth in per capita consumption slipped to 2.2 percent a year in 1976–80 (as opposed to 5.1 percent ten years before), with food, housing, recreation, and educational and health services faring the worst. It has been projected to rise by only about 1 percent a year in 1981–85 (it actually fell by 1 percent in 1982) and, unless something changes in the meantime, to stagnate completely in the second half of the 1980s. Agriculture, vitally important to the consumer, remains a weak and volatile sector despite massive infusions of resources under Brezhnev. Net agricultural output, which advanced by 3.7 percent a year in 1961–70, was up by an anemic 0.9 percent a year in 1971–79 and was so far below planned levels in 1979–82 that the Soviets withheld production statistics. Though some recovery was evident in 1983, lines outside shops for food and consumer goods are more prevalent than five or ten years ago, local shortages seem more common, and rationing of meat, milk, and other food staples has been reintroduced in some Soviet cities.

Explaining the Soviet Union's Problems

What in the Soviet system explains this accumulation of troubles? The underlying difficulties with which members of the Politburo and their successors must grapple can be divided into six categories: the obsolescence of old policy formulas, especially economic ones; the combined challenge of lingering backwardness in key areas and of problems present in a mature industrial society; new doubts about ethnic identity; the widening split between popular expectations and Soviet reality; the turn toward a self-centered morality; and the mixed benefits of the regime's minimal reforms.

Old formulas misfire in new circumstances. As a rule, the Soviet Union addresses its perennial problems with remarkably stable formulas and approaches. It lives by time-tested practice. The catch is that sooner or later old habits generate diminishing returns. This waning effectiveness of inherited solutions accounts for much of the load under which the regime now labors.

Old formulas often lose their efficacy because the conditions under which they were first worked out evolve more quickly than the formula itself. For instance, the Soviet indoctrination network, set up after the Revolution of October 1917 to carry the party's gospel to an illiterate or semiliterate population, has far less impact on today's more sophisticated public. The hospital and clinic system that did well at introducing elementary health care and curbing epidemic disease in a largely agrarian country is less in step with an urbanized and industrialized society with high stress levels, heavy pollution, richer diets, and greater alcohol consumption.

This pattern of declining returns particularly affects the Soviet economy. In Charles Lindblom's apt characterization, the traditional Soviet economic model is "strong thumbs, no fingers."[4] State ownership, central planning, direct administrative control over factories and farms, and periodic campaigns for implementing the latest priorities are its main features. For several decades after being put into operation in Stalin's early five-year plans, the powerful thumbs of the command economy did give rise to a quite acceptable pace of growth. After a certain point, however, they have proven to be maladroit. Not only has Soviet economic growth ebbed; it has also lagged significantly in relation to other industrial economies. One comparison shows Soviet growth, which had outstripped sixteen OECD (Organization for Economic Cooperation and Development) countries by 0.4 percent a year in 1966–70, to have fallen 1 percent behind in the late 1970s. In terms of per capita consumption, the Soviet Union trailed OECD annual growth by 1.4 percent, reversing an earlier Soviet advantage of 0.6 percent. After making some headway in closing the chasm between Soviet and Western standards of living, the Soviets have seen it open up again since the mid-1970s, especially in housing, recreation, health, and education.

Finer, suppler fingers of economic management are needed today because circumstances have changed: the cheap resources around which the original Soviet blueprint for industrialization was drawn up have been largely exhausted. The effect of the coarse thumbs of the classic formula was "extensive" in nature, pressing into service as speedily as possible the Soviet Union's abundance of labor, capital, land, energy, and raw materials. Now, continued development requires an "intensive" strategy, oriented toward the more effective use of scarce resources, with better incentives, coordination, and technological innovation. On all these scores, Soviet achievements have been unimpressive. Total factor productivity in the Soviet economy (the increase in output per added unit of capital and labor input) is the best global measure of this. After rising by 1.5 percent in the 1960s, it inched up by 0.1 percent a year in the first half of the 1970s, then *decreased* by an annual average of 0.4 percent in the second half of the 1970s and of about 1 percent in 1981–82.

Policies are often questioned and revised when their architects pass from the scene. In the Soviet Union, many policy canons devised in the regime's formative years have endured. They have in a sense been written into the operating codes of the huge state and party bureaucracies running the country. In this situation, the administrative apparatus, untroubled by the discipline of the market or by direct accountability to society, tends to act as "a gigantic machine that slowly and inflexibly grinds along in the direction in which it was initially aimed."[5] In principle, Soviet politicians are no less free than any others to attack and re-direct the bureaucracy beneath them. In practice, they have done so only in fits and starts—and were especially loath to do so during the long Brezhnev era.

The problems of success meet the problems of backwardness. Besides perennial problems, such as ensuring steady industrial growth, for which old formulas yield shrinking dividends, political problems of two different sorts have cropped up in the Soviet Union. First, as the leaders have known for some time, the very accomplishments of the country in building an industrial economy and a mod-ern, urban society have brought new problems. "Life goes forward," Brezhnev said as early as 1967. Once the regime's main challenges had been vanquishing internal enemies and laying an industrial base, but now "new tasks stand before us, new not only in scale but in character."[6]

Many of the emergent problems are less economic and technical than social and cultural. Thus environmental pollution, a by-product of unregulated in-dustrialization long passed over by the government, in the 1960s and 1970s became an important issue for widening portions of the Soviet populations, and it is bound to remain so. In big Soviet cities, traffic congestion, in its own way a proof of economic advancement, poses a serious concern. The profusion of huge tracts of high-rise housing, welcomed by all as a needed response to the apartment shortage, has created a faceless and monotonous milieu. Soviet dis-cussions of what to do about it remind one of inquiries in other developed countries.[7] In natural science, Soviet breakthroughs in molecular biology and recombinant DNA research have raised the same issues of technique and con-science found abroad. The foreign reader of Soviet debates on genetic engineer-ing "is increasingly struck by the similarity of these discussions to the ones that have been occurring in the West."[8]

What is fascinating about the Soviet Union today is the simultaneous eruption of these problems associated with progress and of a second set of problems usually linked with economic and social backwardness. Difficulties that the regime thought it had resolved, or at least held in check, have in recent years come back to haunt it. This reanimation of dormant problems has multiple

causes: exceptionally clumsy or ossified policies, the reduced allocation of resources, and bills coming due for what might be called deferred social maintenance—all accentuated as short-term gains are traded for long-term effectiveness.

Examples abound. The rise in death rates points to a regression in the health-
care system, and perhaps in the general quality of Soviet life. Since 1969 the
completion of new apartments has failed to keep up with the number of new
families, thanks to the housing lobby's poor showing in the budget wars after
Khrushchev's fall. Soviet urbanologists, who for some time had devoted their
pens to more complicated and subtle matters, such as the esthetics of mass housing and the impersonality of city life, have begun to write again about the quantitative shortage of housing with a plaintiveness not heard since the 1950s. Some
Western experts think that the Soviet farm system entered a period of absolute
decline in the 1970s. Certain of the regime's own actions lend credence to such
a conclusion, notably its decision in early 1979—before the latest string of bad
harvests—to make mandatory what had been a spontaneous move toward re-
establishing subsidiary plots and gardens at industrial plants and other nonfarm
enterprises. Most of these woefully inadequate facilities had been phased out
decades before. For the average Soviet citizen once again seeing a cabbage patch
or chicken coop in the courtyard of his factory or institute is a throwback to the
lean 1930s or wartime years and a sad commentary on the collective and state
farms. Some take it as an omen of worse times ahead.

New questions about ethnic identity. The roots of the regime's difficulties are
also found in the multinational composition of Soviet society. The 137 million
Russians, though by far the largest single group, constituted a bare majority (52
percent) of the Soviet population in the latest, 1979, census. Some one hundred
nationalities, still concentrated in their ancestral territories, are arrayed in a great
arc around the Russian heartland. The Russians' fellow Slavs (Ukrainians and
Belorussians) account for 20 percent of the population, with the other major
European groups representing 8 percent. Of the remainder, the biggest bloc by
far is the 17 percent of Moslem heritage, based mostly in Central Asia, Kazakhstan, and the Transcaucasus. Among the twenty-one non-Russian nationalities
numbering more than a million, the majority of the members of all but two
speak mainly their mother tongue.

The temperature of Soviet ethnic politics has heated up perceptibly since the
early 1970s. In Khrushchev's day, the regime spoke optimistically of eliminating
ethnic divisions and eventually assimilating the minorities into the Russian majority. Now the Soviet view emphasizes the stubbornness of ethnic identities
and the hazards of ethnic conflict. In the most straightforward acknowledgment
of the problem to date, Andropov declared in December 1982 that the economic
and social development of ethnic communities "is inevitably accompanied by the
growth of their national self-consciousness," not by its decline. The ideal of
fusing the Soviet nationalities into one has not been discarded, but it has been
relegated to the remote future, after the construction of a classless and fully com-

munist society. In the meantime, Andropov said, "problems in the relations among nationalities will not be crossed off our agenda. They demand the special concern and constant attention of the Communist Party."[9]

There are several symptoms of Soviet ethnic dissension. First, as Andropov's remarks attest, the regime itself now takes the problem more seriously than in the past. It has accepted the need for what he labeled "a well thought-out, scientifically based nationality policy," and to this end has sponsored frank empirical research on nationality questions and solicited advice from experts in the field.[10]

Second, there has been an acceleration of protest over issues of nationality, spearheaded by members of the emerging middle classes of the non-Russian groups. Ethnic grievances have become a major theme in political dissent in non-Russian areas, and charges have been leveled against local politicians for sympathizing. Pyotr Shelest, the head of the large Ukrainian branch of the party, for example, was dismissed and indicted as a closet Ukrainian nationalist in 1972. There have also been mass public demonstrations against Moscow's cultural and linguistic policy in several areas, notably in Lithuania in 1972 (where paratroopers had to be called in to suppress the crowds) and in Georgia during the discussion of the republic's constitution in 1978. Strange though it may sound, even the Great Russians, or at least many intellectuals among them, are feeling a similar frustration and pent-up nationalism. Like Lithuanians, Georgians, and Uzbeks, "they too are concerned about the right to express their national identity [and] about the homogenization of their culture.[11]

Third, ethnic emotions seem to intrude increasingly into the economic and socioeconomic spheres. This is true in the competition for investment resources, which has become keener as Soviet economic growth has subsided. Partisans of big regional projects — like the exploitation of Siberian oil and gas, rerouting of northern rivers to parched Central Asia, and the rehabilitation of the Ukraine's Donbass coal fields — have invoked national pride and rights along with narrowly economic arguments. Similarly, rivalry between Russians and non-Russians over professional and administrative jobs has intensified in the minority areas, despite an "affirmative action" policy favoring native personnel for most positions. Crackdowns on local corruption rings have also sparked ethnic controversy, producing "false lamentations that merciless criticism of negative phenomena somehow infringes upon national honor."[12]

Finally, demographic trends cast a long shadow over the future of Soviet ethnic relations. The most alarming from the Russian vantage point is the enormous asymmetry in fertility between the European population and the other Soviet peoples. The rate of births per 1,000 population is now two and a half times greater in Central Asia, where large families are favored by culture and climate, than in the Slavic republics, where the average couple intends to have one child. Whereas the Russian population will increase by 2.4 million between 1979 and 2000, the Moslem total is expected to grow by 20 million. By the turn of the century, the Russians, with 47 percent of the population and only about 40 percent of all 0-to-9-year-olds, will no longer be a majority.

The growing expectations gap. Never is there a perfect match between what a government does and what its public expects it to do. What counts politically is the size of the gap and the direction in which it is moving. One element in the Soviet regime's present predicament is that a large and widening gulf has opened between performance and aspirations.

To the ultrarepressive Stalinist state of a generation ago, Soviet citizens did look for some minimal benefits, as interviews with refugees at the time established. From this low starting point, partly because of the regime's own rhetorical excesses, popular aspirations escalated rapidly in the wake of Stalin's death. The boast of the Communist Party Program of 1961 that Soviet prosperity would eclipse that of the United States by 1980 was perhaps the most hyperbolic of such claims. (As it happened, the Soviet GNP per capita was only one-third of the American in 1980.) Of more consequence was the tacit but clear pact with society that, with the shedding of both indiscriminate political terror and social utopianism, the regime was henceforth to be judged by its ability to "deliver the goods" to the people.[13] Though the Brezhnev leadership muffled the Khrushchevian sloganeering, it left the basic vow intact.

Mass aspirations have also been aroused by the rising educational profile of the population, which has stimulated young people to desire respected and rewarding careers in which their knowledge can be used. Another factor has been the unlimbering of communication within Soviet society, both among professionals and at the level of the mass media — especially television, which came into general use only under Brezhnev. Television has spotlighted the regime's specific failings and contributed to a broadly based yearning for more and better consumer goods. Enriched contact with the outside world has also played a role. Here, even more effective than awareness of the West's wealth has been the example of the communist states of Eastern Europe, to which Soviet citizens have had far greater exposure and where Soviet-like institutions generally serve consumers better than in the USSR.

The regime's performance since Stalin in meeting mass èxpectations has been satisfactory in a fundamental sense. But it is also true that the regime has been losing ground: the distance between its actions and society's aspirations is now increasing. On many issues, including consumer goods and food, the slide is associated with the later phases of Brezhnevism. On others, it began somewhat earlier.

Possibly, some in the regime console themselves with the notion that poor performance by Soviet institutions has sometimes acted to depress expectations. One problem has been widely studied by Soviet sociologists: ambitious Soviet youths' diminishing access to high-status occupations. In the early 1960s, 57 percent of all secondary-school graduates were being admitted to higher education, the stepping stone to a professional career. A decade later, as many more tenth-graders jostled for entrance, only 22 percent were being admitted. Following their initial disappointment, many young people adapted to the new conditions by entering technical and vocational programs. Once in the work force, they often "feel themselves in social terms to be no worse off than those who became [university] students and acquired a diploma. . . . Youth is quite tactfully grasping the change in the real situation."[14]

The larger problem, however, is not self-correcting. For one thing, expectations thwarted in some areas are being diverted into others. In 1975 one sociologist noted that the young person denied entrance to the university tends to seek out satisfactions "that would compensate for his loss," including higher pay and better leisure.[15] Nor do expectations seem to be ebbing nearly as quickly as regime performance. Studies of Soviet buying habits observe that consumers now feel entitled to more and better goods than in the past, that "the demands of people have significantly grown, and industry trails along behind them."[16] Over the whole gamut of issues, particularly those touching on consumer welfare, it is fair to say that the expectations gap has been stretched out during the last decade.

Another telling fact about expectations is that under present conditions the continued wilting among the population of hope and belief in the future is apt to be extremely damaging to the regime itself. In a system where the state is simultaneously employer and provider of goods and services, popular pessimism can limit the state's ability to realize its own goals. While some puncturing of unrealistic expectations has been expedient, it can be counterproductive if it undermines people's willingness to work. Many in the Soviet Union think that this divide has already been reached, that disaffected workers and managers are simply working less on the job. This "social factor," as it is often called, is the final link in a vicious circle: society gets and expects less, so it gives less; the state promises and gives less, so it gets less. One Soviet economist has said that inducing the worker-consumer to produce in a low-growth economy with a flat earnings structure "now forms a unique 'solar plexus,' the center of all the socioeconomic problems of our society."[17]

The reach for private solutions. Because of the regime's faltering capacity to satisfy popular demands, Soviet citizens increasingly seek gratification from other sources. This interest did not originate in the last ten or fifteen years, but it clearly gathered momentum during that time. The partial withdrawal of citizens from public life takes an array of forms, compounding the Soviet system's many other difficulties.

Greater independence and self-centeredness characterize most Soviet political dissent, including the movement for Jewish emigration. They have also become a compelling force in culture and the arts. The most notable feature of Soviet literature, once devoted to preaching the virtues of collectivism, is now "its preoccupation with private human concerns."[18] Recent novels and poetry dwell on individual melancholy, fatigue, and solitude.

The common people exhibit the same spirit when, the blandishments of the regime to the contrary, they follow their own lights in making the key life-cycle decisions. Divorces, abortions, and illegitimate births—all legal but frowned on — are increasing. In the European regions, women have fewer children than the government wants, in Asia more. Choices about employment and location are weakly regulated and costly to Moscow's plans, all owing to "the fact that migration depends on the personal element, on the taking by the individual of the voluntary decision to change his place of residence."[19] Escape of a different nature is provided by vodka, the consumption of which climbs at a rate disconcerting to the leaders, the medical profession, and many others. Soviet per capita consumption of alcoholic beverages, rated in liters of pure alcohol, rose 50 percent between 1965 and 1979, one of the highest rates of increase anywhere; purchases of state-produced alcohol (not counting moonshine) account for 15 percent of total disposable income.

Individualism thrives particularly in the Soviet economy. Since cash incomes outrun the supply of desired goods and services and the prices of most essential commodities are frozen, Soviet consumers are withholding unprecedented amounts of income from the flow of spending. By 1976 bank and other savings that had accumulated from the past were equivalent to two-thirds of the population's money income and 84 percent of retail sales that year. This large reserve of funds available for spending gives a claim on future production, a reminder of popular disenchantment, and a disincentive to hard work. Hoarding of scarce commodities has also become more widespread, especially since the mid-1970s. The upshot is artificial shortages and the feeding of black markets.

"Colored markets" of every tint — black, gray, pink, and others recognized in the argot of the street — have swelled in the Soviet Union, testimony to the inability of official structures to accommodate individual ingenuity. As one Soviet discussion put it: "The person is not at all a bolt that can be snapped into a machine and forced to work there. He does not simply adjust to the system of economic relations. He also actively studies it, finds if necessary its weak spots, and tries wherever possible to use them."[20] In Soviet industry and agriculture, there is more barter outside the plan, often resulting in what the Soviets term "protectionism," or networks for exchanging nonpecuniary favors. Facing the low ceiling on earnings set by wage egalitarianism, more of the able and restless members of society enter the illegal "second economy," as Western analysts call it. Frustrated consumers buy more of what they need on the side (*nalevo*) from friends, free-lancing producers and middlemen, sales clerks, waiters, and so on. Choice goods are either stolen from store shelves or manufactured from scratch by underground entrepreneurs. They find ready buyers at inflated prices because, by Andropov's admission, state production is often so bad "that people prefer to overpay the speculator for articles that are good and made with taste."[21]

Dishonesty among Soviet officials has also been on the ascent, as numerous official and unofficial sources indicate. The economic slowdown and the unremitting pressure to fulfill production quotas have spawned more false and padded reporting (*pripiska*) by managers. This in turn, as the Communist party's theoretical journal noted recently, has a demoralizing effect on the work force: "Where there is lack of correspondence between the visible, real results of production and the announced results, such as is completely obvious to the collective, this dispirits workers . . . negatively affects the attitude toward socialist property . . . stimulates the erosion of moral values."[22]

Most menacing to the regime has been the heightened incidence of outright corruption. Neither regional purges nor repeated editorial scoldings have made large inroads into it. Admonitions to officials feathering their nests became especially piquant in the early 1980s, some hinting that malefactors were finding protection from the police and from political bigwigs. "The use of state and public property and official position for the purpose of personal enrichment" was a major motif in Yuri Andropov's early pronouncements as party leader. The policeman or bureaucrat on the take, he stated on one occasion, is striking "nothing less than a blow at the very essence of our system."[23]

The mixed blessings of minimal reforms. A final cause of the present Soviet malady lies in the regime's preferred way of coping with its problems. The minimal reforms typical of the Brezhnev era, diffident and unhurried as they were, have worked on balance to the benefit of the regime and the population. But they have also engendered costs and frictions that the new leaders will be obliged to come to terms with one way or another.

Again it is the economy that drives the point home. Here the superficial revision of structures and operating rules since the mid-1960s has been much less disruptive than the spasmodic renovations of the Khrushchev years. Yet, tinkering changes, followed by efforts to fine-tune inadequate measures, are "becoming a part of the problem, rather than contributing to its solution."[24] Under Brezhnev, the leadership frequently resorted to local experiments, launched in one sector or place and then slowly extended elsewhere. While the pragmatic and consultative manner in which the pilot projects were formulated and executed was often preferred to past ways, the aggregate effect has been to complicate the administration of the economy without significantly improving it. The experiments have siphoned time and energy off into monitoring, reporting, and analysis. Most of them, after many dry runs, have not been comprehensively introduced. Expensive equipment imported to assist in local innovation operates at a fraction of its potential because the Soviets have not provided the necessary supports. Computers — hooked up without the proper software, telecommunications, and maintenance facilities — are the most conspicuous case.

Irresolute reforms have been most in evidence when it comes to consumer welfare. Agriculture excepted, the regime has attempted to satisfy popular demands for housing, soft and durable goods, and personal services without reallocating budgetary resources in any emphatic way. It has also shrunk from creating potent new organizations able to do the job on their own. Instead, institutions with entirely different missions are ordered to add consumer-directed tasks to their existing repertoires. Industrial construction firms are obliged to build housing; truck factories and radar plants produce refrigerators and televisions; and, in some remote towns, industrial enterprises operate bus and streetcar lines. Established organizations do these things with neither enthusiasm nor efficiency. Hence consumer programs are poorly funded, weakly coordinated, and the first to be harmed when something goes awry.

The production of consumer goods for private purchase, a sore point made more tender in the late Brezhnev years, is a good illustration. Soviet light-industry plants, which manufacture mostly for the mass market, still find themselves at the end of the supply queue. The resultant slack in production is taken up by heavy industry, which makes half of all nonfood goods, including all vehicles and most home appliances. In spite of years of exhortation, heavy industry executives generally have "the attitude that the production of articles for the consumer is something of secondary importance."[25] Subject to little direction from above, they produce a jumble of models that are designed within individual plants, mutually incompatible, and frequently out of touch with consumer needs and tastes. They thus inflict upon the Soviet household no fewer than 130 refrigerator models (most of them obsolete), 70 kinds of vacuum cleaners, 56 different television sets, 50 table radios, 40 sewing machines, and 34 electric razors. With the manufacturer accepting almost no responsibility for spare parts or servicing, the consumer is left to fend for himself if, as often happens, something goes wrong.

A uniquely perverse outcome has come about in the field of low-priced household goods, known in Soviet parlance as "goods of the simplest selection, not centrally planned." For about 85 percent of these approximately 3,000 items, central control consists solely of assigning global quotas, expressed in rubles and not in physical units, to the industrial ministries which are then given carte blanche to decide what to make and distribute. "No one," a retailing official grumbled in 1982, "is occupied with coordinating the production of the whole range of the simplest commodities, and in this lies the source of many omissions and failures."[26] Salt has been rubbed in this old wound since the mid-1970s as plant managers, pressed to meet their basic plans, arbitrarily cut back on the manufacture of household goods. Faced with targets reckoned in gross ruble terms, they have often opted for shorter runs of larger, costlier items and produced fewer of the cheaper but often more necessary articles. This explains the recent proliferation of shortages of inexpensive but irreplaceable consumer goods, such as paper products (of which there is a permanent shortage), toothbrushes, underwear and lingerie, baby blankets and diapers, low-wattage light bulbs, ink, glue, small bottles, aspirin, bandages, light footwear, needles and thread, inexpensive radios, kitchen utensils, ironing boards, axes, spades, garden hoses, wood stools, key rings, hinges, bolts, shoe polish, electric switches, spark plugs, piston rings, typewriter ribbons, bath soap, and detergents.

Minimal reforms with this result may be worse than no change at all. An individual might, after all, be philosophical about not owning a washing machine; when the machine he does own cannot be repaired or stands idle for lack of detergent, he is apt to be less forgiving. Such experiences beget popular disillusionment, fuel the underground economy, and prod demands for more fundamental revisions of policy.

The Danger of Crisis

What can be concluded about the Soviet Union's problems and their underlying causes? Some in the West suggest the USSR today is a society in crisis, that it has come to a turning point in which the very continuance of the Soviet order is at stake. This thesis is wrong. It understates the rulers' resources and overstates their problems.

In surveying the Soviet regime's worries, one must not lose sight of its strengths and assets. The Soviet system is now in its seventh decade. Having weathered more than its fair share of trials and shocks — civil strife, forced-draft industrialization, the great purges, a devastating war with 20 million casualties, de-Stalinization, and the overthrow of Khrushchev — its resilience can hardly be doubted. Its stability is based in large part on sturdy instruments of control — the single-party system, the political police and armed forces, censorship, denial of free assembly, comprehensive political education, and the like — none of which shows signs of cracking. The telltale mark of a political system in mortal danger is violence, and political violence has been kept to a singularly low level in the Soviet Union. There have been impromptu strikes, an occasional street demonstration, and scattered acts of terrorism; but little blood has been spilled, and the authorities have with relative ease limited the fallout from such incidents. Among the forces aligned against the regime, hardly anyone either advocates its forcible overthrow or sees any realistic chance of this happening.

The regime's solidity rests also on a record of positive achievements. Whatever its shortcomings, it has made the country a world military power, safe for the first time from foreign invasion. At great sacrifice, its economic programs and science have moved peasant Russia into the space age. Economic development and free public schooling have drawn millions of Soviet citizens from humble backgrounds into attractive professional and administrative careers. Cradle-to-grave social services and safeguards, extended under Brezhnev to the peasantry, give Soviet citizens a security few would happily surrender (and that most emigrants from the USSR seem to miss dearly). All told, the regime's accomplishments represent a store of political capital on which it can draw for some time. Recent Soviet failures, it must be remembered, have in the main been failures at the margin. Many would not have happened without previous successes. Economic growth has slowed down, but the economy has not ceased to grow, let alone given indications of breaking down. There is a shortage of steak but not of bread, of blue jeans but not of work boots, of living space but not of basic shelter.

Granted that it has been jarred by recent events, basic support for Soviet institutions has thus far not really been weakened. As one observer put it, "there is no evidence that [the] perceived legitimacy of the system has lessened . . . among any but the relatively small contingent of dissidents and critically minded intellectuals." Though there has been a welling up of pessimism, especially in the middle class, there is still a residue of optimism about the future, "a feeling that in the very long run things will turn out all right." Present discontent is directed at the performance of the Soviet system and not its existence.[27]

Before being carried away with the trouble the Soviets are in, it is useful to compare their difficulties with those of other countries. It may be overstating it to say, as did one American commentator, that talk of declining growth and structural problems in the Soviet economy "could describe any country in the world."[28] Still, it is all too tempting in reciting the litany of Soviet woes to forget the recent Western recession, that cash wages in the United States (adjusted for inflation) are below what they were ten years ago, and that there are more than 25 million men and women out of work in Western Europe and North America. The Politburo's headaches do not include, as those of the cabinets of the liberal democracies have lately, sky-high budget deficits, key industries ravaged by foreign competition, race riots, or separatist movements. Making due allowance for its deficiencies, the USSR still possesses the second largest economy in the world, leading all other countries in the production of steel, cement, and many types of machinery. With enormous reserves of natural gas, oil, coal, and hydropower, it has by far the most favorable long-term energy balance of any industrial power.

None of this is to slight Soviet problems. They are real, they are worsening, and they are having a cumulative effect. While the Soviet system has not arrived at a crisis, it is clearly going in the wrong direction, with grave trouble ahead. Some Soviet leaders have guardedly conceded as much. Writing in the party's theoretical journal in 1981, Chernenko, then Brezhnev's closest ally in the leadership, enjoined the party to recognize anew the importance of serving "the proper interests" of all segments of society. With Poland obviously in mind, he warned that otherwise "our policy risks losing its firm social base, its support on the part of the masses." Poor analysis of social problems and disregard of the interests of particular classes and groups are, he said, "fraught with *the danger of social tension, of political and socioeconomic crisis.*"[29] Andropov several times struck a similar chord during his brief leadership. "It is necessary to pay dearly for one's mistakes in politics," he told the Central Committee in June 1983. "If the party's bond with the people is lost, into the resultant vacuum come self-styled pretenders to the role of spokesman for the interests of the working people"–a pointed allusion to Lech Walesa and Solidarity.[30]

Which problems are most capable of shearing "the party's bond with the people"? Which will command priority attention because they have the potential of realizing the admitted danger of a general crisis of the Soviet system? For a problem to be critical in this sense, it must satisfy two criteria. First, it must be severe enough to affect the essential well-being of society and the cooperative relations among its members. Second, it must be urgent, calling for prompt action.

Some of the problems on the Soviet agenda, while far from trivial, fail to qualify as critical by the touchstone of severity. Genetic engineering, pollution, traffic tie-ups, and city planning will agitate many officials and citizens in the years to come, yet they are not likely to be a great burden to the top leaders. They may act as a drain on resources needed to resolve more basic problems (as concern over pollution does in relation to some kinds of industrial growth), but they are not of sufficient weight to alter the leadership's core agenda. The problems of health care, disgraceful as they are, are also noncritical from a political perspective. They have provoked little reaction outside a restricted circle of administrators and experts, and there is evidence that the Soviets managed in the middle and late 1970s to reverse the downward trend in at least one major field (infant mortality). Answers in this instance are probably a simple matter of resources. There can be little question that Soviet health standards can resume their historic upward movement, provided that the necessary allocations are made to treatment, research, and prevention.

Still other Soviet problems do not meet the test of urgency. One is demographic issues. What Soviet leader in the 1980s is going to worry about family-planning decisions that will not be reflected in manpower levels until after the turn of the century, long after he is out of power? The same holds for the reduction in opportunities for Soviet youth to enter desirable careers. Once a society has passed through the early stages of industrialization and the most prized occupational slots have been filled (and the children of the winners given a head start in competing for favored positions in the next generation), it is difficult if not impossible to retain the high rates of upward mobility realized at the outset. For the individuals involved, the problem may be severe; for the government, it cannot be urgent, for there is no tangible remedy short of endangering other policies (such as job security for qualified incumbents).

The Soviet Union's problem of ethnic relations is often discussed by foreign observers in apocalpytic language, sometimes as if the Soviet multinational state were on the verge of collapsing. But careful reflection suggests that the problem is not critical. The Soviet regime has been extraordinarily adept at using sticks and carrots to keep the non-Russian minorities in line. Two or three generations into the future, population dynamics alone may make fundamental change inescapable. Over the next decade, however, and even several decades beyond, the problem seems readily manageable.

Russian hegemony in its present form is in no serious peril for several reasons. First, demographic trends, distressing though they may be to the Russians, will leave them and their Slavic cousins in an ascendant numerical position well into the twenty-first century. Russians, Ukrainians, and Belorussians will constitute 65 percent of the USSR's population in 2000, three times the Moslem proportion. Second, political leverage will not automatically spring from demographic growth. Political power is an independent Russian resource, and it will be used to ensure that as much of it as possible is passed on to future Russians. Third, the dominant Russians will continue to enjoy the advantage of territorial and political coherence and priority. The ethnic minorities will remain on the periphery, penetrated by large Russian settler communities (24 million Russians lived in the non-Russian republics in 1979, making up almost a fifth of the population there), relatively isolated from one another, and able in most cases to communicate with one another only in Russian. Fourth, Russian tolerance of native traditions, successful economic modernization, and other factors should keep the region that poses the greatest demographic challenge — Central Asia — long receptive to Soviet rule. The vast majority of Soviet Central Asians seem content with the regime and would find the arguments of an Ayatollah Khomeini, which have wreaked such havoc across the Iranian border, "very difficult . . . to understand, let alone endorse."[31] Fifth, Moscow will have the opportunity to build on the one great success of nationality policy under Brezhnev: Russian-language training. Between 1970 and 1979, the proportion of non-Russians speaking Russian as a first or second language rose from 49 to 62 percent; the ratio is much higher among urban residents and younger people. An intensified teaching program unveiled in the late 1970s and affirmed in May 1983 by Andropov's Politburo should keep the trend in train.

One item on the Soviet agenda, however, is truly critical and could lead to a general crisis of the regime. That is the faltering economy and the social ramifications of economic stagnation.

Economic difficulties are by far the most common precipitant of political trauma and change. In almost all industrial societies today, economic and socioeconomic issues dominate the political debate. The Soviet Union is no different: elite and mass opinion alike take it as a given that economic and related problems are and will continue to be of overriding importance. The regime's rhetoric, programs, and anxieties all revolve around the economy. The population, for its part, judges the state today more than ever by how it delivers the goods in industry and agriculture.

Moreover, the health of the economy has a direct bearing on many of the noneconomic issues facing the Soviet system. Prized foreign-policy goals are implicated, since high military expenditures and international prestige are harder to sustain in a sluggish economy. At home, almost all major interests would be poorly served by continuing economic malaise. Soviet communists have been no less inclined than American liberals to see economic growth as a surrogate for painful, redistributive choices among competing priorities. The worse the economy does, the more those conflicts — guns versus butter, schools versus hospitals, and the holders of jobs versus the aspirants to jobs — have to be resolved. A worsening economy will also injure ethnic harmony, because retarded growth in an unreformed Soviet economy would exacerbate the competition for investment funds that pits region against region. Ethnic and regional imbalances in labor supply add to the problem. The entire increment to the Soviet work force in the 1980s will occur in the Moslem areas, whereas the number of persons employed in the built-up Russian and Ukrainian republics will decline. Unless economic productivity and growth prospects are improved in the established

European regions, the regime will face two options, either of which is likely to inflame ethnic relations: involuntary importation of millions of Central Asian workers into the Slavic republics, which could both anger the Central Asians and create ethnic ghettos in Slavic cities; or, equally unpalatable, redirection of new investment and maybe even of some existing industrial plant into the Moslem regions.

It is on economic and socioeconomic issues that the gap between regime performance and popular expectations has grown most dangerously in recent years. To make matters worse, it is here that the Soviets seem now to be the victims of several vicious circles, that is, negative economic trends that feed on themselves. Two of these have already been mentioned: the contribution of inadequate rewards to poor work motivation and therefore to low productivity, which in turn reduces the total available for rewards; and the substitution of private for public responses to economic needs, spinning off worlds of activity not under the regime's direct control and in conflict with its values. A third vicious circle involves economic investment, which is now desperately needed to replace aging capital stock in manufacturing and transport and to bring on stream new sources of energy and raw materials, many of them in locations remote from the thickly populated European territory. Although by world standards Soviet investment is high (over 30 percent of GNP), its rate of growth was halved after 1975 (from 7.0 percent a year in 1971–75 to 3.5 percent in 1976–80) and is set at a sickly 1 percent a year for the planning period 1981–85. Force-fed with capital for half a century, the Soviet economy is now being put on starvation rations because the economic growth that sustains the production of capital goods is wavering and because, in circumstances of declining growth, the political leadership was unwilling to rank investment ahead of maintaining levels of mass consumption and military spending. To many Soviet and Western experts, this decision, without compensating measures, makes official growth projections more a wish list than a firm plan and heavily mortgages future recovery.

There can be no grounds for the Kremlin's hoping that within a few years the economic crunch will give way to a period of new and easy prosperity. Most speculation to this effect, in the Soviet Union and abroad, has turned on the question of manpower supply. Even if more cheap workers could bail the economy out of its difficulties (a dubious proposition), the latest Soviet predictions, done after the 1979 census, show no relief in sight. The supply of new labor will improve briefly after 1990, only to worsen quickly after 1995. Net additions to the working-age population in the 1990s as a whole will be 1 million persons fewer than in the stringent 1980s and almost 17 million fewer than in the relatively benign 1970s.

To sum up: the agenda of Soviet politics is indeed a disquieting one. Dwindling payoffs to old solutions, the combination of the novel problems of success and the resurgent problems of neglect, the accentuation of ethnic tensions, the inability of the reigme to meet rising expectations, the spread of self-seeking behavior in such forms as corruption and the second economy, the failure of fainthearted reforms — are all harbingers of more trouble ahead. The Soviet system is not yet in crisis, but unless its new leaders can slow downward trends, especially in the economy, the time may not be very far off when it will be.

NOTES

1. *Pravda*, 23 April 1982.

2. Ibid., 22 Dec. 1982.

3. Murray Feshbach, "The Soviet Union: Population Trends and Dilemmas," *Population Bulletin* 37 (August 1981):30.

4. Charles E. Lindblom, *Politics and Markets: The World's Political-Economic Systems* (New York: Basic Books, 1977), chap. 5.

5. Anthony Downs, *Inside Bureaucracy* (Boston: Little, Brown, 1967), 160.

6. L. I. Brezhnev, *Leninskim kursom: rechi i statyi* (*On the Leninist Course: Speeches and Articles*) (Moscow: Politizdat, 1970–83), II, 99–100.

7. Timothy J. Colton, "Making Policy for Soviet Urban Development" (Paper delivered at the Annual Meeting of the American Association for the Advancement of Slavic Studies, Monterey, Calif., Sept. 1981).

8. Loren R. Graham, "Reasons for Studying Soviet Science: The Example of Genetic Engineering," in *The Social Context of Soviet Science*, ed. Linda L. Lubrano and Susan G. Solomon (Boulder, Colo.: Westview Press, 1980), 235–36.

9. *Pravda*, 22 Dec. 1982.

10. Paul A. Goble, "Ideology, Methodology, and Nationality: The USSR Academy of Sciences Council on Nationality Problems" (Paper delivered at the Annual Meeting of the American Political Science Association, Washington, D.C., Aug. 1980).

11. S. Enders Wimbush, "The Russian Nationalist Backlash," *Survey* 24 (Summer 1979):37.

12. V. Z. Rogovin, "Sotsialnaya politika i yeyo vliyaniye na obshchestvennyye nravy" (Social Policy and its Influence on Public Mores), *Voprosy filosofii*, no. 8 (August 1978), 12.

13. Walter D. Connor, "Generations and Politics in the USSR," *Problems of Communism* 24 (September-October 1975):27.

14. *Literaturnaya gazeta*, 8 Jan. 1975.

15. Ibid.

16. *Trud*, 30 May 1981.

17. T. I. Zaslavskaya, "Ekonomicheskoye povedeniye i ekonomicheskoye razvitiye" (Economic Behavior and Economic Development), *Ekonomika i organizatsiya promyshlennogo proizvodstva*, no. 3 (March 1980): 19–20.

18. Maurice Friedberg, "Soviet Letters Under Brezhnev," *Problems of Communism* 29 (May-June 1980):53.

19. T. I. Zaslavskaya and L. L. Rybakovskii, "Protsessy migratsii i ikh regulirovaniye v sotsialisticheskom obshchestve" (Migration Processes and their Regulation in a Socialist Society), *Sotsiologicheskiye issledovaniya*, no. 1 (January–March 1978), 62.

20. Zaslavskaya, "Ekonomicheskoye povedeniye," 28–29.

21. *Pravda*, 16 June 1983.

22. S. Kheinman, "XXVI syezd KPSS i strategiya intensifikatsii" (The 26th Congress of the CPSU and the Strategy of Intensification), *Kommunist*, no. 3 (February 1982), 27.

23. *Pravda*, 16 June 1983.

24. Gertrude E. Schroeder, "The Soviet Economy on a Treadmill of 'Reforms,'" *Soviet Economy in a Time of Change*, prepared for the Joint Economic Committee, U.S. Congress (Washington, D.C.: GPO, 1979), I, 313.

25. *Ekonomicheskaya gazeta*, no. 32 (August 1982), 7.

26. *Sovetskaya torgovlya*, 12 Oct. 1982.

27. John Bushnell, "The 'New Soviet Man' Turns Pessimist," in *The Soviet Union since Stalin*, ed.

Stephen F. Cohen, Alexander Rabinowitch, and Robert Sharlet (Bloomington: Indiana University Press, 1980), 181–82, 187.

28. Lester C. Thurow, "A Useful Mirror," *Atlantic*, Feb. 1983, 102.

29. K. Chernenko, "Leninskaya strategiya rukovodstva" (The Leninist Strategy of Leadership), *Kommunist*, no. 13 (September 1981), 10–11; emphasis added.

30. *Pravda*, 16 June 1983.

31. Martha Brill Olcott, "Soviet Islam and World Revolution," *World Politics* 34 (July 1982):499.

The Soviet Economy

HENRY S. ROWEN

Confusion regarding the Soviet economy abounds. This confusion, however, results not so much from disagreement over Soviet economic performance as from uncertainty as to how to interpret that performance. Western observers have tended to describe Soviet economic performance as "poor" or "deteriorating" at a time when Soviet defense spending continues to rise, overall Soviet gross national product in real terms continues to increase, and the Soviet GNP is second in size only to that of the United States.

These characterizations are not wrong. Given past rates of economic growth, the gap between Soviet performance and plans, as well as the marked departure from standards of economic efficiency, the record compiled by the Soviet economy in recent years has indeed been poor. Results that are unsatisfactory when measured by this yardstick, however, do not mean that the Soviet economy is losing its viability as well as its dynamism.

In fact, we do not consider an economic "collapse" — a sudden and sustained decline in GNP — even a remote possibility. Our projections indicate that growth in GNP will remain slow but positive. Growth is being retarded by a combination of factors. Some are beyond Soviet control, and some reflect the weaknesses of the Soviet economic system that even the Andropov regime was not able to change. Other factors holding down economic growth represent policy choices — for example, the allocation of resources to defense — that could be modified but are unlikely to change much in the near term. Nevertheless, we expect annual growth to average 1 to 2 percent for the foreseeable future. Per capita consumption could level off or even fall slightly.

Statement of The Honorable Henry S. Rowen, Chairman, National Intelligence Council, Central Intelligence Agency, before the Joint Economic Committee, Subcommittee on International Trade, Finance, and Security Economics, *Central Intelligence Agency Briefing on the Soviet Economy*, 1 December 1982. Some stylistic changes have been made for this publication.

Soviet Economic Objectives and Priorities

Soviet economic activity has always focused on building military power, but the Soviet leadership has also always placed great stress on rapid economic growth. The good life for the Soviet populace, in the form of a rising standard of living, has been of importance to Moscow too for almost thirty years. But improvements in the welfare of Soviet consumers have generally been subordinated to the demands of the military and to the high rate of capital investment necessary to ensure fast GNP growth. It appears, though, that consumer interests are now being treated somewhat less cavalierly. Breaking precedent, the Eleventh Five-Year Plan calls for capital investment to grow more slowly than consumption.

In pursuit of these national objectives, successive regimes have given heavy industry priority status because it is the source of military hardware and investment goods. Meanwhile, despite some experimentation with decentralized forms of economic administration, the Soviet leadership has remained firmly committed to strict central planning and management of most economic activity. The justification has been that rigorous centralization is required for fulfillment of national objectives.

Soviet economic performance in terms of the objectives and priorities established by the leadership has been mixed. The Soviet Union has built an exceedingly powerful military force. Under Khrushchev the emphasis was on strategic nuclear programs, but Brezhnev presided over an across-the-board expansion and modernization of all Soviet forces. Since the mid-1960s, the USSR has increased its arsenal of intercontinental nuclear delivery vehicles nearly sixfold — overturning United States quantitative superiority — and giving itself an assured nuclear retaliation capability. During the same period, Moscow has more than tripled the size of its battlefield nuclear forces, reducing the credibility of NATO's nuclear weapons as a counterweight to the Warsaw Pact's larger conventional forces.

Meanwhile, the Soviet Union has more than doubled the artillery firepower of its divisions, increased ninefold the weight of ordnance that tactical air forces can deliver deep in NATO territory, and reduced the West's qualitative lead in such key areas as tank armor. At sea, the USSR has introduced new, heavily armed surface ships, nuclear-powered submarines, and naval aircraft and quadrupled the number of missile launchers on ships and submarines. Meanwhile, under Brezhnev, the USSR expanded its military activities in the Third World — ranging from arms sales to Soviet forces in defensive roles and support of Cuban forces in combat to intervention in Afghanistan.

While developing its military power, the USSR has until recently been able to maintain a rapid rate of economic growth. Soviet GNP, as measured by the CIA, grew at an average annual rate of 4.6 percent from 1950 through 1981. During the same period, the United States GNP increased by 3.4 percent a year. Soviet growth, however, has steadily slowed during this period — especially since 1978. The average annual rate of increase in GNP was about 6 percent during the 1950s, 5 percent during the 1960s, and nearly 4 percent between 1970 and 1978. In 1979–81, yearly growth averaged less than 2 percent. In 1982, GNP growth was under 2 percent. To a remarkable degree, the slowdown in Soviet economic growth has a parallel in Organization for Economic Cooperation and Development (OECD) countries. During the first three years of the seventies, OECD GNP increased at the rate of 5 percent a year. The crisis induced by Organization of Petroleum Exporting Countries (OPEC) oil prices brought OECD growth to a halt in 1974–75. Then in 1976–79, GNP resumed a respectable rate of growth of 4 percent a year. In 1980–81, however, GNP growth in the OECD collapsed to 1.2 percent a year.

The slowdown in the USSR in part reflects four consecutive poor or mediocre harvests. But most sectors of the economy have been sluggish, especially industry. In large measure, industrial performance has been held back by the emergence of serious bottlenecks unconnected with agriculture. Growth in industrial output, which averaged almost 6 percent a year in 1971–75, fell abruptly in 1976 and in 1976–81 averaged just slightly over 3 percent annually. The decline in growth has been steady. Industrial production grew by only 2 percent in 1981 and is expected to rise by 1.5–2.0 percent in 1982. The higher priority accorded to military strength is suggested by the continued rise in defense spending at the average annual rate of 4 percent that has prevailed since the mid-1960s. Growth in defense spending has continued in spite of competition for resources that might ease strains in the rest of the economy. Defense spending is now about 13 to 14 percent of GNP. At the same time, leadership concern about consumer welfare seems to have somewhat diluted the commitment to growth. The share of Soviet GNP allocated to fixed capital investment — the driving force behind Soviet economic growth — has more or less stabilized in the last few years at about 26 percent (factor cost), compared with about 20 percent in 1960. Slowing investment growth is explained partly by bottlenecks in sectors providing building materials and machinery. But it probably also stems from a political decision to protect Soviet consumers in a time of tightening economic constraints. Nonetheless, consumption still accounts for only 55 percent of Soviet GNP, far below the share in most noncommunist industrialized countries.

The Eleventh Five-Year Plan

The results of the last several years must have been most disappointing to Soviet leaders. It is already clear that most of the important goals of the Eleventh Five-Year Plan cannot be met. The plan was excessively ambitious from the start. For example, both industrial production and agricultural output were to grow by about 5 percent annually, even though production in both sectors grew at much slower rates in 1976–80. Performance was far below plan. The small increase in agricultural output in 1982 did little more than offset the decline in 1981, while stagnation or falling output in key industrial branches threatens to intensify already serious bottlenecks. Production of steel and steel products continues to sputter, with output in 1982 little changed from two years ago and below the peaks reached in 1978. Cement production, meanwhile, fell below the 1980 level, and freight-car production declined in 1982 for the sixth consecutive year.

The slump in steel is particularly damaging to machinery production. Along with shortfalls in the output of building materials, it also threatens to curtail growth in construction. Even the moderate 1981–85 investment targets could be in jeopardy. From the beginning, the Eleventh Five-Year Plan goals depended on large productivity increases. Underfulfillment of the productivity plans has been striking, however. The rise in industrial labor productivity, for instance, averaged only 1.4 percent a year in 1981–82, far below the 4.5 percent-a-year increase called for by the plan. The unrealistic, almost fantasylike character of the plan can be illustrated by comparing production goals with investment plans. Incremental capital output ratios — that is, the amount of additional capital needed to produce an additional unit of output — have been rising steadily and steeply in the USSR for many years, with little prospect that the rise will soon end. Yet, based on little more than admonitions that productivity must rise, capital investment targets in conjunction with output goals imply a decline in these ratios.

Bright spots in economic performance in 1981–82 are hard to find. But there have been a few. On the production side, natural gas continued to rise at a rapid rate — 7 percent in 1981 and nearly 8 percent in 1982. Overall energy production might be considered a plus. In 1982 at least, output of all major forms of primary energy rose. Oil production continued to inch ahead — by about 0.9 percent in 1982. And coal output, reversing a three-year decline, evidently will rise by about 2 percent. At best, however, it will barely exceed the 1981 level.

The USSR also substantially improved its hard-currency balance of trade in 1982. The hard-currency trade deficit in 1981 was about $4 billion, causing some anxiety in Western financial circles. Judging by the first-half 1982 results, the deficit will be reduced to perhaps $2 billion. The central authorities, with their total monopoly of control over foreign trade and the allocation of key resources, sharply raised the volume of oil exports to the West, despite softening prices in world markets. At the same time, they held the value of hard-currency imports steady. The result was a trade deficit in the first half of 1982 that was almost $4 billion lower than in the same six months of 1981. The already relatively small hard-currency debt — $11.5 billion at the end of 1981 — will rise little if at all.

The Soviets have paid a price for this success, however. The increase in oil exports to the West came at the expense of deliveries to Eastern Europe and domestic consumption. In holding the value of imports steady, Moscow also accepted a reduction in the volume of hard-currency imports. In particular, it scaled back purchases of Western equipment and consumer goods needed to help modernize Soviet industry and meet consumer needs.

Basic Strengths of the Economy

The sheer size of the Soviet economy, reflecting the substantial growth since World War II, is one of its strengths. Soviet GNP in 1982 equaled about $1.6 trillion, roughly 55 percent of United States GNP that year. Per capita GNP is almost $6,000. The population is also large, currently numbering about 270 million. The labor force totals about 147 million and, by world standards, is well trained and well educated.

Literacy is by now almost universal in the USSR. The education level of the population has been rising rapidly. Twenty-three percent of those over sixteen in 1979 had completed at least a secondary education (tenth grade in the Soviet Union), compared with only 14 percent in 1970. In 1979 an additional 7.5 percent also had completed higher education, compared with 5 percent in 1970. A particular effort is being made to expand the education of the indigenous nationality groups in the Central Asian republics. The USSR wants to upgrade the skills of the relatively large pools of labor available there and possibly encourage outmigration by assigning these better educated young people to labor-short areas. Graduates of higher, specialized secondary, and vocational-technical schools receive compulsory work assignments at specific enterprises where, it is hoped, they will continue to work. The emphasis on mathematics, engineering, and science in Soviet schools is also a plus for the technologically oriented Soviet society. About one-third of total instruction time in secondary schools is devoted to mathematics and science. There are serious flaws, however, in Soviet education, including too much rote learning and, at the university level, narrow specialization early on.

Another of the strengths of the Soviet economy is the tremendous accumulation of capital assets that has occurred since World War II. The value of gross fixed capital assets — buildings, machinery, equipment, and the like — amounted to over 1.74 trillion rubles in 1980, according to Soviet published data. The value of Soviet capital assets expressed in constant prices increased almost 11-fold between 1950 and 1980 and about 4.4-fold from 1960 through 1980 — long after the USSR had recovered from wartime devastation. This phenomenal expansion reflects the allocation of a large and, until recently, rising share of Soviet resources to capital investment. The rapid growth of capital assets has resulted in a more than 3-fold increase in the amount of capital per worker. The rise was almost 3.5-fold in industry and over 5-fold on state and collective farms. Two-thirds of the stock of capital assets is concentrated in industry, agriculture, transportation and communications, and construction. Only about 15 percent of total gross fixed capital consists of housing or is used to provide services to the population, such as health care and education. Although the rapid accumulation of capital assets is one of the Soviet Union's strengths, the capital stock includes a disproportionately large share of worn-out and technologically obsolete equipment. Soviet policies have kept retirement rates of existing assets artifically low and have prolonged their service lives through repeated capital repairs.

The USSR is exceptionally well endowed with natural resources. Beginning with energy, the Soviet Union has about 40 percent of the world's proven reserves of natural gas — the 30 trillion cubic meters under Soviet control exceed the reserves of all industrialized nations combined. Soviet reserves of coal account for 30 percent of the world's total recoverable reserves and are sufficient to ensure over 200 years of output at current rates of production. The Soviets do not publish figures for oil reserves, as they do for gas and coal. Our estimate is that oil reserves, at least in West Siberia, are substantial, though increasingly difficult to exploit.

The USSR is abundantly stocked with other important raw materials. According to Soviet studies, iron-ore reserves amount to about 60 billion tons — some 40 percent of the world's total. With as much as one-fifth of the world's forest resources, the USSR has a virtually inexhaustible source for producing wood and wood products. In addition, the Soviets claim — and may well have — the world's largest reserves of manganese, nickel, lead, molybdenum, mercury, and antimony. They also say that reserves of chromite, gold, platinum-group metals, zinc, and copper are among the largest in the world and sufficient to support Soviet mine production for many decades. The Soviets also have substantial reserves of potash and phosphate rock — raw materials for the production of chemical fertilizers — although a large proportion of the newer phosphate deposits consists of poor quality ore.

With its wealth in human, capital, and material resources, the USSR is highly self-sufficient — another of the economy's major strengths. The high degree of Soviet self-sufficiency in vital raw materials is shown by its position as a net exporter of a large number of these materials. Net exports of energy — mostly of oil and natural gas — now total about 4 million barrels a day, equivalent to about 15 percent of total energy production. The Soviets are major exporters of precious metals, ferrous and nonferrous ores and metal products, chemicals, and timber. Because of expected gains in output, the Soviets will be able to expand sales of key minerals, such as platinum-group metals, nickel, cobalt, manganese, chromite, and gold during the 1980s. We also anticipate major increases in the Soviet exports of ammonia, nitrogen, and potash fertilizer and methanol.

Though highly self-sufficient, the USSR is not autarkic. Indeed, for at least the last decade, trade with the West has been an important element in the USSR's efforts to modernize the Soviet economy and render it more efficient. The Soviets now must rely on Western imports of capital and technology to increase or maintain production of some of the raw materials in which they are abundantly endowed and self-sufficient. Imports from the West have become critical to Soviet efforts to improve, or simply maintain, the quality of the Soviet diet. In 1981, imports of grain and other agricultural products reached almost $12 billion, or about 40 percent of the USSR's total hard-currency purchases. But despite the large-scale expansion in agricultural imports, the Soviet Union remains basically self-sufficient with respect to food. These imports are intended mainly to prevent a decline in meat consumption and are not essential to maintaining an adequate quantity of food consumption. At 3,300 calories, the average daily food intake is equivalent to that in developed Western countries. Grain production is more than sufficient to meet consumer demand for bread and other cereal products.

In considering fundamental strengths, the highly centralized, rigid system of administering the economy — while perhaps the Soviet Union's major economic millstone — has had its advantages in enabling the leadership to mobilize resources in crash programs to achieve priority objectives. The prime example of this capability has been Moscow's success in building up its military might. This has been achieved through centrally directed mobilization and allocation of the USSR's highest quality human and material resources and a rigorous system of quality control in military production that prevents the shoddiness so characteristic of Soviet civilian output.

Centrally directed concentration of resources does not of course work everywhere. Agriculture is an example. Even though over a quarter of total investment has been allocated to the farm sector for many years, agricultural output continues to be a disappointment to Soviet leaders. There are many reasons for this, but one overriding reason is that effective central supervision of an activity conducted over so vast a geographical area is virtually impossible. Another is that economic administration by fiat is singularly ill-suited to a sector where incentives to individual producers are a crucial determinant of output.

Natural gas has been a major Soviet success story. It will play a pivotal role in meeting the energy needs of the economy in the 1980s, particularly as a substitute for crude oil in industry and in home use but also as a potential hard-currency earner. The nuclear-power industry, although it has not met the full expectations of the leadership, has also done quite well. We estimate that the annual increase in nuclear-generated electricity will increase by about 17 percent a year during 1981–85 and supply about 11 percent of the country's electricity by the end of the period.

The development and production of some Soviet natural resources are proceeding at respectable rates, despite the obstacles of remote location and conditions that make extraction exceedingly difficult. The USSR is second only to South Africa in the production of gold. Production in 1981 was about 325 tons. Its stock of gold is about 1,900 tons, worth over $25 billion at current prices. Soviet production of platinum-group metals, nickel, and cobalt will jump sharply during the 1980s. Output of these resources will be adequate to meet domestic needs and also to provide increasing quantities for export. Prospects for the production of those resources located in more easily accessible regions look even better. Rich new deposits coming on stream in Kazakhstan and Georgia should generate sizeable increases in the production of both chromite and manganese.

Basic Weaknesses of the Economy

Soviet economic performance has been hurt in recent years by declining increments to the labor force and by the increasing difficulty of extracting and transporting vital energy and other raw material inputs. Because of lower birthrates in the 1960s, an increase in the number of workers reaching retirement age, and a rising mortality rate among males in the twenty-five to forty-four age range, increments to the working-age population have been declining since the mid-1970s. The falloff became particularly sharp starting in 1980, and increments will remain very low throughout this decade.

From 1971 to 1981, the working-age population increased by about 23 million. In 1981–91, it will increase by only about 4 million people. The decline in growth of the labor force — that is, of people actually employed — will be less, largely because of a rise in the share of the population in the twenty to thirty-nine age group, where labor-force participation rates are highest. But the decline in growth will still be substantial. The increment to the labor force in 1981–91 is expected to be only 9 million, compared with 19 million in 1971–81. With participation rates in the labor force already very high, there are few unemployed people to draw on to offset adverse demographic conditions.

Other factors will aggravate the labor shortage. Large-scale migration from the countryside to urban areas, formerly a rich source of labor supply to the rest of the economy, has slowed considerably in the past decade. The agricultural sector itself faces shortages of qualified manpower in most areas. This problem is compounded by the fact that rural residents in the Central Asian republics, where increments to the working-age population will be highest and where there is still substantial redundant labor, are reluctant to migrate.

Although the Soviet Union is blessed with enormous quantities of a large array of raw materials, these materials are increasingly inaccessible, and thus the cost of exploiting them has been rising sharply. This has been strikingly true of Soviet energy resources. Since the decline in production in the Volga-Urals oil fields in the mid-1970s growth in Soviet oil production has come from West Siberia, much of it from the giant Samotlor field. However, production in this field has probably peaked, compelling the Soviets to seek oil in even more remote and forbidding regions. In 1981–85, just to achieve the slowest growth rate planned in oil output since World War II will require greatly expanded drilling and pumping operations.

Decades of mining have depleted the underground coal mines of the European USSR. The Soviets must tunnel deeper shafts and mine thinner seams just to maintain coal output at current levels. During 1976–80, for example, more than 80 percent of new-mine output was needed to offset depletion at older underground operations. Even the extraction and distribution of natural gas has grown considerably more expensive. Natural-gas deposits in the old producing areas — North Caucasus, Transcaucasus, Ukraine, Volga-Urals, and western Turkmenistan — are severely depleted. More and more gas must be piped from

Central Asia and especially Tyumen oblast to replace exhausted local supplies. Such long-distance transmission of natural gas requires the construction of lengthy pipelines and many compressor stations, a very expensive operation.

Easily accessible supplies of many nonenergy raw materials have also been exhausted. The Soviets have largely depleted reserves of copper, nickel, and bauxite in the Ural Mountains and are beginning to tap deposits in northern Siberia or, in the case of bauxite, are exploiting nonbauxite ores and boosting imports. Similarly, the richest deposits of phosphate rocks in the Kola peninsula have been depleted, forcing the Soviets to move to lower-quality deposits in Siberia. In the case of iron ore, the Soviets have depleted their richest deposits in the western USSR. To compensate for declining ore grades, increasing amounts of investment must be devoted to ore-enriching facilities, raising both production costs and manpower requirements. The Soviets are also faced with the depletion of forests in the traditional logging areas of the northwestern USSR. Government planners have chosen to overcut these forest tracts beyond the point of natural regeneration so that, at least temporarily, the scale of operations in Siberia could be held down. But when loggers are forced to expand operations in Siberia — and the Far East — recovery costs will be high because of the distances involved, the harsh climate, and the lack of infrastructure.

The increase in fixed capital investment has also slowed markedly in recent years. This deceleration can be seen both as forced upon the leadership by shortages of key inputs and as a conscious policy choice. Growth was 7 percent a year in 1971–75, slowed to about 5 percent a year in 1976–78, and fell sharply to an average annual rate of only about 1.5 percent in 1979–80. Growth picked up in 1981 — fixed investment rising by 3 percent — but the Eleventh Five-Year Plan calls for investment in 1981–85 to rise by less than 2 percent a year. This is by far the lowest planned rate of increase in the post-World War II period. The rise from 1971–75 to 1976–80 was nearly 30 percent.

Because of tightening demographic, investment, and resource constraints, the traditional Soviet economic-growth formula of relying on a lavish use of labor, capital, and material inputs is no longer applicable. The Soviets themselves have long recognized the need for a new approach. For at least a decade they have been stressing the necessity of switching from an extensive to an intensive pattern of growth. This means essentially that growth must largely spring from productivity gains — from more efficient use of resources for any given level of technology and from faster technological progress. But the productivity of capital has actually been falling for several years, and labor productivity has been rising at steadily declining rates. For this, shortcomings in the Soviet system seem largely to blame.

The Soviet economic system is peculiarly ill-suited to promote efficiency and technological progress. Four features of the system help to explain why. First, economic planning and management are highly centralized, with resources allocated mainly by administrative fiat. Reforms aimed at increasing the degree of enterprise autonomy have generally come to naught. Indeed, central control over economic activity has been on the increase for the last several years, as indicated by an increase in the number of commodities that are allocated in physical terms according to central planning decisions. The arbitrary nature of central decisions on allocating inputs and assigning outputs, which is aggravated by the absence of prices that accurately reflect relative scarcities, precludes efficient planning.

Second, the goals the central authorities impose on the economy have generally been unrealistic. Faced with a gap between what they want to do and what is possible, Soviet leaders have tended to call for productivity gains and material savings that are beyond the system's capacity. The economy thus chronically operates under conditions of strain and shortage. With inputs regularly hard to come by, enterprises have a strong incentive to hoard. This intensifies bottlenecks and leads to more hoarding, in a depressing cycle of waste.

Third, overcentralization coupled with unrealistic planning has meant that the behavior of factory directors is largely dictated by the urgency of meeting the plan imposed by higher authorities. Fulfillment, however, is generally measured by multiple and often inconsistent "success indicators" of varying degrees of priority, such as physical volume of output, gross value of output, value added, material savings, and productivity. The principal drawback of this system is that managers often strive to meet the target even at the expense of what is economically rational from the standpoint of the central authorities and society as a whole. For example, if gross value of output is a prime goal, waste is encouraged, as managers seek to make their production as material-intensive as possible.

The Soviet Union is currently elevating value added in production to the position of the prime success indicator. Though probably less perverse a target than gross value of output, it, too, is subject to abuse. For example, it could induce managers to increase employment at a time of labor stringency.

Fourth, Soviet economic performance has long been impaired by the separation of research, development, and production into different organizations. Each organization operates according to different planning targets. Scientific research institutes do basic research and are paid for successful completion of research projects, whatever their practical benefit to the economy. Design bureaus develop the blueprints for new equipment and are largely rewarded for the successful testing of the prototype. Rewards are only loosely linked to successful incorporation of the new product into serial production.

Production plants, meanwhile, are rewarded for increasing both physical output and the value of output. The introduction of new products at a plant initially disrupts serial output, jeopardizing plan fulfillment and resulting rewards. The Soviets have no competitive marketplace to force both developer and producer to introduce better products and technologies. Indeed, hostility to technological change at the producer level is characteristic of the Soviet economy. Because of this division of labor and the system's rewards, Soviet products remain in production for an inordinately long time, new products frequently embody only minimal change, and the fruits of truly advanced research impact on serial production only with great delay. Over the last decade and a half, the Soviets have reorganized development and production establishments to deal with this problem. But the problem persists.

Historically, agriculture has been the economy's leading problem sector. Its performance in recent years has strengthened its claim to that dubious distinction. After peaking in 1978, farm output fell steadily through 1981, when it stood more than 10 percent below the 1978 level. In 1982, production rose but by only about 2 percent. The grain crop, which reached a record height of 237 million tons in 1978, has not reached 190 million tons in any subsequent year. In 1981 the grain harvest was so low that Moscow never announced a figure, although unofficial statements put the crop at 158 million tons. Production of meat — a key commodity in the regime's drive to better the Soviet standard of living — has also fared poorly. It reached 15.5 million tons in 1978 but has been below that level since, ranging from 15.0 to 15.3 million tons in the following four years.

Bad weather has been a major factor in the decline in agricultural production since 1978, but harsh weather and unfavorable geographical conditions constitute a permanent threat and obstacle to agriculture and only partly explain why Soviet efforts over the years to boost farm output have not yielded more dividends. Mishandling of the sector by the Soviet authorities has also had much to do with its disappointing performance. Management and planning processes are much too centralized. Farm efficiency is seriously handicapped by constant intervention of unqualified officials regarding what to plant, when to plant, when to harvest, and the like. Prices of both farm inputs and outputs set by the central authorities are encouraging an assortment of output that is inconsistent with the national plan. At a time when Moscow is striving to expand the output of meat, milk, and eggs, relative prices are such that farmers find it more profitable to concentrate on growing crops.

Though the investment in agriculture has been heavy — more than a quarter of total investment outlays has gone to the farm sector for many years — much of it has been misdirected. There has been too much emphasis on construction, not enough on equipment. Furthermore, the quality of farm machinery is low, with the incidence of breakdowns high. Deliveries to the agricultural sector of needed material inputs, such as fertilizers, have been insufficient, while the proportion of aged and unskilled workers in the farm labor force — which accounts for about 20 percent of the total labor force — is high. The regime has also failed to take maximum advantage of the potential of the private sector in agriculture, even in periods, such as the present, when it is encouraging expanded output there.

In recognition of the rising popular demand for quality food, Brezhnev told the Central Committee in late 1981 that food was the most important "political and economic problem" of the Eleventh Five-Year Plan. The increase in demand reflects rising consumer expectations and incomes. The inability to satisfy that demand is a function of both stagnant output of most livestock products and the regime's unwillingness — reinforced by Poland's experience — to raise prices in state stores. The leadership has attempted to ease the imbalance between supply and demand by allowing various local rationing schemes under which customers may purchase only limited amounts of certain foods in state stores. But long lines for meat, milk, and milk products remain widespread. To soften the impact of shortages on the work force, the regime has redirected substantial amounts of quality foods from public state retail outlets to special distribution outlets in factories and other economic enterprises.

Against this background, in May 1982 Brezhnev unveiled his Food Program — in preparation for a year and a half. The objective of the program was to boost Soviet food production and reduce dependence on imports — quickly. The Food Program attacks agriculture's problems from three directions. First it reorganizes the agricultural administration by creating commissions at all levels of government to coordinate agricultural operations and all related activities, ranging from sectors providing supplies to agriculture to the processing, distribution, and marketing of farm output.

Second, without significantly raising previous targets for total expenditures, the program seeks to redirect investment to weak links in the food-production chain. Investment in sectors producing machinery for agriculture is to rise sharply. To reduce waste, investment in on-farm food processing and storage facilities has been given top priority. More investment in rural housing and roads is scheduled to improve farm-to-market transport and stem the flow of younger workers to the cities. Upgrading the plant and equipment in food processing is another major target.

Third, financial incentives are to be raised. Prices paid by the state to farms for a large variety of agricultural products increased on 1 January 1983. At the same time, prices paid by the farms for equipment, fuel, and fertilizer were lowered.

For the most part, however, the Food Program represents relatively minor variations of old policies. One exception is the reorganization of agricultural administration, which — by increasing friction and confusion within the bureaucracy — is likely to cause more problems than it solves. The basic defect of the program lies in its omissions. It does nothing to reduce day-to-day bureaucratic interference in agriculture, and it does not do enough to restructure prices or to change the incentive system so that rewards are directly keyed to performance.

As recent meetings of the Communist Party Central Committee and the Supreme Soviet made clear, there are very serious problems in other sectors as well. The Soviet steel industry, for example, has become a major bottleneck. Shortages of steel, especially high-quality products, are holding back the growth of civilian machine building and other priority sectors of the civilian economy. The appetite of the Soviet economy for steel is probably unparalleled — and a reflection of its relative technological backwardness. In 1981 the USSR with little more than half the GNP of the United States used 103 million metric tons of rolled steel products, compared with United States consumption of 94 million tons. The shortages of steel will not be remedied quickly. Investment requirements to cope with the declining quality of ore are escalating rapidly, and new capacity requires long gestation periods before it can be brought on stream. In addition, supplies of coking coal and iron ore are likely to continue to be tight in the next several years.

Transportation is another sector responsible for recent poor economic performance. Snarls on the railroads — the backbone of the system — have disrupted economic activity across the board but most particularly in the delivery of raw materials, such as coal, iron ore, timber, scrap metal, and chemical fertilizer. The Soviet economy requires a large volume of transport services, not only because of its size and complexity but also because the country's resources and people are spread widely over a very large land mass. Compared with North America and Europe, the USSR is poorly served by year-round water transport, and government policy has held back the development of an adequate highway system. The brunt of the transport burden, therefore, has fallen to the railroads. The railroads, however, appear to have reached their capacity ceiling with present technology and facilities. Consequently, the transportation sector will find it difficult to support economic growth through the next several years at least.

In the energy field the leadership faces rather different problems in the coal and oil industries. Coal production, which dropped during 1979–81, has been hampered by deteriorating underground mining conditions at larger, established mines, by shortages of labor and declining labor productivity, and by insufficient capital investment. Oil production continues to increase, though slowly. Even the very small growth of the last few years has required an enormous effort.

Finally, shortages of raw materials and the depletion of fuel and power supplies have caused a marked slowdown in the production of construction materials. Current output, for example, increased by less than 2.0 percent annually during 1976–80, compared with nearly 5.5 percent annually in the preceding five-year period. Shortfalls in the production of cement, roofing materials, construction resources, and wall materials have restricted construction activity throughout the economy.

As emphasized earlier, the Soviet economy does not depend on trade for survival. Total imports equal about 12 or 13 pecent of GNP, those from the West only about 5 percent. But, because of the difficulties just enumerated, the elimination or easing of critical bottlenecks and the achievement of key elements in Soviet development plans are closely tied to imports from the West.

The USSR will have to import a broad range of Western oil and gas equipment if it is to minimize the fall in production in fields where depletion is at an advanced stage, to increase output elsewhere, and to help locate and develop reserves. Pipelaying equipment capable of handling large-diameter pipe is produced only in the West, and we estimate that the Soviets will need to import at least 15 to 20 million tons of steel pipe during the remainder of the 1980s to build the pipelines they have scheduled. They will also continue to need sophisticated exploration equipment, high-capacity submersible pumps for the oil fields, and probably high-powered turbines for gas compressor stations.

Soviet requirements for quality steel should result in annual imports of steel other than pipe of about $2 billion (current prices) at least until the mid-1980s. Imports of chemical equipment and technology will probably continue to be large, reflecting the still antiquated character of some parts of the chemical industry and the importance of the industry for agricultural production. Imports of grain and other agricultural commodities have soared in recent years and almost certainly will remain high. Grain purchases in 1979–82 averaged more than 30 million tons a year.

The USSR's ability to earn the hard currency it needs to pay for its Western imports, however, is already under pressure and may well diminish in the future. The main reason is the leveling off and possible decline in Soviet oil production. Because domestic consumption will continue to rise and because of ongoing demands from Eastern Europe, we expect oil exports to the West—which account for about half of Soviet hard-currency merchandise export earnings—to fall. According to our projections, the rise in hard-currency earnings from stepped-up exports of natural gas will only partially offset the anticipated decrease in receipts from oil.

Other factors have also restricted Soviet hard-currency earning capacity. Primarily because of the softening of energy prices, Soviet terms of trade vis-à-vis the West will be less favorable in the 1980s than they were in the 1970s, when upward-spiraling oil and gold prices brought the USSR windfall gains. In addition, demand for Soviet raw materials will be weak if Western economic activity fails to pick up. Soviet manufactured goods, which are generally not competitive in Western markets, are unlikely to take up the slack. Finally, less-developed countries, including members of OPEC, will probably be less able to pay cash for Soviet arms.

The Soviet capacity to buy from the West is of course backstopped by the USSR's huge stock of gold. But the USSR is reluctant to undertake massive sales of gold in an uncertain market, because of the downward pressure that Soviet sales exert on prices. On balance, the unpromising export outlook suggests that the USSR may have to make do with little if any increase in real imports in the 1980s.

The USSR's relations with Eastern Europe add another dimension of strain. Because it wishes to maintain political and social stability in Eastern Europe, the Soviet Union has given favorable economic treatment to five of the six Warsaw Pact countries—Czechoslovakia, East Germany, Bulgaria, Poland, and Hungary. The exception has been Romania.

This special treatment, or "assistance," has taken two basic forms: subsidization and credits. Subsidies have not been given directly; they have been extended through preferential terms of trade. That is, Eastern Europe's terms of trade vis-à-vis the Soviet Union are more advantageous than those that would prevail if Eastern Europe conducted that same trade with the noncommunist world. In essence, the USSR sells energy, mainly oil, and other raw materials to Eastern Europe for less than world market prices and pays more than world prices for the manufactured goods it buys from Eastern Europe.

Estimates of the cost to the Soviet Union of giving preferential terms of trade to Eastern Europe are rough — and controversial. According to the highest Western estimate we know of, these subsidies totaled almost $70 billion in 1960–80, with about 90 percent of this amount accumulating after 1974. The huge jump implicit in subsidies reflects the explosion in world oil prices in 1973–80 and the large rise in opportunity costs to the USSR of its oil exports to Eastern Europe. The credits come mainly from the trade surpluses the USSR has consistently run vis-à-vis Eastern Europe since the mid-1970s, although the Soviet Union has also given some direct hard-currency assistance to Poland.

Eastern Europe, battling severe economic problems of its own, continues to depend on Soviet assistance. But economic stringencies in the USSR have greatly increased the cost to the Soviets of aiding Eastern Europe. The USSR has apparently decided to give reduced priority to Eastern Europe's economic needs in the future. Soviet oil exports to Eastern Europe were cut in 1982, and the USSR's trade surplus with the area apparently declined. Soviet subsidies will probably fall too. But a drastic cut in exports of raw materials and in trade credits and subsidies is unlikely.

Uncertainties Attached to the Growth Forecast

Andropov's and subsequently Chernenko's advents to power have not altered our assessment of Soviet economic prospects, because the exogenous factors impeding economic growth are not affected by changes in leadership. Major policy changes could lie ahead. For this reason — and for reasons unrelated to leadership changes — our forecast of average annual growth in real GNP of 1 to 2 percent could be off the mark. Growth could be more rapid, for example:

• If the USSR enjoyed a run of good luck with the weather, leading to a succession of good harvests.

• If the new leadership were willing to undertake a substantial reallocation of resources from defense to investment.

• If the new regime could somehow, perhaps by diverting resources from defense to consumption, improve morale and labor productivity.

• Above all, if efficiency could be boosted by mitigating some of the most damaging features of the existing system. Productivity might be raised, for example, without a drastic overhaul of the system through a more balanced allocation of investment to end the neglect of such vital sectors as transport and by stopping the proliferation of success indicators and of overlapping lines of authority that has characterized the "reforms" of past years.

• If Chernenko — his rule securely established — undertook basic changes that significantly reduced centralization and gave substantially greater play to market forces, the prospects would be even better. Such a reform, however, would be constrained by the imperatives of maintaining political control in a large multinational society. Furthermore, attempts to implement reform would encounter stubborn noncompliance by party and economic bureaucrats.

Growth could be less rapid, for example:

• If the bad weather of the last few years continued, causing a permanent depression in agricultural output. In any case, there is a theory, substantiated by evidence, that the generally favorable weather that prevailed between the early 1960s and mid-1970s was an aberration. Although the weather for crops in the past several years was surely worse than any long-run average, a return to the pre-1975 conditions is unlikely.

• If the new leadership decided to accelerate the growth in defense spending at the expense of investment.

• If the ripple effect of current bottlenecks intensified.

• If public cynicism and apathy deepened markedly or active unrest developed.

Of these possibilities, serious widespread unrest — as the Polish experience suggests — is the one most likely to hit aggregate output the hardest. However, we consider such an eventuality unlikely. It would probably require a steep and prolonged drop in living standards in the first instance. Large-scale labor disturbances might also occur if Chernenko pursued with excessive zeal a campaign to impose greater discipline in the workplace. And, on his record, Chernenko is less likely than Andropov to pursue such a campaign.

Conclusion

Soviet economic growth has slowed markedly in recent years. The slowdown partly reflects declining increments to the supply of labor and the stock of capital and sharply increased costs in producing and transporting vital energy and raw materials. But it also stems from the inability of the system to offset these constraints by bringing about substantial increases in efficiency and productivity. Indeed, economic growth has sharply decelerated even before the labor and energy shortages have reached their maximum severity.

Two consequences of the slowdown are (1) much harder choices for the leadership in allocating resources to consumption, investment, and defense and (2) further invalidation of the USSR's claim that its economy is an appropriate model for the rest of the world, particularly the Third World. In spite of its disappointing performance, however, the Soviet economy is not going to collapse. Indeed, we expect GNP to continue to grow, although slowly. Furthermore, so far, defense spending continues to rise.

Postscript

Economic performance in 1983 was around 4 percent GNP growth — better than it was in 1982. The improved weather not only helped agriculture but also eased transportation bottlenecks. The Andropov campaign for tighter discipline may also have played a role, but its effect is likely to be transient. The performance in 1983 does not provide enough evidence to warrant a change in the above forecast of continued very slow economic growth.

Managing the Soviet Economy: Alternative Models

JOSEPH S. BERLINER

In July 1979, the Soviet party and government issued a decree announcing a variety of changes in what is now called the "economic mechanism."[1] The decree evoked a flurry of interest at the time, but public attention soon turned to other things. There are two lessons in the incident. First, the process of modifying the system of planning and management has become routinized. The public has become used to the periodic announcement, usually in advance of the next five-year planning period, of a series of changes that had been agreed upon since the last such decree. Second, the changes are mostly technical rather than fundamental, involving such matters as new success indicators or revised planning procedures.

The capacity of the system to review its methods of operation periodically and to seek ways of improving them must be regarded as one of its strengths. There is a view abroad, however, that the range of alternatives that have been considered, at least in public discussions, has been too narrow to score a significant advance. The deaths of Leonid Brezhnev and Yuri Andropov and the accession of Konstantin Chernenko now raise the possibility that the range of discussable alternatives may widen. The objective of this essay is to explore the wider range of alternative systems of planning and management that may be considered as the next two decades unfold.

Four models span the range of the alternatives that may realistically be considered for adoption—the "conservative," the "reactionary," the "radical," and the "liberal" models. The "conservative" model consists of the present system projected into the future with minor modifications. The "reactionary" model may be thought of as Stalinism politically modernized—i.e., Stalinism without Stalin. The "radical" model consists of various elements of the "Yugarian" (Yugo-

This essay is adapted from the author's chapter "Planning and Management" in *The Soviet Economy: Toward the Year 2000*, ed. Abram Bergson and Herbert S. Levine, published in 1983, with the permission of Allen & Unwin, Fifty Cross Street, Winchester, Massachusetts 01890.

slav-Hungarian) experience suitably adapted to Soviet conditions. The "liberal" model — a system neither as timid as the "conservative" nor as bold as the "radical" model — may be thought of as a new version of the NEP (New Economic Policy) of the 1920s.

This essay will focus on the most likely of these alternatives — the "conservative" model — concentrating on the economic outcomes that may be expected from its adoption. A conclusion will consider the alignment of political forces in the USSR as it bears on the relative political acceptability of the economic alternatives. And a brief postscript will comment on Andropov's legacy.

The "Conservative" Model

The status quo rarely has passionate supporters — passions normally run on the side of change. Support for the status quo is usually based on a lack of conviction that the untried alternatives will produce a better future than the present. That is likely to be the case if the "conservative" model is chosen as the basis of the future system of planning and management in the USSR. It is doubtful that many people, even among the system's governors, regard the present structure as having great merit in its own right. That was not the case two decades ago, when Soviet economists certainly, and political leaders probably, looked over the world of economic systems and pronounced their own as exceptionally good. Today, the system may still command strong support, but very likely in the Churchillian vein, as a rather bad system "except for all the others."

The "conservative" model would retain all the basic structural features of the present system but should not be thought of as totally rigid. Though the commitment to central planning as the basis of the economic mechanism would remain firm, the recent history of Soviet reforms suggests continued efforts in the future to find better ways of dealing with old problems. Certainly, the planning system will be continually changed by the incorporation of new techniques of central planning. Extrapolating from the past, planning may become more detailed, and with the growth of electronic-data-processing capacity, the number of material balances is likely to increase, although the mounting complexity of the plan-making process may eventually lead to planning of a more aggregate nature. Beyond that, each analyst is free to predict efforts to change whatever he sees as the principal sources of inefficiency in the Soviet economy.

Many of the production associations will likely be dismantled after a period of time, in favor of a system containing a broader mix of large and small enterprises. Even before the production associations, the size structure of enterprises in the USSR was strongly skewed toward large enterprises, compared with the size structure in the technologically advanced capitalist countries. With respect to efficiency and certainly to innovation, there must be some range of activities in which there are diseconomies of scale. There are also likely to be further changes in such perennials as the success indicators for enterprise managers. The indicator newly introduced in the July 1979 planning decree — normative net output—may well prove to be exceedingly costly to administer and is likely to bias decisions excessively in favor of labor-intensive choices in a period of tight labor supply. There may be some renewed interest in profit as a more general success indicator, but the pathological antagonism to the enterprise's appropriations of unearned economic rents will stand in the way; large profits in particular seem to be regarded as prima facie evidence that they were unearned. There may be new experiments in the use of contractual relations, as well as new efforts to reallocate labor among enterprises by various incentive devices. Recent sharp increases in the prices of gasoline and other products suggest that price policy may be called upon more often to ration scarce commodities. Price revisions every few years would continue to keep relative prices from diverging excessively from average branch costs, and there may be some further incorporation of scarcity pricing into the price structure.

Certainly, there would be new measures designed to promote technological progress and the quality of production. Some would attempt to make use of "economic levers" through new forms of incentive payments. But most would consist of "administrative measures"—changing the structure of authority, holding more people responsible for the completion of assigned tasks, and levying penalties for not meeting quality standards.

To accept the "conservative" model is to give up the goal of attaining the technological level of the leading industrial countries. (It is fairly well established that whatever the merits of the Soviet economic mechanism, the promotion of technological advance is not one of them.) But the Soviet leadership ought to be able to accept such an outcome. There is no reason why the USSR cannot maintain a position that lags permanently behind that of the technological leaders in world industry by, say, an average of five years. There would be some loss in productivity because of delayed innovation, but that loss would be offset to some degree by savings in research and development (R&D) expenditures, as well as in the costs of learning-by-doing that the country pioneering in any new development must bear. It would be a reasonable strategy for the Soviets to wait until each new major breakthrough is announced elsewhere and then to proceed to develop their own version on the basis of whatever information can be perused, purchased, or purloined. After all, it is an axiom in the R&D community that the most valuable piece of information in technological advance is the information that a certain result has been successfully accomplished by somebody. The strategy of waiting until the results have been accomplished elsewhere is not only cost-saving but is also appealing to R&D people operating in a risk-averse bureaucracy. Moreover, the Soviets, have shown that technological excellence can continue to be maintained in a few priority areas deemed crucial for defense or other national purposes.

Since the "conservative" model involves no significant changes from the past, the past can serve as a guide to the economic outcomes to be expected from its continued operation. There is little reason to expect any discontinuous increase either in static efficiency or in the rate of growth. None of the major reforms of the past has succeeded in achieving the longed-for quantum leap in efficiency. Indeed, the term *reform* has disappeared from public discussion and has been replaced by the expression "improving the operation of the economic mechanism."

This evaporation of the spirit of reform may reflect the view that the system of central planning and management has now reached the practical limit of its perfectability. An economic system is like a technological innovation. When first invented, a steam engine or an internal combustion machine represents a major advance over its predecessor, but it is a very ineffecient mechanism in terms of its own potential. In the course of time, its efficiency increases, very rapidly at first and more slowly thereafter, with successive waves of "reforms" or "improvements." Eventually, it attains a degree of efficiency that can be regarded as the effective maximum that is realistically attainable within the limits of its basic conception.

The same may apply to the invention of central economic planning as an economic mechanism by the Soviet leadership in the 1930s. Over time, it became an increasingly efficient mechanism, but like all inventions, the possibilities of improvement within the basic paradigm may have been largely exhausted — in this case by the 1960s. It should be noted that the economic mechanism was designed during a period in which the strategy of economic progress consisted of what was later described as "extensive growth." It is perhaps still a reasonably successful model for that purpose. The problem is that the conditions within which the economy operates today are not such as to generate high rates of extensive growth. Three percent a year more or less may be the most that can be expected of an economy designed according to that model.

This judgment may, of course, be too pessimistic. A future government may yet find ways of extending the frontier of the model's possibilities: through the creation of enterprises specializing in production for export, correction of those relative prices that create perverse incentives in agriculture, or granting greater autonomy to small-scale production units within the collective farms. Without abandoning the "conservative" model, the leadership might extend its limits by adopting some of the features of the other models. While a bold move in such a direction might prove that the "conservative" model contains greater potential than its recent record reveals, the history of the post-Stalin reforms does not offer great encouragement.[2] Individual changes in prices and in organizational structures that made good sense in themselves have not produced the desired results, because they clashed with the imperatives imposed by the dominating structures of central planning and management.

If the "conservative" model fails to improve on the results of the recent past, the leadership can muddle through with small variations on old themes only if the rate of growth ceases to decline and eventually stabilizes. A constant rate of growth, even if very low, would constitute a chronic condition; such conditions ordinarily do not lead to disruption. Acute problems, such as an uninterrupted decline, ultimately lead to disruption.

We cannot judge what the minimally acceptable annual rate of income growth is – 3 percent, 2 percent, or 1 percent per capita. However, it is safe to say that it is likely to depend primarily on the consumption level. A threshold level of consumption may be defined in political terms, as the level below which dissatisfaction would result in outbursts of disorder that would strain the authorities' instruments of political control.

It would be an error for the leadership to believe, however, that there is no danger as long as consumption levels exceeded that political threshold. For there is another threshold at which the economy would begin to suffer from an erosion of incentives. If that "incentives threshold," which must be higher than the "political threshold," is crossed, then it will prove to be impossible to maintain even a low level of stable growth. Output and consumption would reciprocally push each other lower until the political threshold were reached. Hence, the key to the question of whether slow growth will turn from chronic to acute depends on whether the rate of growth can be stabilized at a level sufficiently high to maintain consumption above the incentive threshold.

The Soviet leadership may have some notion of the range within which the incentive threshold lies, but outside analysts can do little more than guess. Gertrude Schroeder Greenslade believes – probably correctly – that a steady increase in per capita consumption of 1 to 2 percent a year would "provide consumers with a sense of forward motion."[3] Under the baseline projection of the SOVMOD input-output model of the Soviet economy at the Stanford Research Institute/Wharton Econometric Forecasting Associates, Soviet GNP would grow at 3.1 percent and consumption per capita at 1.2 percent a year through the end of the century. With a bit of luck, that outcome should keep the economy above the incentives threshold. Under SOVMOD's low-productivity scenario, however, GNP grows at 2.1 percent and consumption per capita at only 0.5 percent. At such a rate, it is conceivable that an erosion of incentives would preclude the stabilization of the growth rate and that consumption would decline to the perilous level of the political threshold.

There is a fair chance that the Soviet economy can stabilize at the levels of the baseline projection. The long period of declining growth that it has been experiencing may presage continued decline in the future, but it need not. It may signify instead that the economy has been readjusting from the high growth rates of the past to a new level of low but stable growth rates in the future. If so, poor performance in static efficiency or in technological progress need not compel abandonment of the "conservative" model as long as consumption does not fall below the incentive threshold.

Political Issues

When the choice is finally made, the economic prospects under the various models will no doubt enter into consideration. But it is politics and not economics that will dictate the choice in the end. The "conservative" model clashes the least with the interests that have become vested in the inherited institutions, and it is therefore the most likely to prevail unless one of two conditions obtains. The first is that the rate of growth fails to stabilize at or above the incentive threshold. The second is that succession politics produces a new and younger leader who either (1) develops a power base strong enough to force through a change over the opposition of major vested interests, or (2) wins the support of a major social group for change. No one knows whether either of these conditions will obtain, but perhaps it is worth exploring which of the alternative models might enlist significant political suppport.

The strongest support can probably be marshaled in favor of the "reactionary" model. This model would do the least violence to the interests of groups most closely tied to the regime — central and enterprise managers, the party apparat, and the military. (They might, to be sure, find privileges such as private shops somewhat more restricted.) It would appeal to ideological purists, if such still exist in the USSR. More important, it might seem to satisfy a longing among large sectors of society for the "blessed" Stalinist times, when "there was a rigid discipline in the country, when there were no difficulties, for example, with labor power."[4] The ordinary workingperson is not likely to be particularly affected by a crackdown on corruption and speculators, and is probably favorably disposed toward a policy combining a strong law-and-order stance with xenophobia, nationalism, anti-Semitism, and anti-intellectualism. The tightening of labor discipline might conceivably be palatable to workers if it is presented as part of a great new national campaign, perhaps even combined with a program to raise levels of popular consumption. In the short run, an imaginative leadership could probably make it succeed, although it is more problematic in the longer run.

The "radical" model, by contrast, runs counter to the interests of all the main groups supporting the traditional regime. Central bureaucrats would be out of jobs, as would that large portion of existing managers who would prove incapable of coping in a decentralized, market-type environment. Workers would have to be given assurances regarding job security, which would undermine one of the major areas of potential productivity gains under a "radical" reform. Only the national minorities, a few economists, and perhaps a smattering of the liberal intelligentsia are likely to support such a model, unless perhaps it included extensive decentralization of agriculture as well.

If that conclusion is correct, it raises the interesting question of why the "radical" model enjoyed such support in Czechoslovakia in 1968 and continues to enjoy it in Hungary today. The difference may be that in Eastern Europe the system of central planning is identified with rigid party orthodoxy and, ultimately, with Russian domination. In the USSR, however, the "radical" model will be adopted only if the small band of market-minded economists somehow get the ear of a new leader and convince him of its advantages — not an easy task, indeed, in light of the modest success of the Hungarian reform. Even then, the leader would have no major powerful group on whose strong support he could count, and he would have to concentrate in his hands the power of a Stalin in order to carry out that reform. But Stalins do not decentralize.

It should now be evident why the "liberal" model would command greater support than the "radical." No one loses one's job. It would win the leadership the support of the new private sector and also provide a sharp improvement in the quality of life for the average consumer, sharp enough to leave no doubt about the success of the policies or the person to whom the credit is due. Ideologically, a neo-NEP policy could be identified with Lenin himself. In dialectical terms, it could be represented as a new synthesis, appropriate to the historical stage of mature socialism, in which the social task is that of generating new technologies rather than of adopting existing ones.

In conclusion, the prospects for change depend on the performance of the "conservative" model. If growth stabilizes above the incentive threshold, that model is likely to be retained and the Soviet economy will limp on to the end of the century. Chronic cases do not normally evoke extreme measures. But if growth falls below the incentive threshold, accumulated social and political pressures will propel the leadership toward either the "reactionary" or the "liberal" model. The greater economic potential lies with the latter, but if the counsels of political prudence prevail, the lot will fall to the former.

Postscript

Yuri Andropov's brief incumbency will be remembered for two economic initiatives. An experiment was launched to test the possibility of increasing the autonomy of enterprises at the expense of the ministry's authority. The experiment is strikingly similar to the 1965 Economic Reform and is well within the tradition of the "conservative" model. The campaign against corruption and violations of labor discipline appeared to be a tilt toward the "reactionary" model, but it was relatively mild by historical Soviet standards and is well within the limits to which a conservative government might go.

Had Andropov's health not failed, it is possible that he might have moved further in a reactionary direction. There is evidence, on the other hand, that his government was entertaining the possibility of further reducing the authority of ministries, which would have involved some degree of decentralization. The measures under consideration, however, did not extend so far as to modify the system of central economic planning in the ways that would constitute a "liberal" or "radical" reform. Konstantin Chernenko's government has not yet announced any initiatives from which his inclination might be assessed.

Notes

1. *Pravda*, 29 July 1979, trans. in *Current Digest of the Soviet Press*, 22 Aug. 1979, 1–6, 14.
2. A much fuller discussion of the central themes of this essay, including an analysis of the post-

Stalin economic reforms can be found in the author's chapter "Planning and Management," in *The Soviet Economy: Toward the Year 2000*, ed. Abram Bergson and Herbert S. Levine (London, Boston, and Sydney: George Allen & Unwin), 1983.

3. See her contribution to Bergson and Levine.

4. Aron Katsenelenboigen, *Studies in Soviet Economic Planning* (White Plains: M. E. Sharpe, 1978), 57.

Legal Policy in the Soviet Union

JOHN N. HAZARD

Communists look upon law as an instrument of politics, as a means of forming a new society. Lenin crystallized this thinking even before the Russian Revolution with his often-quoted dictum "Law is a political instrument, it is politics." That is, law must lead society toward politically determined ends. It cannot be limited to establishing formal order on the basis of codification of traditional social practices.

Lenin did not advocate legal structures that were unresponsive to social pressures. He recognized that pressures are sometimes too great to be resisted. Yet, as he saw it — and his successors have followed his lead — a retreat is tolerable if forward movement is resumed as soon as the state is strong enough to enforce its leaders' will. He demonstrated his techniques in 1921 when he abandoned the pressure politics of "War Communism" and introduced his "New Economic Policy" (NEP), designed to stimulate private investment. He did not live to guide Soviet society back to his preferred road, but in 1928 his successors returned to what they thought was a direct route to communism.

The NEP was taxed out of existence, and state economic planning of industry and agriculture was introduced. State enterprises began everywhere to produce, distribute, and transport industrial goods. Collective farms were organized as the preferred form of agriculture to replace the individual family farms. Wealthy peasants were ordered "liquidated as a class," and a Model Collective Farm Charter was published in 1930 to stabilize the structure of agricultural production.

Although the advance resumed in 1928, some of the legal creations of the NEP were retained in the law. The most prominent of these was the Civil Code of 1922, which encouraged foreign and domestic capitalists to invest in the reconstruction of the economy devastated by the revolution and ensuing civil war. The content of the code, however, changed somewhat after 1928. Its chapters on private corporations and partnerships had become dead letters with the end of NEP. Nevertheless, it remained a civil code similar to the Romanist codes of Europe. This was remarkable to some philosophers who, following

Marx, had expected that law would wither away in a society in which antagonistic classes no longer struggled with each other in social relationships.

On the contrary, property rights continued to be recognized, although not in means of production, and these required legal norms for definition and protection. There was even a continuing law of inheritance — although socialists had long considered inheritance to be unearned income, which they abhorred. The code's provisions on property relationships had become of continuing necessity by 1930, when Stalin concluded that citizens would not produce their best efforts without material incentives. This decision spelled the end of egalitarianism, which socialists had previously heralded as one of their basic concepts, and it justified the law of inheritance as an extension of the fruits of labor to the next generation.

Perhaps it may be argued that Soviet inheritance laws differ from inheritance laws under capitalism in that the amount of property passed from one generation to the next is limited, because no one may own the means of production — except for hand tools. Further, the property passed to an heir is the result of the testator's own toil. It cannot be the accumulation of generations of entrepreneurs. In spite of these arguments, it has to be acknowledged that the heritage of NEP remains in Soviet law, although it stands alongside norms that are new and designed to mold society into the declared image of socialism.

Underproduction as a Problem

Soviet jurists within the Communist party are currently implementing the USSR Constitution of 1977, which established the broad outlines of what is called "developed socialism." The jurists' task is to identify the problems that law might help solve and the opportunities it might present to a leadership intent upon expanding the gross national product and creating a new type of citizen to be called the "Soviet man."

The problems of underproduction in the industrial and agricultural institutions are thought to be significant. Blame is laid on enterprise structures and also on the individual worker and farmer. The approach proposed by the generalists of the Politburo of the Communist party is multifaceted: (1) restructuring industrial and agricultural institutions so as to facilitate seizure of opportunities to incorporate science and technology into production; (2) strengthening labor discipline to ensure hard work and honesty in handling state property; and (3) stimulating enhanced production through the introduction of increased material incentives.

The revision of structures is, perhaps, receiving the most attention because Soviet policymakers have always been confident that there is a structure that will maximize production if only it can be found. With such a faith, it is well worth the time and trouble to search for it in the research institutes where economists, jurists, and administrators work side by side.

The Parameters of Research

Research in the determination of appropriate production structures does have certain parameters. Although pragmatism has played a part in the formulation of remedial programs throughout Soviet history, the range of choices has been narrowed since 1928. No longer is it conceivable that Communist party leaders would propose to legal draftsmen that they reinstitute in the Civil Code the chapters establishing the norms to be observed in the re-creation of various types of institutions suited to a private enterprise economy.

"Developed socialism," which the Communist party has proudly proclaimed to be constructing since 1967, cannot provide through law the measures of retreat comparable to those of the NEP of the 1920s. The Rubicon was crossed in 1936 when the second constitution heralded the achievement of socialism and prohibited the employment of labor for private profit. Since then, the only private enterprise is the economically insignificant workshop of the individual artisan. Even a lone artisan must obtain a license under the Treasury's regulations and pay a discriminatory tax under the income-tax law.

As a consequence of this doctrinal position, which has its source in the *Communist Manifesto* of 1848, increased productivity may be sought in only two ways: (1) by rearranging the structures of state industrial enterprises and revising the charters of collective and state farms, and (2) by motivating workers in factories or on farms through restructured wage and bonus policies and labor laws that punish loafers. Capitalism is not an alternative.

In keeping with this doctrinal imperative, the choice open to legal draftsmen can lie only within the parameters of the state and cooperative ownership system. Even to suggest a solution through means outside the currently acceptable boundaries may result in prosecution or in the loss of momentum in personal advancement, if the proposer persists in his suggestions. It is difficult to distinguish the line between permissible, constructive criticism and criticism believed to be destructive and subject to prosecution. The Criminal Code of 1958 offered one basis for prosecution, although it was limited to speech designed to overthrow or weaken Soviet authority. While this provision is vague and requires proof of intent, there is little doubt that a sustained attack on social or economic structures will be interpreted as a political weapon.

Because of the need to prove intent—even though circumstantially—under the basic provision, the code was amended in 1961 to penalize speech if the court finds that the author uttered "falsehoods which do in fact harm the Soviet state and social structures," even though no intention to overthrow or weaken was in the speaker's mind.

A number of judicial decisions have indicated that courts have punished persons whom the West calls "dissidents" under this article, even though their criticism of the Soviet system would not seem excessively harmful to a Western mind. Yuri Andropov, who was general secretary of the Communist party, expressed the party's frustration with critics, in 1983:

Regrettably, there are still among us persons who are trying to counterpose their own selfish interests to those of society, of all of its members. In this light it becomes clearly necessary to carry out considerable work in order to educate — sometimes even to re-educate — certain persons, to combat encroachments upon socialist law and order, upon the norms of collective life. This, however, is a far cry from the "flouting of human rights" on which bourgeois propaganda so enjoys hypocritically to speculate, but [constitutes] real humanism and democracy, which stand for self government according to the will of the majority, in the interests of all working people.

Whatever a Westerner may think of the characterization of the Communist party as expressing the will of the majority, the statement indicates that wide criticism beyond present parameters will continue to be unacceptable in the foreseeable future.

The Political Parameters

The limitations on choice, as established by law, extend to the political sphere. In the 1977 Constitution of the USSR, the already existing monopoly role of the small core of the population that is the Communist party was restated in even clearer terms than those used in the Constitution of 1936. The monopoly position could be read obliquely into the 1936 Constitution in the article on the right of association, which stated only that "the most active and politically conscious citizens in the ranks of the working class, working peasants and working intelligentsia" could associate in the Communist party. In practice this most active group is only one-ninth of the adult population. Its majority representation is attributed not to its numbers but to the masses for which it claims to speak.

Although the 1977 Constitution established no limitations on the formation of other political-action groups that could become the basis of a pluralistic political system — even one in which all groups are committed, like the communists, to socialism — since 1918 organized political activity has been limited to the communists, defined as "the leading and guiding force in Soviet society and the nucleus of its political system, of all state and public organizations."

In view of what has been established by law and practice, it is evident that unassailable doctrine excludes economic and political alternatives to the present system. Neither capitalism nor a multiparty political system will be countenanced. Permissible alternatives, however, may be considered. There are still choices to be made, and they are needed. The state economy is admittedly less productive than the generalists of the party can tolerate. Stagnation is inadmissible, and Andropov especially called on his colleagues to innovate within the Marxist parameters, saying that mouthing century-old quotations is not the answer. In his speech to the Supreme Soviet at the end of 1983, he listed examples of mismanagement and lack of labor discipline and urged his colleagues to innovate. Law is expected to play its part in restructuring economic institutions and enforcing discipline.

Restructuring Industry

Restructuring the economic institutions developed during the Brezhnev era has been minimal. Brezhnev's contribution to structural reform was a system of "combines" comparable in some measure to the conglomerates in the United States. His innovation in 1973 was designed to foster decisions relating to operations near the production level, while retaining the centralized decision making on economic plans that had become the hallmark of Stalin's concept of socialist administration. While the "combine" structures have been criticized since Brezhnev's death in 1982, they have been left unchanged.

Party officials have demonstrated that they disagree over where the balance between centralism and localism should be placed. Andropov pressed for increased responsibility below the "combines," that is, on the enterprise directors who are currently subordinate to "combine" directors. Some Western specialists think this means that the days of the "combines" are numbered and that economic structures resembling those favored by Aleksei Kosygin in his reform of 1965 may be restored. At that time, the emphasis was on increased authority for the enterprise directors who presided over institutions at the operating level that were structured legally as self-contained public corporations. To the reformers of 1973 this structure fractionalized decision making so much that the economies of scale were lost. There was too much duplication of supporting services, and, more important, directors showed little initiative in introducing new technologies. Andropov seemed to appreciate that there were shortcomings in Kosygin's approach and to want something less than enterprise autonomy, but at the same time he noted the overcentralization that resulted from the 1973 reforms.

Andropov met with opposition. The chairman of the State Planning Commission, soon after his superior made his remarks, attempted to explain them away by arguing that the strength of the Soviet economic system remains in its centralized planning structure. Evidently, he spoke for the entrenched bureaucracy, and to a degree he had economic viability on his side. Although science and technology must be incorporated into the industrial apparatus, plant directors cannot be expected to have contacts with scientific and technological sources all over the world. These sources have been and in the near future will probably continue to be available only to the officials of ministries and to the specialists in the State Committee on Science and Technology.

Further, even if enterprise directors could establish such contacts, they might — and indeed they have demonstrated in the past that they would — be reluctant to dismantle established production lines in order to introduce new technology. A changeover would inevitably result in a temporary loss of production, which might become permanent if the new technology failed to perform as expected. This would mean criticism from above, a loss of prestige, and a loss of bonuses for high production. To a plant manager the career implications would be threatening.

Soviet jurists have a role in any pending reform because the Institute of State and Law of the USSR Academy of Sciences has long had the responsibility of taking the lead along with economists and administrative specialists in suggesting innovations in the industrial ministerial apparatus. It is likely that legislative reform to meet production deficiencies is even now in progress, and choices within the permissible parameters are being made.

The Collective Farms

Close behind industrial productivity comes agricultural productivity. Structures designed to foster high agricultural yields have been in transition since Stalin's death. In a sense, agriculture has been an Achilles' heel because productivity has been low; but low rates were acceptable during the early 1930s when a major purpose of collectivization — perhaps the major purpose — was to use the collective farm as a "transmission belt to socialism." Stalin saw the farm as a means of bringing the peasantry to a point where they would work together rather than as individual families. Once his political aim was achieved, and this goal was reached about 1935 when the second model charter for the collective farms was promulgated as law, attention was given to production. Collective farms did not stand alone in agriculture. Stalin preferred the so-called state farms, which were organized like industrial enterprises. Yet not until November 1952 did he indicate his plan to convert the collective farms into state farms as the preferred institution of socialism in its developed form.

After Stalin died in March 1953, his heirs proceeded with his plans. First, they brought neighboring farms together into large amalgamated units, gradually reducing their number from more than 200,000 to less than 30,000. This reduction was said to be a desirable way to gain the economies of scale by avoiding the duplication of administrative staffs, by utilizing farm machinery to its full advantage, and by maximizing the services provided by the still inadequate number of agronomists who understood scientific agriculture.

The amalgamation into large complexes required restructuring the governing apparatus of each farm. Members who now numbered in the thousands could no longer meet as a general assembly to choose the administration and to discuss policy. The charter had to be revised to permit the assembly to become representative of its members. Further, discussing job ratings for the purpose of computing the share of farm income that each member should receive was impossible when members of the assembly were not intimately acquainted with all of the individuals concerned. There could be no direct relationship on rational grounds between distribution of income and productivity. Administration became largely "impersonal."

What choices were before the policymakers? Of course, they might have proposed a return to smaller farms. This they did not do, perhaps because their allegiance to economies of scale and eventual industrialization of the agriculture process made such a policy seem politically and economically retrogressive. The first indication of direction came with the introduction of the *zveno* system, which meant that groups of farmers were assigned plots of collective farmland to work as a team. They hoped that this would bring administration closer to the dirt farmers than it was on the large amalgamated farm, and distribution of income could be made on an informed judgment of the productivity of the individuals who constituted the team.

The choice of the *zveno* seems to have found favor with the Politburo of the party, for its current agricultural specialists called in 1983 for introducing the "contract system." Brigades were to be directed by the farm management to execute contracts with it for producing specified crops in specified quantities. Payment would then be made to the brigade as a whole in accordance with the contract terms, and its members would divide up the proceeds in accordance with their assessment of the productivity of each member. Probably the proposal was made with the expectation that when the payments to a brigade depended on the work of all of its members, peer pressure would raise the brigade's total productivity.

Introduction of the contract system may be facilitated by the fact that some features of the collective-farm system have been made increasingly similar to those of the state-farm system. Payments to collective farmers have for some years been called "guaranteed wages." In truth, they are not guaranteed, for they depend on the income of the farm as a cooperative association. Consequently, if the farm lacks income, the payments cannot be made in full. To meet the "guarantee" the farm is authorized to borrow from a state bank, and it is expected to repay the loan when the next good harvest occurs. The government now indicates that farmers have voted themselves payments in excess of farm receipts, have borrowed from the bank, and have failed to repay the loans. Farms are accused of no longer functioning on a business accounting basis, with income and expenditures in balance.

Another choice is swiftly to transform collective farms into state farms, which Stalin proposed in 1952. Since Stalin's death, there has been a strong movement in this direction. So many collective farms have been transformed that the number of state farms now almost equals the number of collective farms. Such a transformation will indeed produce a guaranteed wage as farmers become employees of a state enterprise rather than coowners of a collective. The advantage of an assured income has to be considered, however, against the fact that there will be no assembly of members in a state farm. The directors are not chosen by members but by higher bureaucrats. Farmers express their wishes through a trade-union structure, as they do in state enterprises, and this structure is not always responsive to their wishes or effective in changing administrative decisions. In spite of the disadvantages for the farmers, the trend toward state farming is clearly indicated. It will most likely be the favored choice of the party generalists, although they cannot press hard for universal transformation against a peasantry that remains essentially conservative in spite of decades of indoctrination.

One relatively new institution in the agricultural hierarchy that is receiving the attention of jurists is the "agroindustrial complex." Over the past decade, collective and state farms in selected districts have been contributing capital to create specialized enterprises to process their agricultural products. Herds of animals are fed and prepared for market; fruits are processed; and vegetables are placed in bottles or cans. These enterprises are structured like corporations, but their lines of authority to policymakers differ from those of the state enterprises under ministries. They are directed, not by an official appointed by the minister concerned with their type of activity, but by a manager chosen by the representatives of the farms contributing capital. In a sense, the agroindustrial complex is a corporation controlled by its owners, who might be likened to stockholders.

Of course, the production of such complexes is factored into the national economic plan, but the information flow is from the bottom up rather than the top down. The complexes use the materials available locally to manufacture their produce and then inform the planning committees of what they have to sell. In a sense the complexes introduce features comparable to those known to corporation lawyers in open-market economies, but since the stockholders represent the farmers whose capital derives from their own toil rather than distant nonworking investors, the complexes are considered to be within the parameters of permissible socialist structures. At least, in Soviet eyes the complexes do not "exploit" workers, for they do not siphon off "surplus value" to the benefit of owners unrelated by toil to the production process. To the outsider the line between the permissible and the impermissible may be thin, but the agroindustrial complex demonstrates the range of choices open to structural specialists with a knowledge of socialist principles and the imagination to innovate.

Private-Plot Farming

The thin line between the permissible and the impermissible is further indicated in private-plot farming, which lies between the structures of collective and state farming and the impermissible structures of the private farm of the NEP. Private-plot farming was brought into existence when farming was collectivized. It was to placate peasants reluctant to give up all traditional family farming by the peasant *dvor* (household). The collective- or state-farm management allocated each family a small plot around its dwelling to be used for market-garden purposes, from which the surplus might be sold in the farm market. Only children and the retired farmer could spend full time on the plot: all others had to work on the collective or state farms for the usual day so that the farming of the plot was a spare-time operation.

The private-plot farm has at times been discouraged, but shortly before his death in 1982 Brezhnev and his Politburo colleagues directed collective-farm chairmen to make available to farm members tractors or plow horses, improved seeds, fertilizers, and transportation to the market. This was a sharp change from Khrushchev's era, when farms were urged to reduce the size of these plots, and some managements in their enthusiasm to follow his advice had almost eliminated the plots. Brezhnev had reason to act, because at the time of the policy change the plots were producing most of the potatoes on the market, much of the meat and dairy products, poultry, eggs, honey, fresh fruits, and vegetables.

The private-plot system has been extended to areas around cities, where space is also allocated to workers in industry. The title to the land remains at all times in the state, but its use becomes in a sense "private." It is an acceptable alternative to state or collective methods of operation because it is supplementary only, and there is no "exploitation" of hired labor.

Disciplining Individuals

Stimulation of productivity does not come solely through revised economic structures. Much is being said about disciplining the individual. Andropov began his period of leadership with attacks on laggards and the corrupt. Educational campaigns, labor law, and criminal law all have roles to play in this process.

Stalin had been severe: he linked labor and criminal law and intensified the link as World War II approached. To prevent labor turnover, he penalized workers who left a job without consent. Consent was given only when health reasons required it or a worker had a chance to attend a school to improve his or her qualifications. Absenteeism was defined as tardy arrival or early departure (the limits being twenty minutes). Criminal penalties were applied, with a simplified court procedure to establish fact.

None of these severe penalties survived after the war ended. Managers were instructed to return to the earlier methods of educational campaigns, strengthened by the "labor passport" system, as they had been before the war. Under this system, every industrial worker keeps a booklet with his work record. If he departs from a job voluntarily, that fact is registered. Recruiting officials are urged to take it into consideration and thus discourage "rolling stones." The system has not worked well, since there has been a labor shortage in many industrial regions. But it is preferred to compulsion, because public opinion both at home and in the labor unions abroad frowns on what smacked of slavery during the era of criminal penalization.

Corruption is attacked at its two worst points—stealing state property while on the job and soliciting and accepting bribes. Stalin began the severe phase of the attack on theft with his notorious law of 7 August 1932, under which theft from collective farms became punishable by death. By degrees this was extended to theft from any state or cooperative institution. Death became the penalty for "economic crimes," at least when they involved large amounts of property. After Stalin, a short period with no death sentences was tried, but in desperation Khrushchev reintroduced the death penalty for severe economic and some other crimes, and it is in force today.

Newspapers carry accounts of some thirty executions a year, but outsiders believe the figures are larger. In January 1984 the press carried an account of the execution of two high officials of one of the state foreign-trading organizations for taking large bribes.

The increasing severity of penalties for flagrant economic crimes has been countered, however, by a trend toward greater leniency for the petty offender. This was evidenced by a series of amendments to the Criminal Codes in all the republics in December 1983. Under these amendments, prison sentences are replaced for petty offenses of an economic nature by "compulsory labor" without imprisonment. This penalty has long been available in the codes, but its maximum limit was set at one year. With the 1983 amendments, the maximum is set at two years so as to provide a plausible deterrent outside of prison for those who would previously have been sentenced to prison or hard-labor camps.

In a measure the new amendments represent a return to a policy that Stalin abandoned in the 1930s when he turned away from the penology of the 1920s, which had favored efforts to restore the culprit to life through education and work. Stalin seems to have been frustrated by continuing crimes in a society that had given everyone a job and thus removed the likelihood of penury — the source of crime, according to socialists.

The 1983 amendments are paired with a law on the "labor collective," which calls on the workers in every institution to form a group that will be responsible for improving productivity by stimulating disciplined work. It is this group to which a culprit convicted of a crime and sentenced to "corrective labor" is bound over for reeducation for a given period of up to two years while also being required to pay in court a monthly fine from wages.

Discipline is also enforced through the Civil Codes of the republics. An enterprise may bring a civil suit against an employee who has destroyed the firm's valuables or stolen its goods. The recovery is in the amount of a money judgment for the price of the goods as established by retail tables of prices or, in their absence, by the use of values established by the State Committee on Prices of the USSR Council of Ministers.

The Family as Educator

Discipline is also to be inculcated by the institution that reaches every child at the formative period of its life, namely, the family. Stalin began the reversal of the attitudes of the 1920s and 1930s that had acquiesced in popular demand for easy divorce. The figures demonstrated that juvenile criminals came from broken homes. Various measures were tried to discourage divorce and to enforce maintenance duties on reluctant parents, culminating in 1944 with an amendment to the Family Codes declaring that thereafter only registered marriage would confer legal rights on the spouses and their children. The aim seemed to be to encourage parties seriously to consider their decision to marry, with the hope that such a decision would later discourage them from separating without careful thought.

The goal has not been achieved, for in the early 1980s the divorce rate in European Russia had mounted to nearly 50 percent. This looseness of marriage ties occurred in spite of legal provisions requiring that the parties declare their intention to register their marriage well before the registration day and the practice of lecturing them during the wedding ceremony on the desirability of maintaining a model socialist family.

The party's attitude was evidenced with the promulgation of the new federal Constitution in 1977. For the first time the Basic Law put the family under explicit constitutional protection. It declared as a constitutional principle that motherhood and childhood should receive the material and moral support of the state. This principle has been implemented in laws establishing paid leaves for pregnancy, benefits for all ill children, assistance to low-income families, and payment of the greater part of the costs of nurseries, kindergartens, and schools. Evidently, the choice has been made against bending to popular demand to withdraw state intervention in affairs of the heart.

No Joint Ventures

The Soviet leaders believe that their doctrine bars them from joint ventures with high-technology foreign firms. For the reasons set forth above with regard to private enterprise in the USSR, equity investment by foreign capitalists has been rejected as a way to improve productivity, even if the Soviet enterprises in the venture were to hold 51 percent of the stock and assume the presidency of the venture.

When foreign technology is sought, the legal basis is a licensing of patents and the purchase of know-how on a contract basis. In some cases when the technology is totally unknown to Soviet engineers, a foreign firm will be invited to contract for a turnkey project. The firm builds the plant, provides specialists to put it onstream, trains Soviet personnel both in the home office and on the job, and then delivers the key. Thereafter the Soviet side reproduces the plant with its own engineers and pays the patent owner whatever the contract calls for.

Conclusion

Although Soviet jurists have never held the prominent position of their counterparts in the United States, they do have importance. In their traditional role as technicians, they formulate the laws designed to implement the policies set by the Communist party's leaders.

Yuri Andropov's tenure as general secretary of the party was too short to permit more than an identification of the problems he inherited from the Brezhnev era. Andropov focused attention on low productivity and the lack of personal discipline. The latter problem could be faced quickly by a simple amendment of the Criminal Code, and jurists accomplished this change before his death. Low productivity was another matter, and because of its intractable nature, little was accomplished during the few months of Andropov's leadership. The difficulties were of two kinds: (1) doctrine and (2) experience.

In spite of much Western writing about the fading of Marxist tenets from the list of principles that motivate Soviet leaders, there is no doubt within the USSR that there are doctrinal limitations on the kinds of solutions to the problem of productivity. There can be no return to private ownership of factories or farms. The state enterprise system is firmly rooted in the psyche of communists.

As for experience, the limited choice of solutions is the result of the growth of a bureaucracy determined to retain centralized economic structures. Khrushchev's ouster for "harebrained" schemes in 1964 ended experimentation with massive decentralization of administration. Reform of the industrial structure can hardly be expected to extend beyond a limited increase in the authority of enterprise directors to act without constant reference to superiors in their chain of command. In agriculture the only likely change will be the expansion of the collective and state farmer households' rights to utilize more extensively the private plots assigned for their personal use and the organization of brigades on communally tilled land so as to increase motivation to work by restructuring the law on material incentives.

Andropov's heirs seem likely, therefore, to continue to establish narrow parameters and to maintain traditional parameters within which jurists may improvise to meet productivity problems. Of course, there will be some change, because of discontent with the current situation, and the public will expect some sort of action. But it is unlikely that such developments will require Western analysts to reconsider their characterization of the Soviet system.

Housing in the Soviet Union

HENRY W. MORTON

In the Soviet Union, housing is regarded primarily as a social good, while in the United States it is treated essentially as a commodity. To understand this important difference, it is necessary to examine briefly American housing from a broad perspective.

Historically, housing development in the United States was stimulated by land and real estate speculation, not by the government. Even public housing during the Great Depression was intended primarily to aid the ailing housing construction industry and only secondarily to provide housing for those who were temporarily unemployed. After World War II, however, three federal programs helped millions of Americans to buy homes:

1. The Federal Housing Administration (FHA) and the Veterans Administration (VA) guaranteed mortgages on new homes. Thus, banks could lower their interest rates, significantly reducing housing costs.

2. An extensive, federally supported highway construction program encouraged commuters to buy homes in the suburbs.

3. Tax rebates permitted home owners to deduct the interest on their mortgage payment and local taxes from their gross income.

The housing boom also benefited the construction industry and manufacturers of building materials, the automobile and home-furnishing industries, banks and financial institutions, and the economy in general. But a house has become both a tax shelter and an investment that has greatly appreciated in value in recent years. The revenue loss for such tax deductions will amount to $40 billion in 1984, while direct federal subsidies for public housing will cost only $8.6 billion. The governmental support that home owners receive prompted the late Charles Abrams, a well-known housing authority, to remark that when it comes to housing, "we have socialism for the rich and free enterprise for the poor."

The Soviet Union has also improved its housing conditions since World War II. Indeed, the 1977 Constitution guarantees Soviet citizens the right to housing. Article 44 affirms: "This right is insured by the development and upkeep of the state and socially owned housing; and by assistance for cooperative and individual house building; by fair distribution, under public control, of the housing that becomes available through fulfillment of the program of building well-appointed dwellings, and by low rents and low charges for utility services." But, despite real progress over the past thirty years, the Soviet Union still has a long way to go to reach the level of housing comfort that exists in the United States. Nevertheless, the Soviet leaders, who view housing as a social good, proudly point to the following achievements:

• For the past 20 years at least 2 million units have been built annually in the USSR—more than in any other country in the world.

• It is hard to imagine how long people would have to wait for good new housing if a powerful building industry had not been created.

• Housing is built mainly at the expense of the government and is allocated free to people on the waiting list without any key money or down payment.

• In 1928 the lowest rent tariff in the world was fixed in the USSR; it has not been raised since. In Moscow the average sum that a family pays for its dwelling plus communal services does not exceed 3 percent of its monthly budget. The rent itself covers only a third of the state expenditure on the maintenance and upkeep of housing; the rest is subsidized from public funds.

• Eleven million Soviet citizens move into new dwellings or improve their housing standards yearly. Housing can, of course, be built for profit, but in the USSR it is built to meet the people's needs. Homes are therefore not an object of commerce. . . . Housing is not treated as a commodity.[1]

In assessing Soviet housing accomplishments, however, much depends on whether the USSR is viewed as an industrialized or a developing nation. For a developing nation, these housing accomplishments have been admirable; for a developed nation, Soviet housing accommodations are still among the poorest of any industrialized society.

A Short History

Soviet Russia inherited, along with an underdeveloped economy, a predominantly rural population. Only two cities, Moscow and Petrograd (now Leningrad), had populations of more than 1 million. Before 1917 most of the urban housing consisted of small, wooden, single-story, one-family homes, almost all of which lacked basic utilities.

Housing conditions worsened under Soviet rule. During the 1918–21 Civil War, urban housing fell into ruinous neglect. With no fuel deliveries from the countryside, workers—many of whom lived in partitioned apartments formerly belonging to the nobility and members of the bourgeoisie—ripped up and burned wooden floors and door frames to stay alive during winter. When the war ended in 1921, most municipalities lacked the means to administer the housing stock and make repairs. This forced the new regime to return part of the housing that was nationalized in 1917 and 1918 to its former owners. Even now, much of the housing in the Soviet Union consists of privately owned, single-family homes.

The Stalinist policy of rapid industrialization combined with forced collectivization of the countryside, which began in 1929, drove millions of peasants from their farmlands to new industrial sites and converted small towns into large cities. The urban population increased from 26.3 million (18.9 percent of the total population) in December 1926 to 56.1 million (33 percent of the total) by January 1939. Housing conditions in cities deteriorated precipitously. Many of the newcomers lived in barracks or shacks or — if they were fortunate — in communal apartments with one or more families to a room. By 1981 the urban population had increased to 168.9 million (64 percent of the total). In 1926 the Soviet Union had only two cities with populations of over 1 million; in 1981 it had twenty-three.

The waves of people flooding into towns and cities to work in new industries during the first three five-year plans (1929 to 1941) greatly overburdened the existing inadequate housing facilities. The First Five-Year Plan (1929–32) had projected a 33 percent increase in urban housing space, but only 16 percent was built. Housing production was sacrificed in favor of large investments in heavy industry. This intentional underinvestment in housing and other urban services was a cornerstone of Stalin's industrial policy, as living space declined from 61.3 square feet per person in 1926 to 49 square feet in 1940. Thus, early Soviet housing policy followed the pattern of Western capitalist countries where similar squalid housing conditions existed during the early stages of industrialization.

Investment and Construction

Capital investment in housing for the 1930s was governed by two factors. First, the total investment capacity of the USSR, a capital-poor nation, was severely limited and stretched to the breaking point by the unrealistically high goals set by Stalin. Second, within the confines of the capital investment structure, Stalin gave a low priority to housing construction (as he did to other consumer industries). Gregory Grossman, a Berkeley economist, estimated that the Soviet government purchased two years of industrial investment by permitting a reduction of some 40 percent in the housing standards of urban workers.

The German invasion of the Soviet Union in June 1941 made an already intolerable housing situation even worse. The war caused widespread property destruction in the European part of the USSR. According to Soviet figures, 1,710 cities, towns, and urban settlements were fully or partially destroyed, as were many thousands of villages. More than 25 million people were left homeless. Leningrad, Kiev, Minsk, Smolensk, Stalingrad, and other cities and towns had to be almost completely rebuilt from heaps of broken brick and rubble.

Despite the war's devastation of the housing stock, Stalin's primary goal was to rebuild and expand heavy industry as rapidly as possible. Housing and other consumer comforts had to wait. "It wasn't until Stalin's death [5 March 1953],"

Nikita S. Khrushchev wrote, "that the leadership really faced up to the problem of how serious our housing shortage was."[2] And it was critical. In 1950 the per capita living space in urban areas was 52.7 square feet. That year the state built only 38.4 percent of all housing, consisting chiefly of low-rise apartment units built by conventional construction methods, such as brick-laying and casting in place at the building site.

Khrushchev's solution for eliminating the housing shortage (which the Communist Party Program of 1961 unrealistically predicted would be overcome by 1980) was for the state to build as many urban units as quickly and cheaply as possible. Quality was to be sacrificed for quantity. Khrushchev asked, "Do you build a thousand adequate apartments or seven hundred good ones? And would a citizen rather settle for an adequate apartment, or wait ten to fifteen years for a very good one? The leadership must proceed from the principle of using available material resources to satisfy the needs of the people as soon as possible."[3]

By more than doubling the capital investment in housing for the Sixth Five-Year Plan (1956–60), the number of housing units built increased from 1.5 million in 1956 to 2.7 million in 1959 — the highest yearly total ever achieved in the USSR. Khrushchev built cheaply, mainly four- and five-story walk-ups. He lowered the ceiling to 8.2 feet, made the rooms small and the corridors narrow, and upset the public by combining the bathroom and toilet in one chamber. Although these buildings became known as "Khrushchev's slums," they served an important purpose at that time by easing the housing crunch.

Since 1957 the country has built an average of more than 2 million housing units a year — an enviable achievement in consistency. This eased the housing shortage over the years but did not eliminate it.

Khrushchev also brought radical changes to the construction industry. Standardized prefabricated housing parts and wall-sized load-bearing panels made from prestressed concrete replaced the conventional building materials of brick, steel, and lumber. This change permitted production to continue during the long and severe Russian winter. It also greatly reduced the need for skilled labor, which was in short supply.

The use of standardized prefabricated housing parts increased from 1.3 percent in 1959 to 54 percent in 1980. In cities with more than 1 million population, it accounted for at least 75 percent of all construction. Technological advances in the 1970s made it possible to erect nine-story apartment buildings in large cities. These buildings helped to limit the urban sprawl created by the low-rise Khrushchev model. In the 1980s new apartment buildings in major cities will be primarily twelve and sixteen stories high, with a smaller number as high as twenty-five stories. In large and middle-sized cities the construction of nine-story buildings will predominate.

The post-Stalinist leadership's commitment to eliminating the intolerably crowded conditions under which the Soviet people lived has had dramatic results. A visitor to any large Soviet city cannot fail to be impressed by the multiplicity of new housing districts consisting of medium- and high-rise apartment buildings that dominate an expanding perimeter. However, a closer look at the new housing reveals construction defects, cracks in the panels, unfinished facades, neglected landscaping, and poor drainage causing water to collect on walks and grounds.

Soviet architects, government officials, and citizens are the harshest critics of Soviet housing construction. They complain about the dreariness of building design. "The city was built up in a monotonous, architecturally inexpressive way," concluded the USSR Civil Construction Administration's review of Bratsk, a Siberian city of 200,000.[4] Critics also complain about the poor quality of workmanship in large panel housing construction; cold houses; the wind, water, and dampness that penetrate the walls; and sagging ceilings and floors. One Soviet official explained the situation: "There are many reasons for inferior work, but the most typical is the desire to 'just get done with the project.' The main thing is to hand over the building on or ahead of schedule. That is why quality is sacrificed right and left in the scurry to meet the deadline."[5] To meet the deadline, on which bonuses depend, buildings are routinely accepted for occupancy before they are fully completed, and the new tenant is annoyed when he has to repair defects and install missing fixtures.

Inferior housing construction is a universal problem. But the Soviet Union must contend with three factors not found in the West. First, the Soviet construction industry has been operating in a seller's market for decades. There are no boom and bust cycles. The demand for residential apartments is so great that the prospective tenant will accept anything that is offered. The only ones left unsatisfied in a seller's market are the customers; in this case, the government pays for the housing and the consumer uses it.

Second, the Soviet Union has imposed heavy restrictions on its construction industry. Workers must build large quantities of housing as quickly and cheaply as possible, using prefabricated concrete walls in the process. The use of industrially produced parts, primarily the large panel wall-bearing system, limited the industry to relatively few types of housing and thus brought monotony to new housing districts. The use of concrete as the main building component was also a problem. Concrete does not lend itself to sharp lines. As a result, misalignment, unevenness, and ragged edges are common.

Yet, even within the imposed constrictions, the USSR could build much more attractively designed housing of higher quality; and in some sections of the country they do, as in Vilnius, Lithuania.

Third, and most important, Soviet housing is only one part of a system in which the common denominator of the various products is poor styling and quality. Since the government has a monopoly on housing production, as on almost everything else in the Soviet Union, competitive bids for design are rare. Quality and design, therefore, are unimportant to builders, who are rewarded for producing according to plan. Since housing remains in short supply, and the government is the sole producer, the consumer has little choice but to accept the product when it is offered.

Housing in the USSR consists of three categories: housing owned by the state, housing cooperatives (multiple-dwelling apartment houses) built by the state agencies, and housing that is privately owned. The state owns the land and more than 75 percent of the housing stock in urban areas. It is also in charge of construction and distribution. Privately owned homes are restricted to 645.6 square feet of living space. Since 1964, private homes may be built only in towns with less than 100,000 inhabitants; people living in larger cities are limited to apartments. Consequently, a home with a garden is not a viable alternative for Soviet citizens.

The financing of public housing construction and other urban services in many cities and towns comes primarily from central government ministries, not from city governments. Many communities are company towns. Their destiny is chiefly in the hands of directors of factories belonging to large national ministries. In many instances, these factories, not the city, are in physical control of urban services, particularly in new towns. Since the factory directors' job security depends on productivity, housing construction is a low priority for them. Exceptions are found in cities like Moscow, Leningrad, and the republic capitals, where officials have greater control over revenue sources; but even there a significant proportion of the financing originates from ministries. As a result of such ministerial control of housing and other city functions, there is a serious constraint on a city government's ability to plan and improve urban services.

Housing in the USSR is primarily measured by the number of square meters of "living space" per person (and not by the number of persons per room, a common yardstick in the West). It includes bedrooms and the living room but not the kitchen, bathroom, corridors, and storage space. Living and nonliving areas make up the aggregate "useful housing space" of a dwelling—which accounts for about two-thirds of the total. Each of the fifteen republics has determined by law the minimum housing standard for its citizens.

In the 1920s, when the per capita living space was 61.3 square feet per person, the legal minimum for the Russian Republic was 96.8 square feet, a small area by Western standards. In 1983 the norm was raised to 129.1 square feet, presumably because the minimum was finally but not uniformly achieved nationwide. Of twenty-nine major cities or republic capitals in 1982, fifteen averaged more than 96.8 square feet of living space. Moscow and Tallin (the capital of Estonia) led all cities with 121.6 square feet; Tashkent (the capital of Uzbekistan) and Dushanbe (the capital of Tadzhikistan) came in last with 75.3 square feet.

The Housing Shortage

Soviet citizens suffer from the poorest housing of any industrialized nation, principally because so many households still live communally. (A household is defined as a married couple, a parental pair with children, a single parent with children, or an individual.) Furthermore, housing is no longer the government's primary consumer priority.

According to *Pravda* (2 December 1980), about 80 percent of the urban population in 1980 lived in separate apartments. This meant that at least 20 percent lived communally. But the report left unsaid that about 5 percent more (mostly singles) live in workers' dormitories or barracks. The fact that conditions were worse in 1960, when 40 percent of all families lived communally, is of little comfort to large numbers still living in inadequate conditions. A numerical comparison of units to households is crucial in measuring Soviet housing needs, but this information is not published. The statistical gap is not an oversight. The *UN Statistical Yearbook* provides such figures for every European country except the USSR.

Since the numerical relationship between households and dwellings is not available, the next best indicator is a comparison between yearly marriages and the number of housing units built. If more housing units are built annually than marriages registered and the country possesses an equal or superior number of dwellings over households, then the basis for a good housing situation is present. It does not mean that the nation's housing problems are solved. It does signify, however, that a basic goal has been achieved and that other pressing concerns can receive a higher priority, such as the ability to pay for comfortable housing (in the USSR this applies to cooperatives, private homes, and summer homes, and to the use of bribes to acquire accommodations in state housing), the size of a dwelling, the facilities with which it is equipped, the desirability of the neighborhood or a house, the time it takes to get to and from work, and so on.

Between 1973 and 1982, however, 6,175,226 more marriages were formed in the Soviet Union than housing units built. Only Kiev and Minsk in 1982 registered more new dwellings than marriages — 3,643 and 863 respectively. Moscow's "deficit" was 43,947 units and Leningrad's 26,000 units. Needless to say, newlyweds have little chance of moving into their own apartments and are destined to live with in-laws, perhaps for decades.

The urban housing deficit is really much larger than the figures show. With a zero vacancy rate in Soviet urban areas, a household's desire to live in an apartment of its own is strictly (if not always successfully) monitored by the authorities. If a family's per capita sanitary norm of some 96 square feet of living space has been satisfied, getting on the waiting list is virtually impossible except through connections. To discourage new households from forming, singles who wish to live apart from the extended family will frequently be denied a place on the list. Also denied will be the many who have to live beyond the city limit and commute to work. Many of these suburbanites are the "urban poor" of Soviet society — not because of unemployment (the Soviet Union has been particularly successful in achieving full employment at low pay) but because there are few urban amenities. They are not allowed to move to the large population centers, such as Moscow, Leningrad, and Kiev, to prevent these cities from being overrun by rural and provincial migrants. Permission to move there is rarely granted. Moscow is the most severely restricted of all.

Families living in a large city, in a highly subsidized public housing unit equipped with modern conveniences, near a subway station and not more than thirty minutes from work, have no housing problems to speak of. But permission to move to Moscow, Leningrad, or Kiev without sponsorship from a governmental agency or with no apartment to exchange from another city is rarely granted. Even if it is, many difficulties have to be overcome, which can take years. A sponsoring agency has to provide an apartment or room for the newcomer, because residence must be established before a *propiska* (residence certificate) can be issued. Chances of receiving a *propiska* improve if two families of approximately the same size in different cities agree to exchange comparable apartments.

City residents who have a *propiska* but live in cotenancy, subleased apartments, or dormitories and wish to improve their poor housing situation by moving into better quarters are entirely dependent on the housing authorities, who determine waiting-list eligibility. If a family's per capita norm of 96 square feet of living space has been satisfied, permission can be arranged only through connections. Eligibility usually begins with less than 75 square feet, but this differs from locality to locality. It is difficult to get on the waiting list. Figures are rarely published, but for Moscow 180,000 families, or 590,000 persons, made the list in 1974. At that time 60 percent of them averaged less than 54 square feet of living space.

Individuals or couples with a residence permit but with no lease on an apartment or room have no housing to exchange; they therefore have few options. They can rent a room or an apartment, but that is also difficult and expensive because of black-market prices. Or they can try to join a construction cooperative, but first they have to get approval from the housing authorities by showing need. Cooperatives are expensive and require a downpayment of 5,000 rubles (more than double an industrial worker's yearly pay). Even at those prices, co-ops are at a premium.

To engage in a housing exchange, a person must have a room or an apartment registered in his or her name. It can be state or cooperatively owned. In either case, it becomes that person's "working capital" to try to exchange current quarters for more suitable housing. A public housing unit thus becomes a commodity. To succeed in the exchange market, a Soviet citizen needs ingenuity, tenacity, patience, luck, influence, and cash; and it can take years. The Bureau of Housing Exchanges maintains a card file (for a three-ruble fee per entry) of citizens who wish to exchange their housing. Notices also appear in the *Bulletin For Housing Exchanges*, which most large cities publish. The Moscow edition appears weekly and carries more than 1,000 listings.

Because exchange bureaus provide little help, a lively, open-air "stock market" trading in rooms and apartments operates in all kinds of weather just outside the central exchange bureau's office. In Moscow it is located just off Prospekt Mira in one of the oldest sections of the city. Every Sunday, its most active day, hundreds go there eager to make a deal. Exchanges involving a chain of families are seldom equal. Some will accept a decrease in living space; others will give up a desirable, centrally located district for one that is on the city's outskirts; and so on. Those who stand to gain from a transaction will privately pay their exchange partners a sum of money mutually agreed upon. Such illegality is winked at by the housing authorities, who will approve an exchange as long as the same number of persons exchange roughly similar amounts of space.

Just as the housing market has led to a score of illegal practices in the USSR, so have the *propiska*, the housing allocation process, and the constrictions placed on private home ownership. Since government officials monopolize the supply of housing, it is understandable that housing bureaucrats will be offered bribes. Persons on the waiting list are tempted to jump the queue, because doing so can reduce their waiting time from ten years to zero. For such an act to succeed, *blat* (influence) or a bribe or both are needed. It is one of the most frequently cited violations in the housing system.

Another common form of corruption occurs when local party and government officials, plant managers, and other well-placed bureaucrats with connections build and equip oversized homes (far in excess of the permitted 645 square feet of living space) on illegally assigned plots, using stolen building materials, state-owned construction machinery, and labor on the public payroll. Sometimes they own several private homes (though only one is legally permitted to each household), while maintaining a state-owned apartment in the city.

Housing is an integral part of the reward system of the Soviet society. State agencies, holding a monopoly in the distribution of housing, ration out new units on the basis of occupational work and influence — only secondarily on need. Thus housing is increasingly becoming stratified between the haves and have-nots and is also becoming segregated in the cities as different professional groups cluster together in housing complexes financed by their ministries and organization.

The poorest housing class in the USSR, the "least favored," are the millions clustered beyond the limits of large cities who seek to be let in. In the city, the housing poor are the "less favored," living communally or in dormitories. Possessing a legal right to live in the city, they hope that they will receive an apartment of their own. In the meantime, they can profit from the advantages that city living offers in the form of shopping, medical care, and educational and cultural opportunities. Households living in self-contained apartments in newly erected housing districts are much better off. They are the "more favored," even though they are located far from the center. Commuting to work may take an hour by crowded bus or subway, and shopping where they live is difficult. "Most favored" are the families living in their own apartments in or near the center of town. Generally, they are the Soviet political, military, security, economic, scientific, cultural, educational, and worker elites. They are the most heavily subsidized because they are paying the same low rent rate as those living communally. Thus the most advantaged become the beneficiaries of redistributed wealth that they can pass on to their children.

Economic and Social Consequences of the Housing Shortage

Poor housing conditions in the USSR have contributed to the acute labor short-age and high labor mobility. Factories and offices cannot import labor if there is no place for workers to live. Moscow's most serious problem, according to its mayor, is not lack of funds but a severe shortage of workers and employees whose skills are in great demand but for whom accommodations cannot be found.

Soviet society is aging, particularly in the European part of the USSR. The capital and other major cities have a large number of retired people. In Moscow they constitute more than one-sixth of the population. Pensioners do not con-sider leaving large urban centers for overcrowded resort towns in the South, like Sochi, and moving to a small town or a rural area is not an attractive alternative because life there would be much more primitive.

The labor turnover rate is high. About 15 million workers in industry and construction leave their jobs yearly, and millions of workdays are lost. Labor mobility is highest among singles under twenty-five. Singles who do not live with their parents find accommodations in subleases and crowded dormitories of factories. Few singles receive an apartment, and they have no hope of getting on the waiting list unless they marry. One reason for their frequent change of jobs is poor housing accommodations.

Cramped housing conditions also contribute to a decline in the birthrate. Soviet leaders, because of a labor shortage and for military reasons, view their aging population with concern. It has been demonstrated that couples will have their first child even if they live in cotenancy, but they are less likely to have a second or a third if it means greater crowding and a lowering of their living standards.

Conclusion

After years of neglect, in the mid-1950s the Soviet regime launched an ambitious residential construction program with the stated purpose of eliminating the severe housing shortage that had forced the majority of urban households to live communally, with numerous families sharing an apartment. Now, almost thirty years later, the majority of urban families live in modern apartments of their own—a significant improvement.

However, more than 20 percent of urban households still live communally or in dormitories. Therefore, the promise that every family would have an apart-ment by 1980 has been postponed until 1990, because the number of dwellings still lags behind the number of households. The rate of construction, which peaked with 2.7 million units in 1959, has leveled off to 2.0 million in the 1980s. Since 1969 it has fallen significantly below the yearly number of marriages, compelling most newlyweds to live with their parents, often indefinitely. Housing conditions would seriously deteriorate if large urban centers were not legally closed to would-be immigrants, many of whom work in the cities.

The ever-present housing shortage is the government's responsibility. It invests heavily in industry, attracting workers and managerial personnel, yet under-invests in housing construction and other consumer services. It restricts consumer choice to high-density apartment-style living in cities and prohibits consumer initiative for private home building in urban centers with a population of over 100,000.

In the United States, where most dwellings are privately owned, housing is rationed by price. The home or apartment that one decides to rent or purchase depends on the price that the buyer can afford. The choice quickly narrows to the type of housing and location that is both desirable and affordable; this is "democracy by the buck." Those who live in relative comfort in a location that is their second or third choice believe that they, not the market, made the decision. Those who perform poorly in a market economy might prefer living in tax-financed housing, but in New York City, for example, the waiting list for public housing numbered 165,000 families in March 1984.

In the USSR the rationing of urban housing is primarily by allocation. More than 70 percent of all urban units are owned by the state. Bureaucrats decide when, where, and how well one will be housed. A Soviet family living in a modern apartment with a reasonable number of rooms near work and good shopping areas is undoubtedly well satisfied with its housing situation. The apartment, though government owned, is for all practical purposes theirs. It can even be passed down to the children, if they remain registered in it, even though they are married and living elsewhere. The fact that housing is distributed free and rent is minimal is very attractive to Soviet urbanites, who do not realize that they are paying higher prices for clothing and other consumer goods to support the state's huge housing subsidy. The many dissatisfied families with little hope of having an apartment assigned to them have few choices. They can try to buy into a housing construction cooperative (still few in number and expensive), use influence, attempt a bribe, or enter the housing market in which it is difficult to trade up unless one has good housing to exchange. This group might prefer to purchase private homes in large urban areas. Such opportunities exist in Bulgaria, Czechoslovakia, and Hungary but will not be offered in the Soviet Union in the near future.

The United States and the Soviet Union have addressed the housing problem from different ideological viewpoints. But whether housing is viewed as a social good or as a commodity, the people at the lower end of the economic and social scale in both countries are poorly served.

NOTES

1. Alexander Andreyev, *Housing in U.S.S.R. Today and Tomorrow* (Moscow: Novosti Press Agency, 1979), 2–16.

2. Nikita S. Khrushchev, *Khrushchev Remembers: The Last Testament* (Boston: Little, Brown & Co., 1974), 102.

3. Ibid.

4. *Izvestia*, 6 June 1973.

5. Ibid., 17 May 1974.

Soviet Health Problems

MURRAY FESHBACH

At the Twenty-Sixth Party Congress of the Communist Party of the Soviet Union held in February–March 1981, the general secretary of the party, Leonid Brezhnev, addressed the issue of health conditions and delivery in the country. Brezhnev indicated that improving the health of Soviet citizens was among the most important social tasks. He noted that a major decree was issued 22 September 1977 on measures to improve health in the country and that the capacity of polyclinics had increased by 500,000 since the Party Congress held five years earlier. He then confronted the negative side of the health-delivery issue:

> The work of polyclinics, dispensaries, and out-patient clinics which handle 80 percent of all the sick must substantially improve. Unfortunately, in a number of places they lag behind the possibilities of medicine, there is a cadre shortage, especially of middle- and junior-level personnel, equipment is out-of-date, modern medications are insufficient [in quantity]. Hospital and health unit construction plans are poorly fulfilled. . . . Letters are received about the factual infractions of service duties by individual medical personnel, about inattention to people. . . .

This statement is far from unique and serves to confirm even clearer lower-level statements about health-care problems in the USSR.

In 1980, the Supreme Soviet of the RSFSR passed a resolution that made specific reference to the 22 September 1977 decree. Its report was more explicit about the poor response by the republic health, governmental, and industrial authorities in meeting the requirements of the decree. The report also indicated that the problems were republicwide. Lags in providing specialized medical care, particularly for women and children, were noted in addition to the insufficient quantities of medicine that Brezhnev was to cite one year later. The train-

Adapted from Murray Feshbach, "Issues in Soviet Health Problems," *Soviet Economy in the 1980s: Problems and Prospects*, pt. 2 (Selected Papers Submitted to the Joint Economic Committee, Congress of the United States) (Washington, D.C.: GPO, 1983), 203–27.

ing, utilization, and supply of personnel were termed inadequate and insufficient. The turnover rate among medical personnel, particularly those assigned to rural areas, was considered excessive. Sanitation and hygienic problems in schools were not being rapidly eliminated as decreed in 1977. The production of specialized food for children by various industrial ministries of the republic needed improvement. Air, water, and land pollution continued "in several places," partly because antipollution equipment continued to be produced in insufficient quantities. And so on.

Background

The basis for these statements, evaluations, and concerns lay in the overall demographic trends that reflected remarkable turnarounds in officially reported successes for many years. Reductions in fertility meant that the health of each new increment to the population and labor force was more important. The population of the Soviet Union grew by 1.7 percent a year over most of the 1950s. The rate is now about 0.8 percent a year. By the end of the century it should be about 0.4 percent a year, sharply below the rate expected only seven years ago, when projections for this period were 0.6 percent a year. But not only fertility is down; so also is life expectancy. The implication of these forecasts is that the Soviet population will probably total less than 300 million in the year 2000. In the early 1970s, the Soviet Central Statistical administration projected a figure of some 340–350 million. Although the ethnic composition of the Soviet population due to differential fertility rates is beyond the scope of this essay, it needs to be mentioned here as one of the underlying causes for concern about health in the Soviet Union, particularly because of the excessive death rates among Slavic and especially Russian males.

According to the official Soviet data, the crude death rate (the number of deaths per 1,000 population, unadjusted for changes in age structure) increased from the low point of 6.9 in 1964 to 10.3 in 1980. A remarkable achievement was attained in lowering the rate for deaths among children aged 0–1 per 1,000 live births from 80.7 in 1950 to 22.9 in 1971. Unfortunately, infant mortality rates, as well as life expectancy and other major measures of Soviet health conditions and services, are no longer published by the Soviet authorities. The last figure officially reported for life expectancy of males, for example, was sixty-four years, down two years from the previous reported high of sixty-six. The current estimate is only 61.9 years of life expectancy at age 0 for males, or 11.5 years less than that for Soviet females — an unprecedented gap among developed countries.

Such figures should not be interpreted to ignore the remarkable Soviet achievements in reducing the level of infectious diseases and deaths existing at the time of their accession to power. For example, Frank Lorimer's report to the League of Nations noted that from 1917 to 1923 more than 3 million persons died from typhus, typhoid, cholera, and dysentery; this no longer occurs.

Nonetheless, after remarkable successes in these and other individual areas of medical discoveries, services, and treatments, and despite the high quality of various professor-doctors or individual physicians, something has gone awry in the scale, structure, and direction of Soviet health indicators.

Cause-of-death data show part of the problem: the leading cause of death in the Soviet Union, as in other industralized countries, is heart-related diseases. These diseases account for 51.3 percent of all deaths. The high percentage is related to the aging of the Soviet population as fertility drops in the Slavic and Baltic regions, to alcoholism, and to hypertension as stress and other urban-related problems increase. Indeed, coronary heart disease in the Soviet Union reached epidemic proportions in the last two decades. While deaths from heart disease in the United States are still quite high, the trend is downward. In 1960, the United States rate was 515 deaths per 100,000 population. But in 1979 it was 440, a decline of 15 percent. In the Soviet Union in 1960 the rate was 247.3 per 100,000, and in 1979 it was 500, or an increase of more than 100 percent. Simultaneously, the share of ischemic heart disease, alleged in some recent analyses to be linked to alcohol consumption, has grown from 39 percent of all heart-related deaths to 54 percent. One eminent Soviet health commentator, Yu. Lisitsyn, stated that one-third of all coronary heart disease is related to alcohol abuse, with the rate rising among persons thirty years of age and over, especially those thirty through forty-nine years old.

Cancer-related deaths increased from 115.5 per 100,000 in 1960 to 137.3 per 100,000 in 1978. Some one-third of these deaths were caused by stomach cancers that are more typical of less-developed countries. For men, the second most prevalent incidence of cancer-caused deaths is respiratory and the third, lymphatic and blood cells. For women, the second is cancer of the uterus and the third, of the breast.

The third leading cause of death is "accidents, poisoning, and injuries," especially prevalent among children two to three years of age, women under forty, and men under fifty. M. S. Bednyy noted that this is the specific cause of death for 12 to 14 percent of all male deaths regardless of age and 80 percent among males ages twenty through twenty-four who died in 1970. Alternative sources indicate that alcohol abuse was the underlying cause of about 50 percent of these deaths. In 1976, alcohol poisoning was the cause of 39,800 deaths in the Soviet Union, eighty-eight times that of the United States rate.

Deaths related to respiratory illnesses are next in order, but no data are available. More recent information indicates that the rank order of this cause of death may have jumped to third place.

The Soviet Union has also seen an unusual increase in infant mortality due to causes other than those noted above. The increase of more than 20 percent in the officially reported rates between 1971 and 1974, before such data were terminated in primary statistical sources, combined with the secondary report of a phenomenal increase in one year of 2.9 per 1,000 live births (up to 30.8 in 1975, according to the current minister of health and his coauthors), demonstrates that children were at much risk in their first year of life. Based on very recent information for Tadzhikistan, the infant mortality rate for 1977 was 90 for the republic as a whole, decreasing to 63 in 1979. If the reported rate of 28 in 1961 is at all accurate, or even twice that level, the increase was over 60 percent of an assumed 56 per 1,000, or over 200 percent if the original figure was approximately correct. M. S. Bednyy, writing in 1979, noted that in the 1970s there was "an increased frequency in the number of children born with congenital anomolies."[1] He referred to reports that this had been caused by "gene mutation due to exogenous factors impacting on mothers." Among the causes were "influenza epidemics, German measles, alcohol abuse, abuse of medical preparations, smoking, and ionospheric radiation."

Further, diabetes is more frequently afflicting younger women, and this, he noted, had a negative impact on their offspring, leading to more premature births and a consequent increase in infant mortality in the first month of life of such children. In February 1982, the newspaper of the medical sector contained an article entitled "State Concern for Protecting the Health of Mother and Child," which reveals the range of problems in reducing infant mortality:

> The task of further reducing the infant mortality rate continues to be important. Key factors in achieving this goal include prenatal protection of the fetus, attention to the growth and development of the health of an infant during its first year, proper diet, the prevention and treatment of prenatal pathology and broncho-pulmonary, infectious and allergic ailments, and thorough study of the medical and social determinants of infant health. Greater demands must be placed upon the research institutes of several republics with regard to these matters.
>
> Pediatric, obstetric and gynecological institutes and institutes for maternal and child health protection should devote particular attention to studying the diagnosis and treatment of perinatal brain damage, infectious and inflammatory diseases and congenital and hereditary pathology. The problem of resuscitation of newborn and premature babies is in need of serious scientific study.[2]

Medical Issues

Without a doubt there has been a vast increase in the number of doctors, the number of hospital beds, and the amount of money expended for health and a significant reduction in infectious diseases since the time of the October Revolution. However, the numbers conceal other problems in the training, the types of doctors and their location, the behavior of the medical profession regarding their duties and patients, the supply of medical equipment and medicines, and the increase in mortality rates described earlier. This array of problems undoubtedly underlies Bednyy's comment in the July 1981 issue of Sovetskaya meditsina that "in the past 10 years there is no satisfactory correlation observed between increasing material and personnel resources of public health, on one hand, and changes in the state of health and demographic indicators, on the other hand."[3]

In 1980 Izvestiya reported a shortage of medical personnel everywhere. But the shortage was not limited to the supply of middle- and lower-level personnel, as Brezhnev indicated at the 1981 Party Congress. The Ukrainian minister of health noted the shortage of doctors as well as middle-level staff in his republic. Former Minister of Health B. V. Petrovskiy wrote in a recent book that the overall supply of doctors for pediatric sections filled 95.9 percent of the authorized slots by 1978 (up from 92.6 percent in 1975). This assertion is difficult to reconcile with the information that in the twelve pediatric districts of the city of Labinsk (in Krasnodarskiy Kray) there are only seven doctors at work. In the eight rural-district hospitals in the region, only one has a pediatrician. Medical facilities and their personnel are grossly overworked, given the report that the current polyclinic work norm calls for 260 patient visits a day, while they see 1,300. One hopes that the situation has improved in Georgia, where it was reported that in 25 rural hospitals and 127 out-patient clinics there was not a single doctor. However, an editorial in *Pravda* on 12 June 1981 contended that there still existed a "substantial number of treatment sections which are not fully staffed with physicians in certain provinces of the Russian Republic and in Georgia and Uzbekistan."[4] In Kazakhstan as well as in the Russian Republic the local health agencies apparently concealed the shortage by appointing district physicians with only a secondary medical education.

The education of doctors as well as middle- and lower-level personnel has also been subjected to serious criticism. As Dr. William Knaus, an American physician who has written on Soviet medicine, noted, Soviet medical schools teach by a system of protocol, not by problem-oriented techniques. Many physicians have difficulty diagnosing nonstandard conditions on their own. Erroneous diagnoses even of standard conditions appear to be a problem.

For example, from 1971 through 1976 incorrect diagnoses were found in the RSFSR in 25.8 percent of cancer cases, 18.0 percent of circulatory (heart and blood-related) diseases, 15.7 percent of digestive-organ illnesses, and 10.2 percent of respiratory diseases. Soviet medical schools, like those in the United States, have come late to the teaching of geriatrics and gerontology but did introduce such subjects into their curricula beginning in 1978. Radiologists reportedly received little training in the capabilities of their equipment or how to reduce levels of radiation dosage. One hopes that the training received by new physicians will be sufficient in genetics so that more doctors will be able to answer questions correctly. A report in 1975 indicated that of the 500 doctors asked "elementary questions on genetics, only 2 gave the correct answers."[5] Practical instruction time assigned to students is usually carried out in a "perfunctory way to get a check mark," according to an article by a member of the Chita Medical Institute published in *Izvestia* on 31 January 1981. Given its publication in the national newspaper, the frequency of this experience may be more worrisome if large proportions of "the young people go to the hospital, hang around there in groups for an hour or two, and then leave for home. . . . They cannot even give injections properly — carefully, painlessly, with a kind word."[6]

Since the early 1970s little progress appears to have been made — despite public acknowledgment, decrees, and growth in production—to resolve the problem of producing sufficient medical supplies, distributing them equitably, and maintaining their quality. Acknowledgment of the problems ranges from published complaints from individual institutions to the minister of medical industry to the deputy director of the CPSU Central Committee's Department of Science and Scientific Institutions. Just before Brezhnev's report at the 1981 Party Congress, which referred to outdated equipment and shortfalls in modern medications, a joint session of the Academy of Sciences and the Academy of Medical Sciences was convened on 19 November 1980. Among those who spoke at this session, the minister of medical industry, A. K. Mel'nichenko, reported medical-equipment supply problems, presumably including medicines.

In the spring of 1977, Minister of Health Petrovskiy wrote about supply problems in the national trade union newspaper. According to David Shipler's summary of the article, Petrovskiy stated:

> Only a few dozen of the 30,000 clinics in the country have artificial kidney machines. . . . Much x-ray equipment is obsolete, only 75 percent of the needed x-ray film is being produced, anesthetic equipment and artificial breathing machines are being manufactured in only half the required amounts and surgical instruments are inadequate in quantity and quality.
>
> Even such a basic tool as the thermometer is in short supply, Petrovskiy complained. Although 30 million are needed annually . . . 23.6 million were produced in 1976, and this year (1977) 24.1 million are planned—"much less than our order."[7]

Shipler added that economic planners generally cut the medical institutions' orders for technology in half.

Perhaps Petrovskiy was being unusually frank, as preparations were undoubtedly under way for issuing a major decree on health plans in September 1977. But his list was incomplete. *Literaturnaya gazeta* revealed in October 1976 that patients in major cities could not obtain insulin because the Ministry of Railway Transport would not deliver small packages except by slow train, and Yakutiya was short of novocaine. The minister of medical industry responded to "justified complaints" about shortfalls in the supply of equipment and medicines in August 1976. The 1976–80 plan called for substantial increases in the production of hormonal, antimicrobial, antitumoral, and antibacterial medicines and X-ray contrast agents—an overall increase of 48 percent of synthetic preparations, 59 to 60 percent of vitamins, and more than 50 percent of ready-to-use medicines. But he added, in a complaint heard to this day, that an insufficient amount of raw materials was being supplied by other ministries. In all, in 1976, only 70 percent of the requirements of the Ministry of Health for medical equipment were met.

The 1977 demand must have also been unmet, if the 22 September 1977 decree reflected current shortfalls when it announced that the Ministry of Medical Industry did not "fully provide for the requirements of the population . . . for medicines, eyeglasses, medical equipment, ambulances and specialized motor vehicles, medical furniture, and small mechanical tools."[8] Even in October 1980, the Ukrainian minister of health decried the shortage of specialized vehicles, especially for rural hospitals in general and for every feldsher-obstetrical unit in the republic. When available, many of the vehicles are apparently poorly maintained or are used for other purposes, such as providing transportation for staff members or hauling cargo in Moldavia and in the Tatar ASSR. The shortage of spare parts for emergency ambulances obliged the stripping of a large number in the Tatar area to keep them operating or were sent out without full complements of authorized equipment. Bifocal eyeglasses are delivered even in Moscow with an average delay of nine and one-half months. Other problems include hearing aids that are banned from production by the State Standards Committee because of poor quality or because they are declared "unsuitable for mass production." Shortages of cotton bandages, disposable syringes, needles, and the like are widely reported.

The 1981 Party Congress authorized a 40 percent increase in the level of output of the medical industry. In the 1976–80 period, production was expected to grow by 48.6 percent. But output levels never seem sufficient. If production of medical equipment is lower than required, then the production of medications seems to be on a yet lower scale. There is abundant evidence that this problem of shortfalls in production is almost a "permanent crisis." Reports of an insufficient supply of aspirin, as well as of the complex medicines needed for semisynthetic antibiotics for patients with heart disease, blood substitutes, and flu vaccines persist, despite official declarations that medications are being produced at a higher rate. In 1982 the health and social security commissions of the two houses of the Supreme Soviet authorized further measures to "remove insufficiencies" in the work of the Ministry of Medical Industry in order to increase the production of medicine. Candidate member of the CPSU Central Committee Politburo and first deputy chairman of the Presidium of the USSR Supreme Soviet, V. V. Kuznetsov, participated in the joint session, underscoring the seriousness of the situation and high-level interest in resolving this matter.

Evidence is accumulating that a large number of new facilities are being built in the Soviet Union for medical research and treatment. The types of facilities reflect current concerns over specific illnesses or problems, but they appear to be concentrated in Moscow, to be funded from extra-budgetary sources in a number of important cases, and to be insufficient to meet current requirements.

In his report to the Congress of the Medical Personnel Trade Union at the beginning of 1983, L. I. Novak included the expected statistics on changes in medical facilities during the previous five-year-plan period (1976–80). He noted that hospital-bed capacity increased by 323,000 beds. Polyclinics could now accommodate 650,000 more persons per shift. About 100 large multipurpose and specialized hospitals of between 500 to 1,000 beds each were opened, and 119 maternity homes and obstetric units were also opened. Presumably, the minister of health's comment early in 1977 that work was proceeding slowly in Armenia, Georgia, and the Ukraine, and had not even begun in Turkmenistan, was still true in 1981.

Petrovskiy noted that many units were being constructed with funds from the All-Union Communist Saturday (i.e., Voluntary Workday), earned by "free labor." A similar pattern also applied to medical facilities for maternal and child-care. An All-Union Scientific Research Center for Maternal and Child Health Care was opened in Moscow in 1979, with the equipment paid for by the earnings from the Volunteer Day honoring the one-hundreth anniversary of Lenin's birth. Earnings from the April 1981 Volunteer Day were earmarked for construction of maternity homes, obstetrical-gynecological units, female consultation centers, children's hospitals, children's polyclinics, and out-patient services, sanitoriums, and homes for children. In all, 116.9 million rubles so earned were allocated for this purpose, as were 11.2 million rubles for preschool child-care institutions.

The Forty-Sixth General Meeting of the USSR Academy of Medical Sciences in March 1982 was devoted to problems of health delivery to mothers and children. The minister of health informed the participants that three other all-union centers for fetal and infant care had been opened, one for genetic consultation, another for the diagnosis of congenital pathology, and a third for prenatal diagnosis. Moreover, an All-Union Infant Resuscitation Center and an All-Union Center for Surgery of Congenital Heart Defects in Children were organized, the country's first premature-infant resuscitation and intensive-care division. This list is impressive. In the case of the pediatric surgery center, the need is profound. More than 30,000 children are born with congenital heart diseases in the USSR every year. Whether one new center can handle a large proportion of this number is doubtful, but at least a beginning has been made. Similarly, the reported opening of the first neonatal intensive-care unit is significant, but many more are needed. The United States had 485 of these units, according to the 1980 edition of *Hospital Practice*.

The addition to medical facilities for complex heart surgery can be put on a comparative basis. By 1980, a cumulative total of 800 open-heart bypass procedures had been performed in the USSR. According to a report in the *U.S. News and World Report*, in 1967 some forty such operations were performed in the United States, but by 1975 the number had risen to 57,000. In 1982, more than 135,000 were expected to be conducted. Even if an excess number of surgical procedures are performed in the United States, as frequently asserted, the availability of opportunities for such corrective techniques are on a vastly different scale for the two nations.

Insufficient-capacity problems are also provided by the example of the optical laboratory of the Research Institute of Child and Adolescent Hygiene, under the direction of Yu. A. Utekhin. This laboratory developed a technique for the use of bifocal sphero-prismatic glasses to treat myopia. According to *Pravda*, some 50 million Soviet citizens suffer from myopia. Many had been advised to go to this laboratory for corrective glasses. However, in 1980 the waiting list was cut off when it totaled 10,000 persons! Minister of Health Burenkov cited a new national-level genetic consultation center as the first item on the list of new medical institutions. The origin of this facility can probably be traced to the call in 1969 for the establishment of medical genetics consultation offices throughout the USSR. The report late in 1975 that the RSFSR had organized five consultation offices, the Ukraine two, and (explicitly) one office in each of the remaining thirteen republics indicated that the overall program was fulfilled. But Soviet analysts deemed the twenty consultation offices "hopelessly inadequate," and almost all were understaffed, had makeshift premises, and lacked laboratory facilities and equipment.

The head of the RSFSR Health Ministry's Institute of Pediatrics and Children's Surgery indicated that "in recent years 50,000 children have been found to be suffering from phenylketonuria (PKU), a hereditary metabolic disorder," and "if it is detected early enough, these children can be, if not cured, at least made full-fledged members of society."[9] But tens of thousands of people visited the consultation offices, and "unfortunately, many of them did not go there for prognosis but for treatment of an already advanced disease." It is unclear whether all of these young people had PKU, yet it seems that they appeared for treatment at a late stage and could not be cured. The lack of training knowledge of genetics by almost all doctors, as mentioned earlier, adds to the possibility of a late diagnosis of such illnesses.

Other facilities opened in recent years include the first clinic for the "Comprehensive Treatment of Neuroses." The establishment of this clinic, as well as a number of social service and psychological-aid offices throughout the city of Moscow, underscores the growth of a stress syndrome in urban areas of the Soviet Union. This problem is growing, and these facilities are meeting a real need. The growth of stress, as well as reports of mounting hypertension may have also contributed to the rise in coronary heart disease and consequent mortality increases.

Reports on poor service in the open medical system are so rampant that a few citations from the Soviet press should suffice; very little is available about the closed health-delivery system available for the leadership or for the institutional networks available only to staff members, such as that for the Academy of Sciences. A prime complaint is the poor quality of diagnostics. A. F. Serenko, the leading social hygienist of the Soviet Union, wrote in the summer of 1980 a detailed description of the problems of district general physicians. They lacked contacts with other specialists, were not supervised properly, and were overworked. One-third had not undergone retraining or upgrading of their skills for more than five years, and less than half had "skilled categories" of knowledge. Low standards of hygiene in hospitals were likely to lead to high postoperative infection rates. According to Dr. William Knaus, about one-third of all patients in Soviet hospitals acquire such infections while in a hospital; a United States rate of 3 percent would be considered high. Thus, in addition to long stays required by medical protocols for patients, time in hospitals is increased by infections, and therefore more beds are needed to provide for the hospitalized population. If urban medical facilities are bad, all reports indicate that the rural facilities are distinctly worse.

Dental services would also benefit from more equipment and training. Dentures are nondurable, and there is a shortage of dentist chairs. In one report, there were only three chairs for every ten dentists and three dentists for every drill. In addition, the quality of dental service was adversely affected by long lines, cramped quarters, inadequately trained dental technicians, and delayed construction of facilities. Other clinics and medical units for individual populations and organizations are to be built with funds from collective and state farms and from industrial enterprises. It is hard to judge how many, where, and what type will be constructed using this approach. While any expansion is all to the good, given the present needs, it is unclear how the new units will be organized or how duplication will be avoided.

It is also hard to judge precisely the meaning of Soviet statistics on the number of new medical facilities. Petrovskiy wrote about the fulfillment of health plans for 1976 and then admitted that "in recent years, 60 first-aid hospitals have been created and incorporated in this medical service network. However, in some cities the hospitals exist only on paper."[10] Is this unique? Does the chartering of an institution allow the medical statisticians to include it as a new facility before actual construction? Very confusing, to say the least.

Novak's report that the number of hospital beds increased by 323,000 is impressive at first glance, especially when compared with the consistent decrease in the number of beds in hospitals registered by the American Hospital Association of the United States. In the United States, the number of beds decreased from a peak of 1.7 million in 1965 to less than 1.4 million in 1978. The Soviet total of 3,201,000 at the end of 1978 and 3,324,000 at the end of 1980 is noteworthy. However, the average length of stay in hospitals is twice as long in the Soviet Union as in the United States. Also, the additional 323,000 beds reported by Novak does not correspond to the data published in the statistical yearbook of the Central Statistical Administration. According to the yearbook for 1980, the increase between the end of 1975 and the end of 1980 was 315,000 beds. More significant than this small discrepancy, however, are the comparative data for increases in the number of beds over five-year periods. Thus, between 1970 and 1975, the increase was 346,000, which is 20,000 or 30,000 larger than the Novak figure. Between 1965 and 1970, the number of beds grew by 437,000, one-third more than the growth in the 1970–75 or 1975–80 periods. The slower current increment is surprising, given the need for more capacity according to Soviet sources.

Achievements in the area of medical research include developments in orthopedics, cancer research, ophthalmology, laser surgery, and other surgical methods (for example, using wire staples to perform lung-tissue repair during surgical procedures, and high-frequency sonar to shatter stones in the bladder without resorting to invasive surgery). Other work includes efforts on the frontier of hypnotherapy, biofeedback, artificial organs, and the retardation of bone decalcification. The annual number of invention and discovery author certificates in the field of health has grown recently. In the RSFSR, the number of applications increased by almost three times between 1976 and 1979 (from 461 to 1,145), and the number of author certificates issued increased by almost four times (from 141 in 1976 to 520 in 1979).

A survey of Soviet medical journals and newspapers found that the greatest amount of research attention in the 1970s was devoted to cardiovascular diseases, oncology, virology, nutrition, environmental hygenic problems, and human genetics. A. F. Serenko, writing in the May 1979 issue of the Academy of Medical Sciences journal, underscored the importance of cardiovascular research, calling it a question that "has acquired special social importance."[11] Also undoubtedly reflecting his concern about negative trends in health indicators, Serenko described the program of research on women and child care implemented since the Twenty-Fifth Party Congress in 1976. The study will focus on "the health status of different groups of women and influence on it of working and living conditions, determination of the nature and incidence of pathology of pregnancy and parturition, causes of gynecological morbidity related to medicosocial factors. . . ."[12] In addition, much more attention is to be given to the economics of health, over and above the recent increase in attention to this matter. He conceded that "the scope of research dealing with public health agencies and institutions is still inadequate."[13] And as for the available statistical data for analysis, "traditional statistics no longer satisfy present requirements of public health management. The main task now is to make use of statistical data, rather than merely gather and process them."[14]

The positive developments in medical research briefly noted above reveal only one side of the coin. The other side deals with reports from the Soviet medical literature regarding the ineffective results in half of the research conducted in the RSFSR, most of which provided for no advance over existing medical methods. The reports disclosed inadequate planning, nonintegration of research, parallelism, and duplication. Moreover, individual-topic Problem Commissions did not follow up research results, nor did they inform the health ministry of any problems in research organization. In addition, integration often carries "a purely formal character." The absence of follow-up data from the practical application of new methods in polyclinics and out-patient clinics reportedly has hampered any evaluation of the breadth and effectiveness of the application of new medical discoveries or treatments.

Late in 1980, a joint session of the Academy of Sciences and the Academy of Medical Sciences of the USSR convened in Moscow. The participants also included the minister of health and the minister of medical industry. Much of the meeting was apparently devoted to the insufficient effectiveness of medical research, foremost of which was the gap between medical and scientific research and its application in practice. In addition, it was noted that many scientific institutes were poorly equipped. Improvements were needed in supplying materials, in planning and coordinating research efforts, and in dispensing information to medical workers about the latest achievements in medical research and medicine. A joint complex problem of research among the two academies at the session was ordered to be prepared, and a long list of research topics in the fields of biological and chemical-technological sciences, in physical-technical and mathematical sciences, in earth sciences, in social sciences, and in medical-biological, clinical, and hygienic sciences as related to health issues was authorized at the joint session.

Whether this program will be successfully implemented remains to be seen. An article published subsequently in *Pravda* about patent applications in the medical field indicated that it was much too early to see any turnaround. Too many "ministries and agencies still do not orient research sufficiently toward the development of fundamentally new treatment methods and medical hardware."[15]

Shortly after the October Revolution, the tradition of physicians' taking the Hippocratic oath was discontinued, because it represented "bourgeois medicine and was considered incompatible with the spirit of Soviet medicine."[16] It was not medicine that was to be the cornerstone of the physician's activity, but his active participation in the building of socialism. Ideology triumphant could not last forever, and soon after the First All-Union Conference on Problems of Medical Deontology (i.e., medical ethics) was held in Moscow in January 1969, a revised Hippocratic Oath was authorized in March 1971 and restored to its traditional place. The oath was restored primarily because of the poor attitude many doctors were showing toward their patients. As Brezhnev noted, attitudinal problems have continued.

The reported behavior of many medical personnel does not refer to all, of course, but the widespread distribution of such comments indicates that it is not localized or anecdotal. In 1977 a *Pravda* editorial condemned "violations of medical ethics, indifference toward patients," and the irregular supply of medicines and long lines in the rural medical units of Moscow Oblast. In 1978 *Literaturnaya gazeta* discussed problems of bribery and the black marketing of scarce medicines in Leningrad, in Krasnodar, and in the Ivano-Frankovsk Oblast, and the Swiss correspondent Reinhard Meier reported on an *Izvestiya* story about a patient in Odessa who "had been constrained to hand out a ruble note to the nursing personnel for literally everything that was done for him — including giving him a thermometer."[17] In 1979, a report about the Ukrainian Supreme Soviet meeting noted that thoughtless attitudes toward patients had been subjected to censure in a number of cities and oblasts of the republic. In 1981 the head of the Kaunus Medical Institute (in Lithuania) complained in *Pravda* about "charlatanism and pseudoscientific substitutes for medical treatment" and widespread "indifference [and] rudeness . . . in medical institutions,"[18] and *Literaturnaya gazeta* reported on the behavior of medical officials and doctors in health units of the Railway Ministry, which was sufficiently bad to require a special inquiry by an Interagency Commission composed of personnel from the Railway Ministry, the USSR Ministry of Health, and the Central Committee of the Railway Workers Trade Union.

Among the long list of correctives to be introduced was the elimination of "negative phenomena such as corruption, drunkenness, and ill-use of office facilities." Later in 1981 *Izvestiya* reported that a doctor in Magadan without any formal examination gave false diagnoses on medical certificates excusing individuals from work; the charge was 10 rubles per excused workday. In 1982 Radio Moscow's service for North America included a statement by a commentator on United States and Soviet health services: "We've had cases of doctors extorting money from would-be patients or their relatives. Even though such cases are publicized, and such physicians are stripped of their doctor's certificate and gaoled, such things do happen."[19] *Izvestiya* reported on 24 January 1982 that a "certain secret statistic" was used to evaluate hospital success and consequently a hopeless, gravely ill patient was not admitted. The chief physician was reported to "give preference to patients who might recover their health."

And then there is Azerbaydzhan. In this republic, problems of medical ethics seem to have reached their fullest proportion. The republic party newspaper, *Bakinskiy rabochiy*, has referred to problems in this sector for many years, reaching to the time of the Azerbaydzhan Communist party congresses in 1971 and 1976, and especially in January 1979. The extent of the unethical behavior appears to have been beyond all reports cited earlier. G. A. Aliyev, a candidate member of the Politburo of the CPSU Central Committee and first secretary of the Azerbaydzhan Communist party, reported to the Forty-third Baku Party Congress on 24 January 1979:

> The Azerbaydzhan Communist Party Central Committee has more than once pointed out serious shortcomings in the work of public health agencies, an indifferent attitude toward patients, and instances of bribery in hospitals, polyclinics, maternity homes and other medical institutions. Unfortunately, [these conditions have been] slow to change . . . because executives of public health agencies . . . have not genuinely joined in an uncompromising struggle against self-seekers and grafters. . . . A recent poll of a large number of working people and a checkup by . . . the republic Ministry of Internal Affairs brought to light new instances of bribery, the theft of medicine and food, violations of state and financial discipline, mismanagement and a criminally negligent attitude toward the use of medical equipment. . . .[20]

And so on and on. In March 1979 the MVD chief for the republic, D. Veliev, reported on an examination of hospital practices. The investigation found financial irregularities, a high degree of corruption, hospital staffs that had been robbing and blackmailing patients, and inaccurate records of stocks of medicines, premeditated violations of regulations, and four hospitals that had no record of 90 percent of their receipts of medicines and bandages during the preceding nine months in 1978. On 16 June 1979 the Azerbaydzhan Central Committee explained the situation and its program for resolving the defects spoken about by Aliyev or published in the press. In addition to all the poor practices and unethical behavior cited earlier, this report included many new issues, such as poor organization of the work of pharmacies, serious shortcomings in preventive measures against infectious diseases, low compliance with sanitary standards at the "majority of the medical institutions themselves," little effort to correct unsanitary conditions at industrial enterprises, public catering, trade, or other consumer-service organizations, as well as indifference to the decline in the number of skilled specialists, scornful attitudes by some toward "observance of the requirements of medical ethics, socialist legality and the principles of communist morality," criminal charges leveled against eighty-one health agency employees, the abetting of illegal actions by relatives and pulling of wires for them by the republic minister of health, G. M. Abdullayev, misplaced indulgence, and so on.[21] One and one-half years later, Aliyev acknowledged some improvements had been made but full resolution had not been achieved and "extreme measures were necessary in order to rectify the situation." Indeed, serious efforts are urgently needed to modify the individual and institutional behavior patterns elaborated here so that more efficient efforts can be directed toward the reduction of mortality and morbidity, the prime business of a health system.

Morbidity

The Soviet health system has marked major advances in reducing infectious diseases and other illnesses since 1917. Even as recently as the 1930s very high rates of certain infectious diseases were recorded. As a prime example, the highest number of cases of malaria was recorded as recently as 1934, when 9,477,007 were registered. By 1965 the national total number of cases of malaria was 392, of which 201 were noted in the RSFSR and 123 in Azerbaydzhan; the remaining 68 were spread throughout the other Soviet republics. The number of cases of trachoma was also dramatically reduced, decreasing from some 265,000 in 1959 to less than 10,000 in 1964. Diphtheria cases in 1955 and 1956 numbered between 145,000 and 150,000 each year (a postwar peak) but decreased to 350 in 1980. Whooping cough, which totaled almost 800,000 cases in 1958, was down to 14,000 cases in 1980. Since 1980, however, new data indicate significant increases in a number of infectious diseases, especially in diphtheria and measles. From the viewpoint of domestic progress, enormous strides have been made, but much remains to be done.

It is not certain how to evaluate the data on the number and rate of infectious diseases when alternative evidence derived from special Soviet medical surveys of the urban population shows twice as many sick people as those registered as sick based on visits to medical facilities. Thus the overall rate of illness among the urban population (per 100,000 population) based on patient visit data was 1,069.9 per 100,000 males and 1,196.9 per 100,000 females; based on medical examination data, the figures should be 2,048.7 for men and 2,447.7 for women. Similar overall data for the rural population are not available. Nonetheless, the relative differentials between recorded numbers and "real" numbers would imply that the health status of the Soviet population is much worse than shown by the standard morbidity data.

In regard to the health of young people, several contradictory statements can be compared. In 1978 *Izvestiya* published a statement claiming that in recent years the health of preschool-age children had shown considerable improvement. Petrovskiy, the former minister, affirmed that the pneumonia rate among children up to age three had decreased from 85.3 per 1,000 children in 1975 to 81.1 in 1978; for children 0–1 years of age, it decreased from 110.4 to 99.8 during that period. These figures stand in contrast, but not necessarily in contradiction, to Bednyy's statement, cited above, that in the previous decade there had been more children born with congenital birth anomalies, that in the RSFSR between 1973 and 1978 the level of acute upper-respiratory-channel illnesses grew by about one-third among children in both urban (37.5 percent) and rural (31.0 percent) child-care institutions. Acute respiratory virus infections and influenza account for 70 to 80 percent of all childhood illnesses. Perhaps Petrovskiy's report is correct for the country as a whole, but it seems to contradict the evidence for the largest component republic of the country.

One of the most startling pieces of evidence regarding the health of young people is the 1980 report by N. S. Sokolova (of the First Leningrad Medical Institute) that in Leningrad — a city one would expect to have one of the better health-delivery systems — only 42.2 percent of all five-year-olds were healthy. Further, 41.7 percent were frequently ill with acute respiratory illnesses, and 16.1 percent either were seriously ill, injured, chronically ill, or had developmental anomalies. A survey of 450 families in Leningrad with children up to seven years of age found that 6.3 percent of these children suffered from rickets and hypertrophy! Evidence on the prevalence of rickets among rural children is available. Among these children, respiratory illnesses — especially pneumonia — occurred 1.7 times more frequently among those suffering from rickets. This illness rate among young children must contribute to the reported 30 million Soviet citizens suffering from influenza each year.

Very revealing reports have been published recently about the negative impact on children of alcoholic parents in the Soviet Union. A sociological and medical survey of forty-five chronically alcoholic women conducted by the Moscow Psychiatric Research Institute found "extremely serious consequences for their offspring." Of the 291 children conceived by these women, only 118, or 40.5 percent, were born healthy; 54 were medically aborted, miscarriages, or still-born; 97 were born mentally retarded; and 22 died in their first two years of life. Thus, of the 237 children born alive, 41.0 percent were mentally retarded, a figure almost as high as the proportion of healthy children. The research of B. and M. Levin reported in 1978 and 1979 found that the rate of alcoholism was growing faster among women than among men, that women's sections had to be opened in sobering-up stations and psychiatric hospitals, that alcohol consumption was increasing among widows, divorcees, and single women, and that females began drinking at a younger age.

A remarkably frank article was published in the newspaper *Cina*, by V. Strazdins, the chief narcotics expert of the Latvian Ministry of Health, on 23 September 1982. This article noted the increase in absolute volume of consumption, the growing share of hard liquor among all alcohol consumption, the high proportion of all expenditures on alcohol relative to consumer goods, and the impact on individual adults and the dramatic impact on children – including their intellectual capabilities.

According to the information provided Dr. Allen Greenberg, former science counselor at the U.S. Embassy in Moscow at the time of the World Health Organization conference on Primary Health Care held in Alma-Ata, Kazakhstan, in 1978, about 50 percent of all hospital beds were occupied by persons whose illness was associated with alcohol-related problems. Abel Aganbegyan, head of the Institute of Economics and Organization of Industrial Production in Novosibirsk, reported that in many of the plants he visited throughout the country, special brigades were formed to keep drunk workers away from the now complex and very expensive machinery. Given the impact of alcoholism on productivity in addition to its social and medical costs, the prevalence of such brigades described by Aganbegyan in the national trade union newspaper in 1982 is serious indeed. The Ministry of Health of the USSR has developed a "Long-Term Program for Scientific Research on Problems of Alcoholism in 1976–1980," in conjunction with the Academy of Medical Sciences. Also, a ban on the sale of liquor has been considered but rejected. According to *Komsomol' skaya pravda*, the newspaper of the Young Communist League, it is feared that *samogon* (moonshine) would make such a ban ineffective.

The importance of the alcohol issue to the health of Soviet society appears to be very serious and of growing concern to the leadership. This issue, as well as those outlined here on medical supplies, equipment, facilities, and ethics, clarifies Brezhnev's statement at the Twenty-sixth Party Congress. They indicate the underlying bases for his unusually strong negative remarks about one of the areas for which the Soviet regime has long – and to a large degree correctly – been praised. Its present status, however, leaves much to be desired, given that the population and manpower trends necessitate an even healthier population.

NOTES

1. M.S. Bednyy, *Mediko-demograficheskoye izucheniye narodonaseleniya* (Moscow: Statistika, 1979), 128.

2. *Meditsinskaya gazeta*, 17 Feb. 1982, trans. in *Current Digest of the Soviet Press* (CDSP) 34, no. 8 (24 Mar. 1982), 22.

3. M.S. Bednyy, "Demographic Processes and the Role of Medical Science and Health Maintenance in Improving the Demographic Situation," *Sovetskaya meditsina*, no. 7 (July 1981), 81–84; trans. in Joint Publication Reading Service (JPRS), *USSR Report, Life Sciences, Biomedical and Behavioral Sciences*, no. 12, JPRS no. 79338, 30 Oct. 1981, 18.

4. Trans. in CDSP 33, no. 24 (15 July 1981), 23.

5. *Literaturnaya gazeta*, 26 Nov. 1975.

6. Trans. in CDSP 34, no. 5 (3 March 1982), 5.

7. *New York Times*, 26 June 1977.

8. *Pravda*, 15 Oct. 1977.

9. *Literaturnaya gazeta*, 26 Nov. 1975, trans. and abstracted in CDSP, 28, no. 18 (2 June 1976), 4.

10. *Isvestiya*, 24 Feb. 1977.

11. A. F. Serenko, "Sociohygienic Problems of Public Health Care in the Light of the Decisions of the Twenty-Fifth CPSU Congress," *Vestnik Akademii meditsinskikh nauk SSSR*, no. 5 (May 1979): 3–10, trans. in JPRS, *USSR Report, Biomedical and Behavioral Sciences*, no. 113, JPRS 73912 (26 July 1979), 51.

12. Ibid.

13. Ibid., 52.

14. Ibid.

15. Trans. and condensed in CDSP, 33, no. 27 (5 Aug. 1981), 19.

16. Cited in Mark G. Field, *The Doctor and Patient in Soviet Russia* (Cambridge: Harvard University Press, 1957), 174.

17. Reinhard Meier, "Soviet Health Care: Myth and Reality," *Swiss Review of World Affairs* (April 1978), 20.

18. Z. Januskievicius, "Health," 1981, p. 3.

19. Vladimir Pozner, Radio Moscow (in English), 2300 gt, 1 Feb. 1982, in BBC, *Summary of World Broadcasts, USSR*, SU/6956/B/3, 17 Feb. 1982.

20. Trans. in CDSP, 31, no. 4 (21 Feb. 1979), 13.

21. Trans. and excerpted in CDSP, 31, no. 31 (29 Aug. 1979), 9–10.

The Nationality Question and the Soviet System

The rise of ethnonationalism in recent years — as widespread as it was unexpected — has made ethnicity one of the most potent and destabilizing forces in contemporary international politics. Neither developing nor highly industrialized systems have proved immune to the pressures of increased ethnic assertiveness. As Joseph Rothschild concluded, "though several newer 'isms' have arisen in the twentieth century, ethnic nationalism, or politicized ethnicity, remains the world's major ideological legitimator and delegitimator of states, regimes, and governments."[1]

As one of the largest and most complex multinational states in the world — comprising some one hundred distinct nations and nationalities, twenty-two of which number over 1 million people each — the Soviet Union seems to be singularly vulnerable to the destabilizing effects of rising ethnonationalism. Yet until quite recently the Soviet system appeared to be comparatively immune to the impact of ethnic self-assertion. Official writings repeatedly insisted that the Soviet Union had brought equality, prosperity, and harmony to its ethnically diverse population. At the Twenty-second Party Congress in 1961, for example, Khrushchev asserted with a characteristic optimism that "the party has solved one of the most complex of problems, which has plagued mankind for ages and remains acute in the world of capitalism today — the problem of relations between nations."[2]

This optimistic assessment, however, has been replaced in recent years by a more somber recognition that from the Baltic republics to Soviet Central Asia rising ethnic self-assertion constitutes a growing political challenge. The nation-

The author would like to express her appreciation to the National Council for Soviet and East European Research and to the Harriman Institute at Columbia University for supporting the research project on which this essay is based.

ality question occupies a prominent place on the current Soviet political agenda. In December 1982, on the occasion of the sixtieth anniversary of the creation of the USSR, Yuri Andropov delivered a major address on national relations in which he reminded his audience that "Soviet successes in solving the nationalities question certainly do not mean that all the problems engendered by the very fact of the life and work of numerous nations and nationalities in the framework of a single state have disappeared. This is hardly possible as long as nations exist, as long as there are national distinctions, and they will exist for a long time, much longer than class distinctions."[3]

In order to understand the combination of satisfaction and concern that marked the sixtieth-anniversary celebrations, it is necessary to review briefly the evolution of Soviet strategy for managing a multinational system. Both the theory and practice of Soviet nationality policy reflect a fundamental tension, the origins of which go back to the two major political ideologies of nineteenth century Europe — nationalism and socialism. Nationalism identifies the nation as the basic human community and the vertical ties that linked its members as the most compelling social identity, while socialism stressed the importance of the horizontal ties of social class that cut across national boundaries and viewed national identities as obsolete and destined to be superseded by a new international community. Indeed, the essence of socialism is its hostility to nationalism; but the Bolshevik revolution of 1917 (and Marxist-Leninist movements in China, Cuba, and elsewhere) succeeded largely because they were able to harness national movements to the cause of social revolution.

But that success created a problem for the new Soviet state. The "Leninist compromise" that brought the federal Union into existence committed the new state to granting political-administrative recognition and limited cultural autonomy to a variety of national groups and to launching a massive program of economic and social modernization that would sustain and promote national development. A highly centralized party organization provided a powerful unifying force against the centrifugal pressures that the federal system might have generated. Nonetheless, this arrangement provided an organizational context, a political legitimacy, and a cultural impetus for the assertion of group interests, values, and demands.

At the same time, economic power and political control were concentrated in the hands of a predominantly Slavic central elite that sought to eradicate ethnic nationalism and to promote the long-term convergence of diverse nations and nationalities in a supranational Soviet state — with all its connotations of Russification. This Soviet strategy, however, undercut the commitment to diversity and provoked intensified national consciousness and self-assertion on the part of non-Russian elites.

Not surprisingly, the dualism embedded in the Soviet approach to managing a multinational state has been the source of a continuing controversy reaching to the very apex of the Soviet leadership. In a December 1982 speech, Konstantin Chernenko, the ideological specialist and future general secretary, referred to "the problem of the relationship between the two leading trends in the development of nations under socialism: their all-sided development and flowering (*raztsvet*) on the one hand and their steady rapprochement (*sblizhenie*) on the other."[4] The Soviet experience thus provides a test case of the degree to which it is possible for a determined, centralizing, interventionist, and modernizing elite, which derives its legitimacy in part from the espousal of national aspirations, to eradicate national identities and loyalties or transfer them to a supranational community based on a commonality of ideological orientations and economic and political goals.

The coercive policies of the Stalinist period, which had temporarily silenced the quest for collective identity and obliterated its leading advocates, fostered the expectation that a combination of repression and co-optation might indeed have succeeded in eroding national attachments. But the relaxation of terror under Khrushchev, and the more benign climate of the "thaw," permitted a revival of national sentiments and claims and made it clear that primordial loyalties would not easily succumb to the combined pressures of modernization and coercion. The growth of the dissident movement, which included an important national and religious component, dramatized the diverse sources of alienation generated by the Soviet system. A rising wave of protest and demonstrations in the Baltic republics, the Ukraine, Georgia, and among the Crimean Tatars — coupled with the large-scale emigration of Germans, Armenians, and Jews — demonstrated a widespread dissatisfaction with the USSR's denial of national rights. More recently, the rise of Islamic fundamentalism in the Middle East, with its possible impact on the burgeoning Moslem populations of Soviet Central Asia, has also brought this region to the forefront of Soviet concern. At the same time, the increasing self-assertion of the non-Russian nationalities has contributed to the growth of a Russian nationalism that views the Russian people as the victims, rather than the beneficiaries, of a Soviet multinational empire.

Thus, in managing the tension between the "flowering" and the "convergence" of nations in a complex multinational state, in controlling a turbulent Eastern European empire, and in seeking to harness national liberation movements in the Third World to its larger political goals, the Soviet leadership has confronted recurrent nationalist challenges. In the process the Soviet leadership has come to recognize that nationalism is a far more significant, prevalent, and tenacious force than it had initially assumed. Moreover, because the USSR was conceived as both the core and the model for a worldwide socialist system, the internal and international dimensions of the "nationality question" were inextricably entwined. Thus, Soviet approaches to this question at home have continually impinged on, and in turn been influenced by, wider foreign-policy concerns.

The Impact of the Nationality Question on the Soviet System

Before examining how the nationality question impinges on Soviet institutions and policies, two fundamental differences between the question and its

American counterpart should be clarified. In the United States, territorially dispersed immigrant communities constitute the major ethnic groups. But in the Soviet Union, territorially compact nations and nationalities have inhabited historical homelands over many centuries and have developed distinct national histories, languages, and traditions. Further, by contrast with the individualistic, meritocratic, and assimilationist strains of American policy, which until recently was based on the assumption that ethnic background as well as religious and linguistic affiliation should be irrelevant in the public arena—a policy reflected in the "melting pot" metaphor—Soviet policy formally recognizes national identity as a major political and social category. Not only is nationality inscribed on Soviet citizens' passports and prominently featured in Soviet statistics, but it is also officially recognized in a Soviet federal system that allows different national republics the right to maintain schools in which children are taught in the local language or to use local languages in the press and other media. Rising ethnonationalism in the Soviet context therefore involves not only growing claims of dispersed but mobilized ethnic groups but also pressures that impinge on the very structure of the Soviet federal system.

The problem of legitimation. Nowhere does rising ethnonationalism raise more crucial problems than in the legitimation of the Soviet system itself. The rise of both Russian and non-Russian nationalism, coinciding with the decline in the vitality and relevance of official ideology, exacerbates a long-standing problem in Soviet political culture: the tension between the internationalist ideology of Marxism-Leninism, which validates key features of the Soviet multinational state, and the unifying force of Soviet patriotism, which derives much of its power and appeal from its association with selected strands of Russian nationalism.

Despite the apparent contradiction of these two ideologies, it is precisely the fusion of Marxism-Leninism—with its powerful sense of historical mission and its universalist perspective—with selective elements of traditional Russian political and cultural nationalism, reinforced by the global aspirations and satisfactions of superpower status, that form the core of Soviet civic culture and endow it with both dynamism and mass appeal. The inherent and inescapable tension between the proclaimed "internationalism" of Soviet civic culture, on the one hand, and its implicit promotion of Russian political and cultural domination, on the other, may be an asset or a liability for the system. It has made possible an exceedingly astute, if delicately balanced, political strategy capable of eliciting the support of both Russian and non-Russian national elites.

At the same time, it risks provoking the dissatisfaction and alienation of both elites. Its Russocentric thrust creates anxiety and antagonism among non-Russian elites, while its internationalism legitimizes the claims of non-Russian elites and inhibits the unconstrained expression of Russian national values and interests. The Soviet leadership must therefore tread a delicate line between acknowledging the legitimacy of a growing national consciousness and curbing what it sees as undesirable manifestations of national egoism, chauvinism, and conflict. The fine-tuning required to negotiate this balance is made exceptionally difficult by the atmosphere of political uncertainty and competition that accompanies a major political succession, particularly one involving generational change at the apex of the Soviet leadership.

The problems of political control. The nationality question creates particular difficulties in maintaining a pattern of political rule that combines centralization of power with responsiveness to local demands. Issues of autonomy and of representation are at the center of current tensions.

The Soviet federal system simultaneously promoted the centralization of power in the hands of a predominantly Slavic elite and provided a framework for, and a legitimation of, the assertion of local demands. It also provided substantial opportunities for indigenous elites to play important roles in governing their regions. The efforts of these elites to enhance both the power and the resources available to them create a pattern of crypto-politics, barely visible to the outside observer, involving attempts to expand the powers and the autonomy of republic governments, to gain greater access by republics to central decision-making organs, particularly to *Gosplan* (the State Committee for Planning), and to gain greater influence over those decisions.

Such political maneuvering also involves national elites' efforts to increase the number of indigenous cadres in the republic, state, and party institutions. Indeed, the growing share of these indigenous cadres in some republic political organs in recent years — including Central Asia — has provoked visible and growing concern in Moscow. Not only does it pose a challenge to central political control, but it also provokes anxiety and opposition among nontitular nationalities residing within the republic, especially within the Russian settler communities, which fear being squeezed out of their traditional positions of dominance.

The problem of devising mechanisms that will offer equitable representation to the diverse constituencies of the multinational state reaches to the highest level of the political system. Indeed, the question extends to the composition of the Politburo itself, where recent deaths have considerably reduced the representation of non-Russians and eliminated the head of the Uzbek party organization, the only "representative" of Central Asia. How the Soviet elite addresses this problem will have important symbolic as well as practical consequences, but the growing evidence of conflict behind the scenes suggests that the issue will be increasingly controversial in the years ahead.

The problem of economic reform. The multinational character of the Soviet state, particularly its federal system, also hinders the management of current economic problems. On the one hand, it is a serious obstacle to centralized planning and management, especially to the treatment of the USSR as a single economic entity. The republics cut across natural economic regions; they enhance the leverage, however limited, of local national elites in promoting local interests; and they add an affective dimension to the interregional competition for resources and power. On the other hand, the symbiosis between regional and ethnonational interests is a barrier to the decentralizing economic reforms that would give the Soviet system a badly needed flexibility in deploying resources.

The endemic problems of localism (*mestnichestvo*) and departmentalism, which subvert central economic priorities and distort implementation, would only be compounded by reforms that devolved significantly greater power from the center to the periphery.

The brief experiment with economic decentralization under Khrushchev, as well as the experience of Yugoslavia in the 1970s, undoubtedly reinforces the conviction of the current central economic and political elite that any dispersion of economic decision making, however essential to economic initiative and the effective use of hidden reserves at the local level, would also subvert central priorities. Indeed, the Hungarian economic model has little applicability to the Soviet scene precisely because of the absence of comparable ethnoregional cleavages.

Regional demographic trends further compound these economic difficulties. Rapid population growth in Central Asia, coinciding with stable or declining birthrates in the more developed European regions of the country, increases the pressure for a reallocation of resources to the southern regions to maintain living standards and social infrastructure at existing levels, and to provide expanded irrigation to sustain its agriculture. Vast new investments are also needed to provide employment for this new generation and to soak up this labor surplus.

However, the ethnic factor also undercuts the operation of conventional economic levers in producing a rational allocation of labor resources among regions. The social and cultural values of the Central Asian population have been a major constraint on labor mobility, preventing the redirection of surplus labor to regions of labor scarcity. Moreover, providing extraterritorial cultural facilities — such as schools and newspapers in the native language — to encourage groups to move from their national homelands to regions of labor scarcity will considerably increase the costs of such efforts. Thus, whether the Soviet leadership will opt for a strategy demanding massive new investments in Central Asia, on the one hand, or will commit itself to a serious effort to shift some of its surplus labor to the east and north, on the other, it will be obliged to allocate substantial resources to the effort.

Language and cultural policy. The status and recognition accorded various nationalities, whether in the treatment of their languages, history, cultural monuments, or customs and traditions, are a further source of policy problems for the current Soviet leadership. Language policy has become especially sensitive in recent years. While basic instruction in the non-Russian republics is guaranteed in the local languages, Russian is the official language, and its study as a second language is compulsory in native schools. Moreover, upward mobility — especially in scientific and political arenas — depends on local elites' mastery of the Russian language and cultural norms, while Russians experience little pressure to master the languages of the republics in which they live and work. Shifts in language policy, which may have been intended to promote national integration, were interpreted as efforts at further Russification and have generated severe resistance and even massive demonstrations.

Moreover, despite the obvious limits placed on this process, Russian and non-

Russian elites alike are engaged in exploring as well as glorifying "roots." The resurrection of ancient and modern folk heroes, including those previously under opprobrium; the purification of national languages and the exclusion of foreign borrowings; the evocation of group achievements; the concern with preserving the group's environment, both cultural and natural; and the defense of local traditions — from religious practices to family behavior — all involve the assertion of developing cultural identities and an effort to convert cultural traditions into a political resource.

Nationality and the armed forces. Soviet management of the ethnic dimension of military policy reveals a high sensitivity to its impact on military performance. The party leadership's strategy is both integrationist and preemptive. Relying on universal male conscription, the Soviet armed forces — more than any other social institution — integrates diverse nationalities, socializes them into common norms of behavior, and imbues them with a patriotic consciousness. How the Soviet military compares with other multinational armies in achieving these goals remains a point of controversy.

Official Soviet claims are given indirect support by the testimony of a number of critics, including the prominent Ukrainian nationalist Ivan Dzyuba, who has described Soviet military service as a "denationalizing" experience that tears young people from their national roots. At the same time, there is ample evidence of ethnic friction and tensions within the armed forces and explicit calls in Soviet military publications for more decisive efforts to curb discriminatory attitudes and practices. The need for more widespread and effective "internationalist" and "patriotic" education has been virtually an obsession in recent Soviet writings, which increasingly emphasize the achievements of Soviet nationality policy.

Further complicating the tasks of the Soviet military is an inadequate knowledge of the Russian language — the language of command and control — by non-Russian conscripts, particularly from Central Asia, and their poorer educational and technical qualifications. As in the case of economic management, these difficulties are compounded by the rapidly increasing proportion of young Central Asians in the conscript pool. Between 1959 and 1970 the Muslim populations increased some 45 percent, compared with 13 percent for the Great Russians. By the end of the century the share of the Muslim population in the all-Union total will not only exceed 20 percent but will also constitute close to one-third of the draft-age cohort. Even if a knowledge of Russian as a second language is rising as rapidly as Soviet census data indicate, all the evidence suggests that the Soviet leadership is concerned about the adequacy of that knowledge. This concern is clearly reflected in Politburo reports, in the stepped-up campaign to expand and intensify Russian-language instruction in Central Asia, and in statements and resolutions that directly link this effort to military as well as to broader economic and social objectives.

Shortcomings in educational and linguistic preparation are also largely responsible for the de facto patterns of ethnic stratification within the Soviet military. Even if there is no discriminatory intent, uniform policies affecting recruitment and assignment will have a differential impact, given variations in education and skills among conscripts. Consequently, Central Asian conscripts tend to be disproportionately concentrated in noncombat units, such as construction battalions, and largely absent from branches that place a premium on sophisticated technical skills. Moreover, because the officer corps remains largely the preserve of Slavic elites, the prevalence of units in which non-Slavic troops are commanded by Slavic officers is a built-in source of tension. An effort is clearly under way to step up the recruitment and training of officers of non-Russian nationalities as well as to combat attitudes prejudicial to their promotion. As a recent article in a Soviet military journal asserted, "the party constantly points to the necessity to be concerned that all nationalities of the country are adequately represented in military training institutions and in the Soviet officer corps."[5]

The preservation of national identity and the policy process. The unexpected durability of national identities not only creates obstacles to the realization of important goals but also vastly complicates the entire Soviet policy-making process. Soviet nationality policy was premised on the expectation that economic development in a socialist society would produce fundamental behavioral and attitudinal changes. These changes would in turn facilitate the erosion of national differences and the gradual rapprochement and ultimate merger of distinct national entities. Much as in Western social-science literature, modernity was treated as a syndrome in which changes in virtually all spheres—from the workplace to family to life-style to religious beliefs—were functionally interrelated and would change together.

The mounting evidence of recent research by Soviet ethnographers has challenged many of these assumptions. It has become increasingly clear that Soviet policies not only reshape national identities but that nationality itself has an independent and reciprocal impact on economic and social behavior as well as attitudes. The recognition of this fact has far-reaching ramifications for Soviet policy making that are just beginning to receive attention.

Unquestionably, Soviet development has brought about growing similarities in the life-styles, behaviors, and attitudes of the population. Moreover, these similarities are greater among younger cohorts than among their elders. Whether one looks at educational levels, occupational patterns, or the knowledge of Russian as a second language, the earlier differences among a variety of national groups have been substantially narrowed.

At the same time, however, a number of areas have seen a relatively slow rate of change. The durability of national languages has been little affected by the spread of Russian as a second language. Endogamy remains the norm despite the increased intermixing of national groups in educational institutions and in the workplace; 75 to 94 percent of the population of major nationalities live in ethnically homogenous families, while mixed marriages tend to be concentrated within the core cultural group. Religious observances, especially where they are closely entwined with national traditions, retain considerable vitality. In Central Asia, for example, nearly all families observe such rites as burial and circumcision, which have communal significance; many observe religious rites; and a somewhat smaller number adhere to social customs of religious origin.

Equally important, attitudes and behaviors among different nationalities vary substantially. Economic and political behavior appears to change more rapidly than sociocultural influences; family and mode of living are especially tenacious. As Soviet investigations have repeatedly confirmed, where religion and national customs are closely entwined, new norms encounter greater resistance. Moreover, situational factors — such as urban or rural milieu, social class, and ethnic environment (Russian, mixed, or native) — help shape the direction and pace of change. Language itself appears to be an important determinant of attitudes and behavior, especially with respect to intermarriage and migration. Finally, Soviet research has demonstrated that attitudes in one sphere do not necessarily carry over into another; there may be no single syndrome of "ethnic modernity."

The implications of this finding for Soviet policy making are both far-reaching and chastening, given the official commitment to directed social change. A distinguished Soviet ethnographer, Yu. V. Arutiunian, has suggested: "If this conclusion is true, it means that there can be no universally valid means of improving ethnic relationships. A given technique may lead to different and sometimes even directly opposite results in different social groups."[6]

The Nationality Question and Soviet Security

The impact of the nationality question on Soviet security is a sufficiently important issue to be singled out for separate treatment. Throughout its history the Soviet regime has been sensitive to the double-edged nature of the linkages between domestic security concerns and foreign-policy objectives. On the one hand, Soviet nationalities and foreign minorities have been important assets in expanding Soviet influence and power beyond its borders. On the other hand, the presence of nationalities and minorities is a source of vulnerability: at a minimum, a constraint on domestic policy; at a maximum, a channel for outside penetration. Not surprisingly, Soviet policy has attempted to exploit these assets while insulating the Soviet system from foreign contagion.

In the recent past (leaving aside the cases of nonterritorial nationalities, notably the ethnic Germans, the Koreans, and the Jews), four important national groups have been particularly affected by developments outside Soviet borders: the Ukraine during the Czechoslovak crisis of 1968; the Baltic states during the Polish events of 1980–82; Central Asian border nationalities during the conflicts between the Soviet Union and China; and the Central Asian Muslim populations in the wake of the revival of Muslim fundamentalism in Iran and the Soviet invasion of Afghanistan. All these cases demonstrate the considerable, but limited, ability of the Soviet system to insulate internal developments from external influences.

The Sino-Soviet case poses the fewest problems for Soviet policy. China's strongly assimilationist treatment of national minorities historically held little appeal for the ethnic groups on the Soviet side of the border. Notwithstanding Chinese efforts to portray the Soviets as "heirs of the tsars" in their imperial proclivities, it is likely that the Mongols, Uighurs, and Kazakhs on the Chinese side of the border are more vulnerable to appeals from the Soviet Union than vice versa. The recent shift in China's policies, and its more tolerant treatment of national minorities, may reduce Chinese vulnerabilities in this area, but in the short run it will not dramatically alter Soviet assets in this competition.

The linkages between Soviet nationality questions and foreign-policy concerns were considerably stronger in the case of the "Prague Spring" of 1968. For at least some Soviet leaders most notably Petro Shelest', then a Politburo member and first secretary of the Ukrainian Communist party, the fear that liberalizing trends in Czechoslovakia would exacerbate liberal and national dissidence within the Ukraine (which shared a common border with Czechoslovakia) was an important motive in their advocacy of Soviet intervention. What made this linkage particularly important was the combination of parallel ideological and political cleavages in both Czechoslovakia and the Ukraine — making the Czech reforms a relevant model — and the factional conflicts within the leadership in both Kiev and Moscow over the handling of such challenges at home and abroad. It remains unclear to what extent Shelest' was responding to genuine contagion and to what extent events offered him a welcome opportunity to crack down. Whatever the appeal of the Czech reform program, Soviet intervention also helped tighten domestic control, effectively ending any further reverberations in the Ukraine.

The impact of Polish developments since 1980 on the Baltic republics had some parallels to the case of Czechoslovakia and the Ukraine; both cases involved a national as well as a sociopolitical dimension in the affected region not found elsewhere in the USSR. Close historical and cultural affinities as well as common grievances against Moscow, reinforced in Lithuania by religious ties (but tempered by mutual animosities), heightened sensitivity to Polish events. Repercussions were most evident in Estonia, where they reportedly triggered work stoppages, youth rebellions, and intelligentsia protests directed at Estonian officialdom. But even there, where a strong sense of national identity provided a potential bridge between workers and intelligentsia and a deteriorating economic situation fueled popular discontent, the failure to develop such a coalition is a reminder of the obstacles to emulating the Polish experience within the USSR. Nonetheless, it is clear even from published sources that the Soviet leadership has been exceptionally nervous about the possible spillover of unrest from Poland and its exploitation by "bourgeois" propagandists and has sought to respond to grievances by a sophisticated mix of repression and redress.

The fourth example of domestic/foreign linkages, involving the Soviet southern tier, remains an open case. The potential impact of a revival of Islamic fundamentalism in the Middle East on the Soviet nationalities of Central Asia has virtually eclipsed the West's preoccupation with the Baltic states and the Ukraine as the potentially weakest links in the Soviet internal empire. A number of commentators have argued that the single most profound cleavage within the Soviet system is the division between its Muslim citizens (using the term to connote a broad cultural identity, rather than religious beliefs) and the rest of the population. Linked by history and culture to the east, endowed by Soviet rule with new resources, skills, and claims, represented by increasingly assertive local elites who, in their view, pay lip service to Soviet values while retaining a strong identification with their local culture, and increasingly aware of developments in the Muslim world outside Soviet borders, these populations pose a serious threat to the future stability of the Soviet system. Indeed, the Soviet invasion of Afghanistan, in this view, was propelled by Soviet anxiety over the danger of contagion—an anxiety that was partly justified when the unreliability of Central Asian troops allegedly forced their early withdrawal from Afghanistan.

Without denying the evidence of genuine Soviet concern about the potential use of Islam to the detriment of Soviet interests, it is possible to exaggerate the concern of the Soviet leadership about the loyalty of its Central Asian populations and underestimate the degree to which it perceives that political instability in the Middle East provides opportunities for, as well as dangers to, Soviet strategic interests. The invasion of Afghanistan increased, rather than diminished, the exposure of the Soviet Union's southern region to contagion from abroad, as does the substantial reliance on Central Asian cadres in building a new administrative and cultural infrastructure in the occupied regions of Afghanistan. While the Soviet invasion was based on a calculus of security concerns in which Islamic fundamentalism was neither a decisive nor a necessary ingredient, it surely reflected a certain confidence that, for Soviet Muslims, exposure to Afghanistan would hold no special attractions. The military difficulties of the initial months of the invasion were largely due to the inadequate combat readiness of the reserve units that bore the brunt of the invasion, rather than evidence of disaffection among Muslim conscripts, and the subsequent replacement of these units was a matter of routine rotation practices.

These four cases suggest that, by contrast with earlier stages of Soviet development, when the presence of national minorities could be exercised on behalf of expanded Soviet control over neighboring states, the multinational character of the Soviet Union now imposes increasingly substantial costs. The greater openness of the Soviet system to developments outside its borders than prevailed during the Stalin years has increased Soviet vulnerability to external influences even as it has brought important benefits. The growing salience of foreign policy on the Soviet political agenda, combined with the presence of important domestic/foreign linkages resulting from the concentration of non-Russian populations on the border regions of the USSR, has created an indissoluble link between the domestic and international dimensions of Soviet nationality policy.

Thus, even if the Soviet system retains its considerable capacity to insulate domestic developments from external influences, and even if the emergence of genuine ethnonational movements with separatist goals remains a highly unlikely prospect—whether in Central Asia or in other regions of the USSR—the nationality question will raise increasingly difficult problems of management for the Soviet leadership in the years ahead. It will constrain and complicate the resolution of many of the key problems that the Soviet system faces in the 1980s and will compel the Soviet leadership to make difficult and unwelcome choices among a limited range of policy options.

Policy Options

A number of Western observers have argued that the scope and intensity of rising ethnonationalism is likely to become unmanageable and that, in the words of Richard Pipes, "sooner or later the Soviet empire, the last multinational empire, will fall apart roughly along the lines of today's republics."[7] Such expectations are exaggerated. The Soviet system possesses important assets as well as liabilities in the management of ethnic tensions, and it is by no means certain that rising national consciousness will culminate in secessionist movements. A sophisticated combination of effective coercion, co-optation of local elites, and partial accommodation of national cultures has enabled the Soviet system to preempt, displace, or exploit national aspirations in ways that have maintained the overall stability of the system. The more difficult but fundamental question is whether the successful management of the nationality question in the years ahead will require costly changes in key Soviet institutional arrangements and policy orientations and how these changes will affect other priorities.

The Soviet Union can address its national relations in one of three ways. The first would be a coercive, centralizing, and Russifying strategy designed to solidify the regime's support by the core Russian population and elites even at the cost of greater alienation of the non-Russian populations. This strategy's ideological expression would be a greater tilt toward Russian nationalism and increased emphasis on the rapprochement rather than the flowering of national cultures. The central organs of power would be strengthened at the expense of the republics and would reassert the dominance of Slavic elites—a deliberate reversal of the trend toward "indigenization" of local party and administrative organs and a rejection of "affirmative action" programs at the present stage of Soviet development. An increase in economic integration and a decrease in the republics' control over economic and social policy within their borders would be accompanied by investment policies designed to shift surplus labor from Central Asia to regions of labor shortage, possibly involving compulsory assignment of secondary-school graduates to work outside their native republics. Cultural and linguistic Russification would be intensified, and the development of local schools and the use of local languages would be sharply curtailed.

The opposite strategy would accommodate the interests and aspirations of the non-Russian populations within the framework of a more genuinely federal system. It would promote greater autonomy, pluralism, and decentralization, in the expectation that a consociational system based on greater equality and reciprocity among national groups would be more stable than one based on hierarchy and Russification. It would build on the internationalist strains of Soviet ideology, giving greater emphasis to the development of national cultures. Political and economic integration would be promoted as a functional requisite of a modern industrial society, dissociating itself from Russocentrism. The status and powers of the republics would be enhanced, the representation of non-Russians in the central political and economic organs would be increased, and — to create a more genuinely federal system — the Russian republic would be endowed (as are all the non-Russian republics) with party organs of its own. A more balanced pattern of economic development within republics would be promoted, even at the expense of a "fraternal division of labor," as well as cultural and linguistic pluralism, including the requirement that Russians themselves be obliged to learn as a second language one of the national languages of the USSR. Needless to say, the perceived costs of such a strategy would be exceedingly high, and its prospects minimal; not only would it challenge fundamental Soviet institutional arrangements, but it would also simultaneously risk alienating the Russian majority and stimulating, rather then satisfying, the appetites and aspirations of the non-Russian nations and nationalities.

A third possible strategy — and indeed one that is most closely approximated by recent Soviet policies — is a bifurcated one, based on a more aggressive approach to core economic and political priorities and their "decoupling" from social and cultural issues, which are considered secondary. It would involve a sharpened focus on political and economic integration, combined with a greater recognition of, and tolerance for, the durability of national identities and a less confrontational approach to national cultural concerns.

The contours of such a strategy were outlined in a number of speeches and articles by key party leaders in the past few years, as well as by the recommendations of several major conferences devoted to national relations. At the top of the list of core priorities is the pursuit of accelerated economic integration and improved efficiency. The effective use of scarce resources requires, in this view, greater freedom of action for central planning agencies and the subordination of regional and republic interests to national needs. The optimal allocation of both capital and labor is likely to lead to greater regional differentiation and to benefit those more developed regions where the returns to investment are greatest or those, like Siberia, that are rich in energy and other resources.

Enhanced political and ideological integration represents a second core priority in this emerging strategy. The term *sblizhenie* is increasingly focused on political and ideological rapprochement rather than on cultural assimilation or Russification. The new emphasis on the "Soviet people" as a social community is intended both to stress cohesion and integration and to distinguish Soviet citizenship from traditional national affiliations. This terminology gives more explicit recognition and legitimacy to the dual identity embodied in simultaneous membership in a national group and in the Soviet supranational community.

At the same time, to the extent that this integration is promoted by the retention of an adequate Russian presence in local party and state institutions, it is associated with muted but unmistakable resistance to the gradual elimination of Russian cadres. The repeated emphasis in recent Soviet speeches on the multinational character of the republics, and on the right of all nationalities to be adequately represented in republic organs, is clearly directed against what is perceived as excessive pressures for indigenization by local national elites.

Accelerated Russian-language training is another key component of this emerging strategy. Instruction is now to begin at preschool levels, and to be expanded both within and outside educational institutions, in an effort to spread effective bilingualism throughout the younger generation of non-Russians. Military concerns clearly occupy an important place in this effort as the demographic explosion in Central Asia alters the ethnic composition of the conscript pool. But it is also linked to efforts to promote a redistribution of manpower from labor-surplus to labor-scarce regions of the country, which in part depends on transforming the attitudes as well as the skills of the younger generation so it will feel more comfortable in mixed ethnic environments.

This more aggressive approach to core economic and political priorities is coupled with an apparent effort to relieve some of the anxieties and tensions in Soviet national relations by less confrontational approaches to some aspects of national identity and culture. The most dramatic element of this new approach is the treatment of the persistence and even growth of national consciousness (clearly distinguished from nationalism) as a natural and lawful process. National identities are now recognized to be more stable and enduring phenomena than had previously been acknowledged, and have even been described in authoritative publications as "in principle . . . indestructible."[8] The revival of the term *sliianie* (merger) under Andropov has occurred in a context that postponed its advent to a very distant communist future and that stripped it of any connotation of biological fusion.

Not only does this new formulation provide official legitimation for a viewpoint that might otherwise be deemed provocative; it can also be used in support of initiatives that seek to accommodate national diversity. Within the military, for example, increased emphasis on Russian-language training has been accompanied by measures that allow the use of non-Russian languages in noncommand situations and allow conscripts (and indeed all Soviet citizens) to subscribe to newspapers and journals in their native languages. Soviet officers as well as party and state officials have been urged to display greater sensitivity to national differences and customs in order to enhance effectiveness. They have been reminded that "negative phenomena" in national relations cannot be treated simply as vestiges of the past "but are sometimes nourished by our own mistakes."[9]

Andropov's call for the development of a "well-thought-out, scientifically-based nationalities policy," together with growing interest in and support for policy-relevant social science research on ethnic relations in recent years, suggests that the leadership is persuaded that ethnosociological research and not merely ideological dogma should play a major role in the further development of the theory and practice of nationalities policy. Top party leaders retain the ultimate power to define the bounds of the permissible, but they are extending the limits of indigenous cultural expression in what may well constitute more sophisticated central management of the Soviet multinational state.

NOTES

1. Joseph Rothschild, *Ethnopolitics: A Conceptual Framework* (New York: Columbia University Press, 1981), 14.

2. *Pravda*, 18 Oct. 1961.

3. *Pravda*, 22 Dec. 1982.

4. Konstantin Chernenko, "Shest'desiat let bratskoi druzhby narodov," *Problemy mira i sotsializma*, no. 12 (December 1982), p. 10.

5. Lt. Gen. Ye. Nikitin, *Agitator armii i flota*, no. 23, (1982), pp. 10–14.

6. Yu. V. Arutiunian, "Konkretno-sotsiologicheskoe issledovanie natsional'nykh otnoshenii," *Voprosy filosofii*, no. 12 (1969).

7. Carl A. Linden and Dimitri K. Simes, *Nationalities and Nationalism in the USSR: A Soviet Dilemma* (Washington, D.C.: Georgetown Center for Strategic and International Studies, 1977), 10.

8. For example, by a key party theoretician and editor of the party's ideological journal, R. I. Kosolapov, "Klassovye i natsional'nye otnosheniia na etape razvitogo sotsializma," *Sotsiologicheskie issledovaniia* no. 4 (1982), p. 15.

9. Yuri Andropov, *Report to the Joint Ceremonial Meeting of the CPSU Central Committee, the USSR Supreme Soviet and the Russian Republic Supreme Soviet, Pravda*, 22 Dec. 1982, p. 1.

Policy Issues in the Soviet Media System

ELLEN MICKIEWICZ

A number of serious policy issues may be identified in the Soviet media system. In large part, these issues have arisen because of the phenomenal growth and spread of the media and the new technologies that have become available. For example, although the Soviet television industry was producing only 960 sets a year between 1940 and 1950, the annual production figure jumped to an average of 3 million a year between 1960 and 1970. By 1976, the industry was producing over 7 million sets a year. National newspapers have a combined circulation of over 80 million copies, and the circulation of all newspapers at all levels is over 175 million. The circulation of daily newspapers is 400 per 1,000 persons, as compared with 282 per 1,000 in the United States. "The Knowledge Society," the leading component of the oral media system, presented over 26 million lectures in 1979. The picture is one of tremendous communications activity, and with that activity have come both successes and problems.

Soviet Feedback Channels

Before the late 1960s, Soviet communications policymakers were confident that they were accurately assessing the efficacy of their system, that they understood media audiences, and that they could evaluate preferences and discontents. They operated on two fundamental assumptions. The first was that the single most important variable was the reach of the media. The persuasive capability of the media, they believed, depended on the citizens' exposure to the messages approved by the officials (and the denial of exposure to unofficial, especially foreign, communications networks). The second operating assumption was a connection between education (expressed in cognitive skills) and persuasion. Under this assumption, Soviet communications policymakers equated the ability to understand messages, whether in the electronic or print media, with the certainty of being convinced by those messages. Only a lack of cognitive skills would keep a viewer, listener, or reader from being persuaded; he or she, unable to understand the message, could not appreciate what should be an evident truth. For recalcitrants, the vestiges of the past—a catchall category used to explain undesirable phenomena as holdovers from before the Revolution—produced an obstruction to understanding and persuasion.

Soviet media officials could have confidence in their assumptions, because they believed they were exposed to ample feedback from the media audience. Every year all the media combined receive some 60 million letters from viewers, listeners, and readers. Each of the thirty-one major national newspapers receives half a million letters a year. In one year alone, the central radio and television studios received more than 2 million letters. This volume of letters is handled by large staffs. At *Pravda,* for example, some seventy people are employed full-time in the letters department. Other newspapers have staffs of similar size. They catalogue, summarize, distribute, and respond to letters. The process is computerized, and reports are produced at monthly intervals. *Pravda* prepares ten to twelve such reports a month for distribution to the Central Committee of the party. On the basis of these reports, culled from the huge sacks of letters delivered to the editorial offices, certain conclusions are drawn about the readership of the newspapers, the audiences for radio and television, and the mood of the nation. With millions of communications a year from the audience, it is easy for the officials to think that they have tapped public opinion. As analysts of Western communications systems understand, the opinion of some of the audience has been tapped in this way, but it is probably far from a representative sample of the audience.

The New Understanding of the Media Public

Since the late 1960s the media officials have questioned their assumptions about the media public. Methodologically sound surveys of the readership of the national and regional newspapers, and then of television, film, and theater audiences, revealed a considerable divergence between the characteristics of those who write letters and the typical receiver of media messages. The Soviet audience surveys found that letterwriters were apt to be considerbly older than the average, much more likely to belong to the Communist party, and engaged in occupations that do not match those of the audience. The surveys produced a picture of the audience that contradicted official operating assumptions. For example, although illiteracy has been eradicated in the Soviet Union, the comprehension of media messages cannot be assumed. One survey asked respondents to define a number of words commonly used in newspaper stories about international affairs. About a quarter of the readers did not know what *colonialism* meant; about two-fifths did not understand the word *dictatorship.* Almost half were unable to define *imperialism,* and almost two-thirds did not understand the meaning of *leftist forces.* Finally, up to three-quarters had no idea what *reactionary* and *liberal* meant.

Thus, even though cognitive skills were much more highly developed by the

1980s, it was clear that the way in which the media expressed themselves was still far too abstruse for most of the audience. Another assumption about education was also crushed by the survey results. It was found that education was inversely related to agreement and satisfaction with the media. The college educated, though the most avid consumers of the media (with the exception of television, of which they are still comparatively low consumers), most frequently disagree with the editorial point of view and are most often critical of what they see and read. To a Western observer, the relationship between critical stance and education is a familiar one. But a key assumption of Soviet media officials — that rising levels of education would be associated with rising levels of persuasive power of the media — has been fundamentally challenged by the survey findings.[1]

The scope of this policy problem is widened by a certain urgency that has entered into official Soviet discussions of media policy. That urgency is related to an increasingly powerful perception of international tensions and what is in Soviet eyes a hostile and aggressive American policy. This thrust, called "unprecedented" by Konstantin Chernenko, the top communications boss before his rise to the position of general secretary, in his June 1983 speech to the party's Central Committee, constitutes a "real information-propaganda intervention." Chernenko, like other party leaders recently before him, advocated a broad program of counterpropaganda and new measures to halt the intrusion of foreign media.[2] Media competition with the West for the domestic Soviet audience is seen by the Soviet leadership as more acute now because the capitalist countries are ahead of the socialist world in the relevant technology. Although jamming continues to affect the Soviet public's ability to hear nonofficial programs, it has been found, according to Western estimates, that in any given week about 20 percent of the Soviet adult population is exposed to at least one of the four major Western broadcasters — the British Broadcasting Corporation, Deutsche Welle (under the Ministry of the Interior of the Federal Republic of Germany), the Voice of America (administered by the United States Information Agency), and Radio Liberty (administered by the Board for International Broadcasting and funded by the United States Congress). Some officially sponsored surveys have asked Soviet citizens about the effect of "bourgeois propaganda" and the efficacy of official responses to it. Only fragments have reported, but once again, higher levels of education remain associated with dissatisfaction.

The intrusion of foreign media has exacerbated the policy problem that Soviet media officials have just begun to acknowledge. Through the faulty operation of the feedback loop, which is almost entirely confined to letters and to the personal impressions gathered by journalists, the true dimensions of audience satisfaction, preferences, and comprehension had been unknown. Thus the efficacy of the media was also unknown. Efficacy has become a much more critical concern as Soviet-American relations have worsened. There is now a concern that the official Soviet message be assimilated and that competing messages be kept out or at least resisted by a public already informed by the Soviet media.

Measures for Improving Media Efficacy

There are several policy implications of the present situation, and it is clear that some actions are being taken by the Soviet leadership. An attempt has been made to open new channels for feedback. At the Twenty-sixth Congress of the Communist party in 1981, a new Central Committee department was described: the Letters Department, with jurisdiction over the Group for Analyzing Public Opinion for Social Research and Development. Leonid Brezhnev, in his speech to that congress, underlined the importance of letters. The Central Committee was said to be receiving over 3 million letters a year. A new department for letters would presumably bring still more letters, activate those who do not write letters, and allow policymakers to see more of Soviet public opinion. When Yuri Andropov succeeded Brezhnev, his first call was for more letters from the population. He urged citizens to write letters exposing corruption and mismanagement in the economy. But the call for more letters, even if enhanced by the creation of a new Central Committee department, is still advocacy of the same self-selected method of feedback — the method that has shown little reliability and yielded only skewed information. In his June 1983 speech to the Central Committee, Chernenko revealed something of the ambivalence that besets the policymakers on this issue. He spoke positively of letters as "barometers of public opinion," as though their traditional place would be preserved. However, later in the speech, he cited three kinds of feedback: letters, questions addressed to speakers at public lectures, and sociological research (understood as survey research). He then concluded that uncoordinated studies of public opinion had to give way to systematic and reliable methods and suggested that a national center for the "scientific study of public opinion" be organized. Now that Chernenko is general secretary, there will probably be considerable movement in this direction.

One might ask why a policy problem so clearly delineated has met with such conservative and fragmented measures on the part of the Soviet leadership. The restrictive, methodologically unsound procedures of the past are clearly less useful than a new, reformulated conceptual framework — one that would rely on scientifically sound methods and result in accurate and reliable projections and measures of efficacy. However, such a move would entail the positioning of the public at the center of attention. To the extent that this occurs, the function of Marxism-Leninism as a guidance system becomes problematic. If media efficacy is to be evaluated in terms of audience response, then the audience is elevated to the commanding position. Although total capitulation to audience (or consumer) demand is by no means necessary, the Soviet media system has not until now had any accurate notion of audience preference at all, and any ground given to the primacy of audience demand is a significant step. Soviet survey analysts, including those in the party organs, have recognized not only that audience preferences must be discovered through surveys, but also that they must be addressed if messages are to be effectively assimilated. Some moves by the Andropov regime suggested a greater responsiveness to audience interests. After the

Korean Airlines flight 007 was shot down in September 1983, an unprecedented press conference was aired on Soviet national television. Conducted by Chief of Staff Marshal Nikolai Ogarkov, Deputy Foreign Minister Georgy Kornienko, and the head of the International Information Department, Leonid Zamiatin, the press conference lasted more than two hours. In April 1983, Foreign Minister Gromyko had held a press conference, but this later performance was remarkable — first, for its responsiveness to a major international story; second, for the extended public appearance of the chief of staff, and third, for the sharp and, at times, emotional questions from the audience, including those taken spontaneously from foreign correspondents. Shortly after, the pilots responsible for the incident explained their story on television. In December 1983, Ogarkov, Kornienko, and Zamiatin once again gave a press conference explaining the Soviets' withdrawal from the intermediate nuclear forces talks in Geneva.

Another recent measure to improve responsiveness is the practice, inaugurated by Andropov, of "covering" the meetings of the Politburo. *Pravda* now carries a summary of the agenda items and describes the major issues discussed and the kinds of measures ordered. Obviously, there is no way of knowing how fully the report reflects the actual agenda, and the coverage is rather general and abstract, but the scheduled review of the workings of the hitherto obscured leadership body is an important change.

The Media and International News

If, in an effort to improve the efficacy of the media, audience preferences were given greater priority, what additional policy changes would be involved? This question underlies much of the ambivalent temporizing concerning the media. The surveys have revealed a widespread lack of interest in the purely instructional fare of Soviet programming. To be sure, all Soviet media are didactic in that their mission is the explicit shaping of social, political, and moral values. However, much of the material in the media is lectures on themes such as industrial production, agricultural harvests, and innovations in the organization of labor. The types of stories and programs that most attract the Soviet public are those on international events and human-interest stories. The latter, which appeal most to people who have not gone to college, are dramas of family life and moral choices in everyday situations. But the former, the story or program on international news, attracts strong interest from all age groups and occupations. To a great extent this buildup of attention to communications about foreign, particularly Western, countries is the result of Soviet media policy.

Although most stories in the Soviet media are about domestic events, much of the material about foreign countries is devoted to stories about the United States and its NATO allies. Almost half of all the foreign news in *Pravda* covers these Western countries. In local newspapers a little more than 41 percent of the coverage on international themes is devoted to material on capitalism. Only about 30 percent is related to events taking place in communist countries. To be sure, these stories tend to be negative — accusations of aggressive policies of imperialism or depictions of the economic crises of capitalism — and the attention to the West is designed to strengthen support by focusing on its constant and pervasive threat to the Soviet Union. However, the policy has also resulted in a desire for stories about international events, particularly those dealing with the capitalist West. Recent surveys show that within this category, readers most want to learn news of military conflicts and problems of war and peace. Television had been seen primarily as a vehicle for entertainment, but the public now considers it to be the chief source of information about life in the industrialized West.

Some Soviet officials have been disturbed by the considerable space and time allocated to stories and programs about their Western adversaries. These officials argue that "the clear, deep demonstration of the strengths of the world system of socialism, of the camp of democracy and progress, should occupy the leading place among articles on international questions."[3] It is possible, too, that interest in foreign radio broadcasts is another consequence of such policy.

However, the policy implications point in another direction as well, and this direction provides opportunities for the media officials to influence the Soviet citizenry. Studies of Western media publics show that the more a story approaches the life of the reader or viewer, the less confidence he or she accords the medium. In other words, the greater the opportunity for independent verification of events — through word-of-mouth or personal observation — the greater the skepticism. On the other hand, the more the story transmits information that cannot be independently verified, the more the source is trusted. Stories about international events are clearly in this latter category — beyond the personal knowledge and observation of readers and viewers. The level of trust and confidence among readers and viewers is higher for the central media and for stories about international events. It is likely, therefore, that a considerable reserve of support for the central media exists. Domestically, the heavy coverage of the emplacement of Pershing 2 and Cruise missiles in Western Europe has, on the whole, successfully communicated the Soviet point of view.

In order to tap this reserve of support and to reduce the potential impact of foreign sources of information, Soviet policymakers must do several things. First, as they themselves acknowledge, they must ensure that events are reported initially by the Soviet media. Soviet specialists are aware that once a foreign information source has put forward its story, the Soviet media have the task of breaking down that story and then building up their own. It is much easier for the Soviet media to be convincing when they are first with the story. In general, fast-breaking news is not given high priority in Soviet newspapers; only about 15 percent of a newspaper's space is devoted to events, domestic or foreign, that had occurred the day before. Thus, responding to the public's strong interest in international news and tapping the support accorded the central media on international issues will require some changes in media practice. The initiatives noted earlier are obvious moves in this direction. However, there are other more far-reaching opportunities that could be taken.

Television news coverage affects the audience more than any other medium. *Believability* and *objectivity* are words often used to characterize television coverage in the West, because visual transmissions are inherently less suspect and more trusted than written words. The notion that the editing of these visual images affects the product has been only dimly perceived. Television's high credibility and appeal to all segments of the population, regardless of education, have not been fully utilized by Soviet policymakers. Although there are about 150 correspondents throughout the Soviet Union and 40 in foreign countries, they rarely appear live and sign off from location. Rather, Soviet television news programs rely heavily on "talking heads." The advantages of on-location, fast-breaking news stories are apparently sacrificed to a principle of tight control and predictable images. Live, on-location coverage — which could include the unpredictable, the censorable, and a potential impact of a very advantageous sort — gives way to a "safe," but decidedly less effective use of the media. Most programs have the static look that Western television had in the 1950s. Although the Soviet communications industry lags considerably behind that of the West, especially in the production of videotapes and videotaping equipment, they do have electronic news-gathering equipment. The decision is a political one, and few steps are being taken to improve the situation.

Audience Preference and Media Efficacy

Reaching the media audience more effectively would necessitate a restructuring of other types of stories and programs. For example, if one compares a rank order of newspaper space by topic and a rank order of the top ten most popular topics for the reader, only two of the topics that are given prime attention by editors reappear among the top ten readers' preferences: sports and trade-union stories. Human-interest stories, articles on crime, and information about capitalist countries would take most of the space if consumer demand prevailed. As another example, the Soviet motion-picture industry produces many serious films with contemporary settings. This kind of film accounts for about a third of all motion pictures produced, the single largest category. But in terms of ticket sales, they are the least popular, outgrossed by adventure, comedy, and musical films. The problem for the policymakers, then, is a familiar one. As audience interest is stimulated, media efficacy is enhanced; but the central control and guidance function is reduced.

Prominent Soviet sociologists maintain with increasing insistence that communication is not simply a one-way channel for the dissemination of information but rather a two-way relationship between communicator and receiver. As one writer put it, the recipient of media messages "perceives and assimilates far from all that is addressed to him; he relates selectively to the influence. This selectivity to transmitted information depends on its content and the significance for the individual. The attention of the person is directed first of all to communications that answer his interests."[4] The official political doctrine of Marxism-

Leninism does not provide specific guidelines. A leading party sociologist in the Central Committee's Academy of Social Sciences wrote recently that the assimilation of media messages can be figured only on a probabilistic basis, the product of interaction with an audience and its predispositions. The political doctrine gives norms without any practical strategy or method to apply. If the methods and strategy of communications are cut loose from the moorings of the political doctrine, then the policymakers must look to other ways of finding out about and responding to audience needs. This recognition, in itself, is a policy change; but how far up into the media officialdom it will go remains to be seen.

Media Organization and Elites

A consideration of Soviet media policy directions and choices must involve an analysis of the media officials. What are their principal functions and how likely is this bureaucracy to respond to a rapidly changing international communications environment? As in other areas of Soviet administration, there is a parallel structure of government and party authority. At the apex, over both structures, the Politburo of the party exercises decisive power. The new Politburo leader, Konstantin Chernenko, has come up through the ideology and communications network. Before 1984, he had taken over the functions of the long-time ideology chief, Mikhail Suslov. Chernenko, having earlier lost the top post to Andropov, settled into this role while building support during Andropov's long illness. Thus, for the first time, the Soviet leader is now a person with long-time experience in the media system. Thus it is likely that changes, both in foreign and domestic media use, will be forthcoming. At the next level of authority is the Central Committee secretary responsible for the media — the propaganda secretary. This post oversees the areas of culture, education, propaganda, and science. The operations of the official censorship agency, the Chief Administration for the Affairs of Literature and Publishing Houses (GLAVLIT), come under its jurisdiction.

Next in line in authority over the media is the head of the Central Committee Propaganda Department. One of the largest departments, it is charged with mobilizing public opinion and is the overall administrator of the media. It has an important voice in the selection of editors and communicates to the individual media the appropriate tone and content to follow. It also allocates budgets and defines the circulation size of print media. Other Central Committee departments, such as the Letters Department, the International Information Department, and the International Department, have some connection with the media. Each of the republics has a counterpart to the propaganda secretary and a republic-level Central Committee Department of Propaganda. These two positions, in close consultation with and under orders from their superiors in Moscow, provide principal oversight for the media at the regional level.

On the government side, administration of the media is performed primarily by the Ministry of Culture and three state committees: the State Committee for Publishing Houses, Printing Plants, and the Book Trade; the State Committee for Cinematography; and the State Committee for Television and Radio Broadcasting. In addition, the telegraph agency (TASS) and the news feature service (NOVOSTI) are components of the media structure. Still another key figure in media policy is the head of the Komsomol, the mass youth organization. The centralization of power is further enhanced by the *nomenklatura* process, which ensures that all appointments of key editors, journalists, and other communications officials are approved by the appropriate party organization at a higher level. In addition, as another part of this system of controls, the Union of Journalists establishes criteria for performance and authorized subject matter. Expulsion from this association effectively closes the door to participation in all official media. The Union of Journalists is administered by party officials, and the majority of the journalists in all media belong to the party.

The censorship system, directed by GLAVLIT, was founded in 1922. It must approve all publications in excess of nine copies. But an informal or self-censorship system has reduced the importance of GLAVLIT. Authors understand what will likely be prohibited and seek to avoid difficulties with the authorities. Therefore, they tend to censor their own material. In addition, the editorial staff of the newspaper or television station checks the material for deliberate or inadvertent evasions of the censors' guidelines. By the time material reaches GLAVLIT, a fine screen has generally removed censorable items.

The officials who direct media policy in the departments, agencies, and committees share certain characteristics. They have had, in roughly similar percentages, one of three types of higher education: technical institute, primarily engineering; university; or teachers college. It is rare for a communications official to have had a journalism education. It is very likely, however, that these officials will have studied at special schools run by the party for midlevel party workers who will be singled out for higher-level party posts. Although less than a quarter of the top national and regional officials have had this experience, about half of the communications group have taken these ideology and management courses under the auspices of two Central Committee institutions — the Academy of Social Sciences and the Moscow Higher Party School. These two-year courses prepare them for professional party leadership; they help to integrate a geographically dispersed elite, bringing them to Moscow and sending them back to positions of regional responsibility, presumably with some managerial training and a common understanding of the political aims of communication.

Since very few of the communications elite have had formal training or on-the-job experience in communications, the party school must provide whatever managerial or specialized training they will receive. To keep current, editors of regional newspapers are occasionally brought to Moscow for month-long refresher courses run by the Institute for Raising Qualifications of Leading Party and Soviet Cadres of the Academy of Social Sciences. They are lectured to by high-level officials of the Central Committee, some of the most important figures in the country. It is unlikely that training of this sort will enable communications officials to master the new technology of the communications revolution and its implications or to understand the issues associated with media efficacy. Clearly, the emphasis is on understanding party requirements and methods of control and administration. If the media officials had had on-the-job experience in the media they now manage, their perspectives might well be different, but, in fact, the large majority have had no real communications experience, having been plucked out of party or youth organization duties and placed at or near the top of the media organizations. A very large number have served in high-level professional positions in the youth organization, and their professional background is related to a function they must perform as overseers of the media — the molding of the youth and the prevention of youth countercultures.

A significant number of these officials are involved in international activities and in agencies with foreign counterparts. This is surprising, if one considers that most of the communications jobs are defined by *domestic* or *internal* duties. Especially at the regional level, it is difficult to imagine how international connections and activities relate to, say, the local television channels or the local motion-picture industry. After all, foreign news is provided to the provinces from the center, and all questions relating to foreign events are set from and communicated by the *apparat* in Moscow. Communications officials, however, are apparently used as spokespersons for the Soviet political system and often travel abroad as representatives of Foreign Affairs Commissions of the parliaments of their republics or of the Soviet Parliament. Equally important is a second function: control. The task of the media officials is, in part, the reduction of the undesirable effects of foreign or nonofficial communications. In their travel abroad and in their attention to the communications brought into their provinces by foreign tourists, they have an obvious connection with the security organs.

The communications cadres received their training and education essentially outside the world of communications. Their functions relate to international propaganda activities; security and control, especially regarding foreign communications; and youth management and the political socialization of the following generations. The group is not particularly skewed toward old age. In fact, the age distribution is rather normal and suggests stability and continuity.

Although predictions based on this type of biographical material are uncertain, it is apparent that the communications bureaucracy will find it difficult to appreciate either the technological breakthroughs of modern worldwide communications or the methodological requirements of determining the efficacy of the media. These issues are of increasing importance for the Soviet media system, but there is little evidence that professionals with the appropriate background are being drawn into the policy-making structures.

The Search for Media Efficacy and Current Dilemmas

The policy issues raised here regarding the Soviet media system may be seen as a series of dilemmas. Media efficacy, now a far more serious issue because of the pressure of foreign messages and the unreliability of the usual performance indicators, involves considerable responsiveness to audiences. But satisfying audience demand would result in the loss of rigid guidance, which is inherently divorced from the information needs and predispositions of the audience. Technology presents an opportunity for greater impact and support and at the same time carries the possibility of transmitting what would be censored if less effective techniques were used. The familiar Soviet media practice not covering events deemed unsuitable for the populace is under attack. If the story enters the public consciousness through an unofficial route, the task for the communications professionals is made more difficult. For this reason, the local media are a particularly thorny problem and are suffering from a crisis of confidence. Because of the prohibition on stories about crime and deviance, and because of the didactic nature of the Soviet media, local newspapers present a certain view of local life—a view that is unreal, stilted, and varnished. Much that goes on and is of interest to the local populace simply goes unreported. People want to know more about matters of specifically local interest: hospitals and health programs, sports, cultural events, retail trade, and shopping. They want accurate reporting, and they can judge stories for themselves, because they may have already received the information first hand or from participants. Only 3 percent of the readers of an urban newspaper said that the newspaper rarely distorts the events it describes.

These dilemmas are, in some quarters, seen as opportunities. According to many Soviet media officials, media efficacy can be studied and measures developed that depend not on methodologically weak indicators, such as letters, but rather on scientifically sound research. Chernenko's public pronouncements, though distinctly ambivalent, do include this point of view. Party leaders recognize, however, that the focus on the West as adversary has had a major impact on Soviet public opinion. An unintended result may be enormous curiosity and interest in the West. Because of the relatively high level of Soviet confidence in the national media, this curiosity and interest could be exploited, and the new moves to make the media more responsive to the citizenry are significant initiatives. The 1980s are a time of change, not only of leadership but also of the communications environment worldwide, of the educational level of the Soviet public, and of the saturation of Soviet households by the new and powerful medium of television. It is likely that more changes will occur, although the dilemmas and the ambivalence will not soon be resolved.

Notes

1. For a discussion of the Soviet media system and audience exposure and preferences, see Ellen Mickiewicz, *Media and the Russian Public* (New York: Praeger, 1981).

2. "Aktualnye voprosy ideologicheskoi, massovopoliticheskoi raboty partii," *Pravda*, 15 June 1983.

3. V. V. Kelnik, "Bolshoi mir i malenkaya gazeta (O vystupleniyakh na mezhdunarodnye temy v raionnoi i gorodskoi pechati)," *Gazeta i zhizn* (Sverdlovsk, 1975), 137.

4. E. V. Vasilevskaya, *Ocherki istorii razvitia televidenia v zapadnoi sibiri*, Novosibirsk, 1978.

Science and Computers in
Soviet Society

LOREN R. GRAHAM

The Soviet Union possesses the largest scientific establishment in the world. In the fields of natural science and engineering, it has about a third more researchers with a Ph.D. degree or its equivalent than the United States. Furthermore, the Soviet Union has for decades devoted a larger share of its GNP to research and development than has the United States.

Of course, numbers do not tell everything. The Soviet Union's quantitative achievement in building the world's largest research establishment has not been matched by equivalent qualitative gains. As Thane Gustafson has observed, "by any measure – whether Nobel prizes, frequency of citation by fellow specialists, origin of major breakthroughs, or simply quantity of publications – U.S. scientists lead their Soviet colleagues in most disciplines, and in many there is simply no competition."[1]

One of the striking characteristics of Soviet science and technology is its qualitative heterogeneity. In some fields, Soviet researchers are among the best in the world; in others, they are mediocre. The disparity in quality in different fields is remarkable, especially when viewed against the background of Soviet efforts to be the leader in many, if not all, fields. To anyone interested in how science develops, its history, and its social foundations, the unusual pattern of strengths and weaknesses in the Soviet Union is a genuine challenge, a set of important questions demanding answers.

By the early 1980s a number of important studies of Soviet science and technology had been published in the West. These studies concentrated on the issue of political intrusion in Soviet science, the relationship of science to Marxist ideology, military technology, Soviet science policy, and the growth of the Soviet scientific establishment. *The Social Context of Soviet Science*, published in 1980, interpreted the features of Soviet science from the standpoint of Soviet politics and culture.[2] Other valuable studies of Soviet research came out of the exchanges and bilateral agreements that flourished in the 1970s, particularly the Kaysen report of the National Academy of Sciences.[3] This report was based on questionnaires submitted to hundreds of American scientists who had worked closely with Soviet scientists. It contains a great deal of valuable information on the strengths and weaknesses of fundamental research in the Soviet Union, and it has the advantage of being based both on quantified empirical data and on qualitative assessments made by leading American scientists.

None of these studies included reports from Soviet scientists themselves. The Kaysen committee had attempted in the late 1970s to involve Soviet scientists in its study of the exchanges, but the Soviet Academy of Sciences refused to permit its researchers to participate. In the 1970s, however, large numbers of Soviet scientists and engineers emigrated to the West and provided an opportunity for studies of Soviet research based on information given by recent native participants. At Harvard and MIT two projects of this type have recently been completed: one, financed by the National Council for Soviet and East European Studies, was based on interviews with several hundred émigré scientists and engineers. The other was the Eyewitness Seminar series.[4] This essay will present an overview of some of the findings from these projects, relying primarily on the series of Eyewitness Seminars.

The goal of these studies was to define the strengths and weaknesses of Soviet science and technology and to explain them in terms of the intellectual, political, and social characteristics of the Soviet Union. Among the strengths of Soviet science and technology that emerged were the following: a strong elementary and high school educational system, continuity in research efforts, a tradition of excellence in some areas of fundamental research, a high esteem for science in Soviet society, and a system of research priorities that permits the government to accomplish many of its goals. Among the weaknesses of Soviet science and technology were the following: a lack of innovation, limited contact between research and industry, political and ethnic discrimination, poor supply and distribution, and inadequate communication — both among Soviet scientists and between Soviet and foreign scientists.

Strengths of Soviet Science

Almost all of the émigrés who were interviewed had a higher opinion of Soviet elementary and high school education than they do of American education; some of them also believed that Soviet university education is superior to American education, especially in mathematics and physics. While the United States has gradually declined in science education, the Soviet Union has continued to build an impressive system. Soviet high school students are given much more work in mathematics and science than American students. Several years ago only a few more than 100,000 American high school students were taking calculus each year, while 5 million Soviet students did so. Perhaps these statistics have changed somewhat, since the United States has tried to improve its system of mathematics and science education, but a severe shortage of qualified high school mathematics teachers has hampered a rapid improvement.

On this topic, there was considerable agreement between the émigrés and Professor Izaak Wirszup of the University of Chicago, who has maintained that "the disparity between the level of training in science and mathematics of an average Soviet skilled worker or military recruit and that of a non-college-bound American high school graduate . . . is so great that comparisons are meaningless."[5]

By concentrating on curricula rather than on results, Wirszup has probably exaggerated the difference in the quality of Soviet and American science education. The impressive and rigorous Soviet science and mathematics curricula do not always succeed on the local level, especially in schools that are far from the major cities. In provincial schools, Soviet education is plagued with problems similar to those of American education: poorly trained teachers, apathetic students, and inadequate resources. Furthermore, part of the deficiencies of American high schools are compensated for in the better universities. Vladimir Kresin, an émigré physicist now working at the Lawrence Laboratory in Berkeley, agreed that Soviet elementary and high school education is superior to American education on the same levels, but he disagreed with some of the other émigrés by maintaining that "on the university level . . . the American system makes a giant leap forward leaving the Soviet system behind."[6] Even if this correction takes place in the best American universities, such as Berkeley, it would not affect the conclusion that one of the strengths of the Soviet Union in science and technology is its educational system on the elementary and secondary levels.

The Soviet system supports specific lines of research over very long periods of time. American researchers have to contend with much greater oscillations of funding from year to year. The NASA budget, for example, increases and decreases in step with national and congressional moods. The same is true for many other areas of American research. The United States lurches from one research fad to another, from "Wars on Cancer" to "Campaigns Against Aging" to "Synthetic Fuels." Furthermore, the system of contracts and grants prevalent in American research, while possessing many strengths, is also time consuming. Several of the émigrés were critical of the American grant system, which they consider somewhat chaotic and inefficient. In the Soviet Union the budgets for most lines of research are rather constant. Few areas of research are dramatically cut, and institutions are almost never eliminated. While this degree of continuity of research strategy leads to conservatism and may inhibit innovation, it also has certain real advantages; Soviet researchers in leading institutions feel free to embark on long-term projects without fear that their budgets will be eliminated before they can complete their work. For example, continuity of research effort significantly helped the Soviet Union in magnetohydrodynamics, an area where the United States discontinued an important line of research only to have to do catch-up work later when it appeared that the Soviet decision to continue had proved correct.

The strength of Soviet mathematics and physics is a tradition that began before the Russian Revolution. Moscow today probably contains more outstanding mathematicians than any other city in the world. The more abstract and mathematical an area of science is, the more likely the Soviet Union is to be a leader in that area. Indeed, Western specialists on Soviet science and technology often speak of "The Blackboard Rule"—meaning that Soviet science is likely to be strong in any area where the main tools of research are a blackboard and chalk and weak in areas requiring material support, sophisticated instrumentation, or close contact with industry. There are exceptions to "The Blackboard Rule," to be sure, but it is often strikingly accurate.

Science as a field of study and scientists as members of a profession are held in high esteem in the Soviet Union. In the United States and other Western countries one often hears of revolts against science, or even of antiscience movements. Such social attitudes are rare in the Soviet Union. Full members of the Academy of Sciences are the most prestigious members of Soviet society, enjoying far more admiration than the top leaders of the Communist party or the government. Soviet television and the Soviet press are filled with features on the lives of the leading scientists. Americans, however, are skeptical of scientists and engineers described as culture heroes, pure in motive and action.

Soviet science also benefits from political leaders' and science administrators' ability to select a few high-priority areas of research and to support them with vast quantities of funds and personnel. The centralized planning system in the Soviet Union does not work well in running an entire economy—especially the consumer economy—but it does operate rather well in choosing a few selected issues for special emphasis, both military and nonmilitary—including scientific research. At the present time the Soviet Union places great emphasis on biotechnology and computers. There are already signs of significant improvement in research and development in these areas, accompanied by difficulties in moving beyond the research to industrial applications. This pattern of strengths and weaknesses is a common one.

Weaknesses in Soviet Science and Technology

As mentioned earlier, former Soviet scientists and engineers now working in the United States often reported that they received a more rigorous education in mathematics and science in the Soviet Union than their American collegues received in the United States. They did not feel, however, that Soviet advanced research in their particular area was superior to that in the United States. Soviet engineers sometimes maintained that although they know much more mathematics than their American coworkers, they had great difficulty keeping up with them in terms of productivity and innovation. In other words, the émigrés believed that Soviet scientists and engineers are better educated than American ones but much less productive and innovative.

A number of émigrés often explained that the most exciting aspect of American research and development is the sense of which topics are "hot" and which are not. Among Soviet researchers, this ability to choose independently which issues are crucial seems to be less developed; Soviet researchers seem to feel that the important products of research are papers and publications. Little thought is given to their relative importance or possible industrial applications. American research is more competitive, more selectively directed toward breakthroughs, and more concerned with developing products that can be commercially utilized. Soviet research is directed toward the building of individual or institutional reputations by producing publications. Once the publication has appeared, the Soviet researcher often loses interest in the topic. To American researchers, publication is frequently viewed as a step toward developing something more concrete, either a commercial application or the next step in the research process. Indeed, Soviet researchers seem to value publication more highly than American researchers — an observation that may amuse Americans familiar with the "publish or perish" syndrome. The difference is that in the United States publication is not the final or only goal. The functional importance of publication to Americans is undermined by other means of communicating research results, such as preprints and telephone calls among the small circle of leaders in any given area of research.

Another obstacle to innovation in the Soviet Union is the economic system, which discourages originality in industrial products and processes. Traditionally, Soviet industrial planners are rewarded for increasing quantitative output, not for qualitative improvements. Despite enormous efforts to change this emphasis over the past thirty years, progress has been very slow. There is no "market pull" for the introduction of innovation in the Soviet Union, only "bureaucratic push." And even the bureaucracy is often afraid of innovation, because it undermines careers and leads to unsettling changes.

Since most of the émigré scientists were Jewish, it is not surprising that many of them reported on anti-Semitism in the Soviet Union. A sobering conclusion that must be drawn from their reports, however, is not only that anti-Semitism exists in Soviet academic life but also that it is growing in significance and has now affected the quality of scientific research in a number of fields.

Most entrance examinations to Soviet universities are oral, and it is at this stage that Jews or politically suspect students are often eliminated. Jews are given much more difficult questions than non-Jewish students. One of the émigrés was denied admission to Moscow University because he could not describe how the Dalai Lama in Tibet is selected. The question was obviously designed to eliminate him, despite his excellent record in mathematics and science.

Since the early 1970s Jewish mathematicians have been virtually eliminated as authors in several of the leading mathematics journals in the Soviet Union. The quality of the strongest areas of Soviet science — mathematics and physics — is being damaged by the growth of anti-Semitism. Although the depth of talent in these fields is so great that the damaging effects can probably be tolerated by the Soviet authorities, the injury that has been done to Soviet intellectual life is visible.

Yet another weakness of Soviet science is the poor supply and distribution system. The Soviet émigrés reported that supply and distribution problems are some of the most significant drawbacks in Soviet science and technology. Shortages of materials extend, at different times, from sophisticated equipment to the most simple reagents — even to nuts, bolts, and paper. Obtaining supplies for research is a never-ending task in the Soviet Union, involving an enormous waste of time and effort. It is not unusual for a laboratory to halt its work for several weeks while searching for rather trivial supplies. And in areas like astronomy, important results are sometimes lost forever because the right kind of photographic plate was unavailable at the required moment.

Finally, Soviet science is isolated from the West and compartmentalized at home. As a result, Soviet researchers suffer from communication lags, learning what is going on in their fields only after researchers in other countries have utilized the latest findings to further their own research. Western journals are received late in the Soviet Union, and they often go first to senior scientists. The more creative junior scientists have difficulty obtaining them early enough for the information to be useful. Furthermore, scientific journals are censored along with all other publications.

Even within the Soviet Union communication lines are weak. Although abstracting and indexing services are highly developed, these services are not computerized to the degree that they have been in the West. Furthermore, new fields and interdisciplinary efforts do not receive attention before it is too late. Western scientists visiting the Soviet Union often find that a Soviet scientist working on a given problem in one institute does not know of the existence of another Soviet scientist working on the same problem in another institute in the same city. The foreigners often bring the two researchers together.

Receptivity to Technological Change

Western analyses of Soviet science and technology usually concentrate on hardware and technology rather than on the receptivity of Soviet society to technological change. Yet the rapidity with which a society absorbs a new technology is a crucial factor in determining the rate at which that technology will develop. The development of computers in the Soviet Union illustrates the importance of this absorptive capacity.

During the early phase of computer development, the major emphasis was on large mainframe computers, which were, by necessity, institutionally controlled and best adapted to centralized functions. These computers were attractive in terms of Soviet ideology, centralized planning, and traditional Soviet tendencies toward "gigantomania." Recently, however, microcomputers and personal computers have been developed with so much power that they are beginning to rival in capacity their larger ancestors. Today one can buy in almost any computer store in the United States an Apple Computer or an IBM PC with internal memory capacities up to 640 kilobytes, or even higher, which only a decade ago would have been a respectable memory for a large mainframe computer. Furthermore, the versatility of these small desk-top computers can be vastly increased by connecting them to larger mainframe computers. As a result, it is becoming increasingly clear that the most efficient use of computers for a great range of applications is based on decentralized systems in which, at the local level, microcomputers can be used either alone (for simpler tasks) or in connection with a larger coherent system (for assignments demanding greater capacity or access to centralized data banks).

The Soviet social and political system is having difficulty adapting to the new trend toward personal computers controlled by private individuals. Every microcomputer or word processor connected to a printer is a potential printing press. In the Soviet Union, private possession of printing presses and even photocopy machines is prohibited; yet a microcomputer can print the desired number of copies. Anyone who remembers how Soviet dissidents of the 1960s spent days typing *samizdat* documents on typewriters stuffed with five or six carbon copies will understand the significance of the new technology. In Poland, some members of the scientific intelligentsia who support the Solidarity movement have turned out political documents on computers in government offices. These computers, however, used old-fashioned tapes instead of disks, were centrally controlled, and were not located in private homes. The authorities cannot permit Soviet citizens to acquire personal computers or word processors without risking the repetition of such events on a much broader scale.

Of course, the Soviet leaders have several possible solutions to this challenge: all computers, like all photocopiers, could be housed in institutions and controlled by institutional officials. Or, if microcomputers were permitted in homes or under decentralized control, they would not be accompanied by printers; printing would take place in a central institutional office where it could be both printed and censored. Or, finally, all microcomputers could be connected to central computers that would record all manuscript files as they are created; if the local computer were unplugged from the central network, it would not work. Thus, security officials would have records on everything that Soviet citizens did with computers. Big Brother would triumph after all.

Soviet authorities certainly have the power and the technical capabilities to try to enforce such rules, and in fact they are doing so already, by requiring all computers to be institutionally housed and controlled. But the Soviet authorities will pay a high price for these regulations by severely limiting the rate of the growth of the computer culture, by hampering the spread of computer literacy among young people, by losing the advantages of economies of scale that the mass production of computers is bringing, by failing to take advantage of the efficiencies in financial transactions — including personal ones — that computers can bring, and by watching the West become a true "information society" that they will be doomed to follow enviously unless they loosen up their society. Furthermore, they can never be sure that someone will not circumvent their controls; if American authorities worry about the teenagers in Milwaukee and Seattle who break *into* central data banks without authorization, the Soviet authorities have the opposite worry that an undergraduate in a Soviet technological institute may break *out* of the central computer surveying his activities, because if he succeeds then by definition he does not leave traces.

A great many factors influence a culture's receptivity to new computers, and in all of them the United States seems to have the edge over the Soviet Union. These factors include: (1) a tradition that successful technologies should be privately owned and controlled if it is advantageous to do so; (2) a tradition of free access to information; (3) a tradition of creating large amounts of reliable and accurate data about the economy and about society; (4) a financial system offering diverse business and consumer services; (5) widespread education in business and technological skills, including typing and programming; (6) excellent telephone lines that can be used for remote access to data bases; (7) close relationships between sellers and buyers of technology, including consulting services, maintenance, and spare parts; and (8) a tradition of entrepreneurship and innovation under which a person who develops a successful product—whether hardware or software—can legally make and attempt to sell it.

The Soviet Union has major problems in every one of these areas. It has a tradition of prohibiting individual control over communication technologies. The most secretive industrialized power in the world, it controls information zealously. Under its financial system, private checking accounts are almost unheard of and individual credit arrangements are extremely cumbersome. Its telephone system is of such low quality that the attempts made so far to establish modem communication have had to rely either on special lines or on a "search" system by which only one out of some twenty possible circuits is deemed good enough for high-speed communication. The Soviet Union's educational system does not emphasize business or "hands-on" technological skills, and typing is not widely taught in Soviet schools; Soviet college-level education about computers is strong on the theoretical or mathematical side but weak on the practical side. A "hacker culture" does not exist in Soviet universities. The technical consultation, maintenance, and spare-parts services that good computer dealers provide in the West are notoriously poor in the Soviet Union; yet computers are so complex that without helpful dealers, start-up and maintenance problems can become insurmountable difficulties. Finally, business entrepreneurship is prohibited in the Soviet Union.

The last point needs elaboration. The most vigorous aspect of the computer business in the United states today is the production of software. Software programming seems to be an activity similar to a cottage industry, but there are no legal cottage industries in the Soviet Union. Rather than allowing a cottage software industry to develop, Soviet authorities have turned software production over to enormous institutes and production facilities, where several thousand researchers work. Yet in the United States even giant companies like IBM often buy their software from individuals or small firms. While the popular picture in the United States of the reclusive genius who descends from his mountaintop twice a year with a new brilliant piece of software may be exaggerated, it is nonetheless true that enormous organizations have not produced the most innovative software. The evidence so far seems to indicate that a wide open, chaotic, competitive marketplace with a staggering variety of contenders is the best environment for producing ingenious computer programs. In Silicon Valley in California about one hundred new high-technology firms—most of them computer related—have been established in the last twelve months. The Soviet Union could not duplicate this environment without contradicting its most cherished economic principle—the elimination of private enterprise.

One of the principles known to every computer specialist is "garbage in, garbage out." That is, the best computer in the world cannot produce a good product if the information fed into it is inferior or incomplete. Some economists doubt that centralized planning of an economy is theoretically possible, but even those who defend it admit that it must be based on accurate data. Yet much of the economic, demographic, and sociological information available in the Soviet Union is inferior and incomplete. Why have the Soviet authorities failed to improve the quality of their data? Within limits, they are trying to do so, but some of the information necessary for social planning would be embarrassing, even if available. Infant mortality rates, necessary for health planning, have not been published in the Soviet Union since 1975, soon after a sharp increase in this vital death indicator. By Western standards, the Soviet Union has a measurable unemployment rate—another fundamental statistic—yet no figures on unemployment are available. Grain production in the USSR has been a state secret since 1981. Other economic data are statistically inferior, at least when compared with those available for Western countries. Local managers may not even want the information to be more accurate, since it could reveal corruption or managerial ineptitude. Rewards exist in the Soviet system for incomplete or false reporting, just as they do in the United States (income tax returns, for example), but in the Soviet Union the tradition of secrecy and the absence of investigative reporting aid the person trying to cover his tracks.

This inadequacy of accurate information decreases the efficiency of the Soviet system while making the application of computers more difficult. After games and word processing, probably the most common nonmilitary use of computers in the United States is financial and business planning, as the popularity of the "financial spread-sheet" programs indicate. Computers increase the velocity of local decision making; and the faster the planner operates, the more important it is that one's data be accurate and that one have the authority to make a quick decision. The centralized Soviet system relying on data of questionable accuracy does not seem well suited for this new business era.

All the above arguments suggest that the Soviet Union will have unusual difficulties in adjusting to the computer revolution. But do these same arguments mean that computers will undermine or destroy the Soviet system? Not at all. The Soviet leaders are experienced in maintaining their control, and they will find ways of containing the implicit threat to their authority that the new computers pose. Complete computer systems and access to international telecommunication networks will not be placed in the hands of individual Soviet citizens. Institutions will control access to the computers.

Conclusion

With the exception of a few fields, the Soviet Union is not a leader in science and technology. For decades it has invested an enormous share of its talent and material resources in science, but it has not yet won the premier place that its leadership has sought. Failure to be a winner in science and technology, however, is not the same as being a loser. In fact, the Soviet Union has a solid record in science and technology as a rather good follower. Again and again, people in the United States have noticed deficiencies in Soviet research and then have gone on to underestimate seriously the ability of the Soviet Union to stay close behind the United States in technical achievements. Being first in technological competition may not be as important as being able to stay close behind the leaders in the areas that count. At the end of World War II, many Americans predicted that it would be ten or fifteen years before the Soviet Union could produce an atomic bomb; it produced one within four years. Then it was said that the Soviets would have difficulty developing the hydrogen bomb, but they produced it at about the same time as the United States. Then it was said that they could not produce accurate intercontinental ballistic missiles, but they soon did. Then it was said that they could not develop MIRV'ed warheads for their missiles, but they did, and now the United States is having trouble living with the results. Then it was said that they could not develop look-down, shoot-down radar, but they now have that, too.

The story of American-Soviet competition in science and technology is not a refrain from the old song "Anything you can do, I can do better," but "Anything you can do, I can do a bit later." This is particularly true in military technology, where the Soviet system of governmentally determined research priorities and centralized control over resources enables the USSR quickly to focus its efforts in any direction it sees its competitors pursuing. This ability should cause the United States to hesitate before opening up new areas of expensive competition in military technology, such as the militarization of space. In military technology the Soviet Union is a very good follower. Being a follower may not be the same as being a leader, but the results are often similar. At any rate, the results are extremely costly for the United States.

The Soviet ability to keep up in civilian technology is much less well developed, which should spur the use of computers in Western economies. In the civilian computer revolution, the Soviet Union will have enormous difficulties keeping pace, and time is on the side of the West. If the United States and its allies can slow the competition in military technology that can so easily destroy us all, and in which the Soviet Union is faring rather well, then the competition in civilian technology that has begun penetrating to the lowest levels of Western societies, and in which the Soviet Union is faring poorly, will give the Western alliance real advantages over its Soviet bloc rivals.

NOTES

1. Thane Gustafson, "Why Doesn't Soviet Science Do Better Than It Does," in *The Social Context of Soviet Science*, ed. Linda L. Lubrano and Susan Gross Solomon (Boulder: Westview Press, 1980), 31.

2. Linda L. Lubrano and Susan Gross Solomon, eds., *The Social Context of Soviet Science* (Boulder: Westview Press, 1980).

3. National Academy of Sciences, *Review of the U.S.-U.S.S.R. Interacademy Exchanges and Relations* (the Kaysen report), Washington, D.C., 1977).

4. The Eyewitness Seminars lasted from 1981 to 1984. They were funded by the Ford Foundation and jointly sponsored by the Program on Science, Technology and Society at the Massachusetts Institute of Technology and the Russian Research Center at Harvard University. The cochairmen were Loren R. Graham, professor of the history of science at MIT and Mark Kuchment, research associate, Russian Research Center, Harvard University.

5. Report of Dr. Izaak Wirszup to Drs. D. Aufenkamp and J. Lipson, National Science Foundation, 14 Dec. 1979, p. 13.

6. Vladimir S. Kresin, "The State of Natural Sciences in the U.S.S.R.: A Physicist's Point of View," Eyewitness Account no. 5, Russian Research Center, Harvard University, p, 24.

Dissent and the "Contra-System" in the Soviet Union

ROBERT SHARLET

A specter is haunting communist Europe. Known by various names in different places, it appears as the "second society" in the USSR, while in Czechoslovakia it is called the "parallel polis." By either name it is an "anti-world"[1] engendered by the continual failures, mediocrity, emptiness, ennui, and immobilism of the contemporary official systems of the Soviet Union and Eastern Europe. Given this dialectical tension, the individual is forced to live a double existence. By day one conforms to the image of a public person nominally committed to the party's goals, while by night one plays the role of private citizen actively pursuing one's own projects in the "antiworld" immanent within the official reality.

In this hidden world beneath a planned environment of acute and persistent scarcity, nearly everyone steals goods from the state, sells one's services on the side, or, if neither is possible, at least "steals time"[2] on the job. In this milieu, Johnny Cash's song about a Detroit automobile worker assembling a car from parts smuggled out of the plant brings forth smiles of recognition. The private car itself is a Trojan horse within the state economy, bringing along with it gypsy cabs, off-the-books servicing, stolen spare parts, syphoned gas, and under-the-table resales. As a vehicle of privacy in the midst of an intrusive society, the car is also "subversive."

Artists paint for their friends, writers routinely send manuscripts abroad, and actors save their best performances for living-room theater. Religious activists, refusing to register their sects with the state, surreptitiously build their own printing presses and preach the gospel on their own terms underground. Ethnic nationalists resist assimilation, promote cultural autonomy, and preserve the past in the collective memory. The young imitate Western fashion, frequent clandestine cabarets and underground concerts, and outrage their elders.

In their antipodal existence, nearly everyone is "bilingual," speaking the standard party jargon in the everyday world and the language of rock music, religion, political dissent, or ethnic chauvinism in their preferred roles. Bilegal-ism is also the norm, as individuals strike deals by one set of rules and earn their paychecks by another.

Alongside the official educational establishment, there exists a shadow educa-tional system where forbidden topics are discussed and banned courses are taught at every level from "flying kindergarten" to "flying university," even to unofficial postdoctoral seminars in science, philosophy, and history. Lecturers appear in apartment "classrooms," and sometimes also in public sanctuaries, such as a church. Instruction is either direct with *samizdat* (self-published) texts or by correspondence with cassette lectures.

Bold individuals practice dissent by publicly criticizing the prevailing order or some part of it. Invariably, for their impertinence, they are cast out of official society. If anything, the role of outcast enhances their sense of personal freedom, and they band together to produce *samizdat* journals, protest injustice, and project alternate images of the system as it might be. Inevitably, many are im-prisoned for these activities, but some of them continue their resistance to the closed official universe from behind the barbed wire or within the cell.

Whether incarcerated or merely ostracized, the dissidents' most significant achievement has been the creation of "private opinion"[3] as an alternative to con-trolled public discourse and an independent information system for uncensored communications with trunk lines running east to west. It is largely through the voluminous transmissions over these lines that the West has become more and more aware of the complex antiworld variously called second societies or parallel polities.

These alternate constructions of reality constitute no less than the reappear-ance of civil society through a process of "reprivatization," or "the reappropria-tion of elements of social life in a form that is responsive to the needs and interests of the population."[4]

The contra-system existed under Lenin and Stalin; Khrushchev tried to uproot it; it flourished under Brezhnev; while Andropov mounted a major campaign to contain it. Yet the contra-system endures and even thrives within the Soviet sys-tem and society as well as in Eastern Europe.[5] A contra-system is an analytic as well as a metaphoric construct that brings together within a single framework seemingly diverse phenomena. Two criteria must be met for a phenomenon to be included within this conceptual constellation:

1. In a significant way, a phenomenon as a whole—or at least substantial parts of it—must represent overt or covert activities, individual or group behav-iors, or strongly held attitudes or beliefs that are "contrary" or antithetical to the official system or one of its parts, the conventional notion of permissible con-duct, or, at least, the publicly promoted modes of acceptable thought and discourse.

2. To qualify for inclusion in the contra-system, a "contrary" phenomenon must interconnect, directly or indirectly, with at least several other contra-phenomena. In this way, a matrix of interrelationships is formed. Similar to the

Marxist base-superstructure relationship, the "second economy" and "privatism," for example, underpin and cut across all other categories in the manner of a contra-base, while dissent and the contra-political cultures represent the contra-superstructure most consistently linked with nearly all other contra-phenomena.

Needless to say, certain linkages are stronger than others, depending on the national or subnational context, such as the interconnection between subterranean religion and ethnic nationalism in Soviet Lithuania, the Central Asian republics, Poland, the Slovak region of Czechoslovakia, in certain republics of the Yugoslav federation, and between Great Russian nationalism and dissident Russian Orthodoxy. Conversely, the relationship between the religious and ethnic variables is weaker, or absent altogether in other instances, such as Soviet Georgian nationalism, Russian Pentacostalism, and the small sect of Soviet Hare Krishna, whose belief is more a function of their social class and educational level than any common ethnic bond in Soviet society.

The level of contra-system development varies from one country to another in the European communist states. As a transnational phenomenon, a national contra-system may comprise several or all of the following components:

• A flourishing, largely illegal "second economy," both in competition with and complementary to the planned economy of the state.[6]

• A "parallel culture" that defies the canons of censorship and orthodox art.

• A vast, subterranean archipelago of religious belief that conflicts with the regime's official atheism.

• An enduring mosaic of unassimilated ethnic nationalism counterposed to the majority nationality or prevailing supranationalism.

• A dynamic youth counterculture that conspicuously diverges from adult mores and life-styles.

• A polarized "bilegality"[7] and dichotomized morality by which the citizen, in chameleon fashion, adapts to the prevailing norms of a dual existence in the official and contra-realms.

• An urban-based, subrosa, "open" educational network that rejects the curricular restrictions of the heavily controlled state educational system.

• A dissident movement that constitutes a small but vocal contra-elite opposed to the theoretically hegemonic party elite and represents a set of alternate political cultures challenging the monopolistic official political culture and the party's tendency to depoliticize and reify large parts of the systemic decision-making process.

• A crosscutting, widespread tendency toward "privatism" that is antithetical to the pervasive statism and incessant propaganda calling for civic participation.

Each contra-phenomenon tends to subsume a range of subtly differentiated parts. Neither the second economy nor the parallel culture, to take two examples, is monolithic. Both contain a broad spectrum of activities. In turn, regime tolerance or intolerance of contra-activity can vary considerably between the wholes and among their parts.

The degree to which particular contra-phenomena fulfill the contrarian and linkage criteria varies from one national or subnational jurisdiction to another, and over time. Take, for instance, working-class protest, a subcategory of dissent in the USSR and Eastern Europe. In Yugoslavia, where strikes over narrow job issues are frequent but neither prohibited nor lawful, labor activism falls only marginally within the contra-system. By contrast, in Romania, where strikes are rare, forbidden, and suppressed, a widespread but shortlived strike of coal miners in the late 1970s can be classified as an episodic manifestation of dissent even though one criterion was overfulfilled while the other was underfulfilled. Although the Romanian miners struck over specific economic issues only, their overt activity, group behavior, and manifest attitudes were profoundly antithetical to, and openly defiant of, the Romanian communist system. Less evident, because of the paucity of information and brief duration of the strike, was the linkage between the worker unrest and other contra-phenomena in Romania. There was some after-the-fact connection within the main dissent category with the Romanian dissident movement of that time, as well as some probable linkage to the Hungarian minority's ethnic activism. We do not know, however, whether a significant number of the strikers were also believers in any of the Romanian underground religious sects.

The period between the summer of 1980 and December 1981, after which martial law was imposed in Poland, constitutes the single most extraordinary episode of labor protest in which both the contrarian and linkage criteria were fully met. Elsewhere in Eastern Europe and the USSR, labor unrest is marginal and fragmented. The tiny, free labor movement in the USSR has thus far been contained by the joint action of the political and legal authorities. Nonetheless, this beleaguered group has fully satisfied the contrarian criterion, though, as a result of official repression, it is difficult to discern much linkage beyond the dissident community within the contra-system.

A regime's reaction to a contra-system within its jurisdiction ranges from a mix of co-optation and containment in Yugoslavia, a combination of decriminalization and marginalization in Hungary, to a generally low tolerance and high level of repression in the Soviet Union. Whether tolerance and repression are high or low (or more often than not, somewhere in between), none of the European communist regimes remains passive in the face of a developing indigenous contra-system. All actively intervene to keep contra-activity, behavior, and attitudes under some degree of official control.

Where the opportunities exist, elimination rather than containment becomes the official objective, though it is rarely achieved. Regimes conduct selective campaigns, concentrating on one or another contra-phenomenon that is especially offensive to official sensibilities or that threatens to get out of control. Rarely is there an across-the-board offensive against a contra-system as a whole. The low likelihood of success would not justify the necessary massive deployment of cadres and resources.

Usually, while maintaining containment with periodic campaigns against certain contrarians, a regime exploits the traditional cleavages in society (say, between workers and intellectuals and between Russians and other nationalities in the USSR). Where this tactic is not possible, a regime generally marshals its personnel to attack linkages within the contra-system. This maneuver is intended to disrupt the cohesion of the contra-system and check its development qua *system*, thereby achieving the minimum objective of dividing the adversaries to facilitate on-going containment.

Origins and Effects of the Contra-System

The sources of the contra-systems in the European communist states can be divided into four categories: (1) sources common to all contra-systems; (2) sources peculiar to Eastern Europe as a region; (3) sources indigenous to individual countries of Eastern Europe; and (4) Soviet sources.

The major sources of the contra-system in the USSR and Eastern Europe are, in order of importance, modernization, de-Stalinization, and détente. In the post-Stalin modernization process, individual self-consciousness heightened, specialization of interests developed, and the differentiation and fragmentation of the mobilized society increased. An effect of modernization has been the revolution in the technology of communication that brought forth television and the photocopier, both of which have become transmission points in the contra-information system.

Television has produced special problems for regimes intent on controlling the "word"—spoken, written, and imagized. Most East Germans receive West German television, while parts of Czechoslovakia receive both West German and Austrian telecasts, and sections of Hungary can also get Austrian television. In the near future, the USSR will confront an even thornier problem when the U.S. Information Agency beams Western telecasts into the Soviet Union via satellite transmissions that are nearly impossible to jam. Unapproved Western images (politics, advertising, and value-laden entertainment) already flood into East Central Europe, and soon they will reach the USSR as well.

Soviet television has produced unintended problems on the homefront. Domestic telecasting has inadvertently sown the seeds of economic discontent among rural viewers who can now view the enormous disparity between urban and rural living in the portrayal of city life on television. Television in the USSR, as in other industrial societies, is beginning to produce a passive "private" citizen, at variance with the official image of an outer-directed, collectivist-oriented public person. Thus the appurtenances and appliances of modernization—the family car, the private apartment, and the living-room television set—all contribute to the privatism that permeates the contra-system.

Other technological offspring of modernization that have an impact on contra-system communications, especially among political, religious, and ethnic dissidents, include photocopiers, cassettes, video recorders, and personal computers. The photocopier is an immediate problem, because it proliferates throughout the bureaucratic systems and unauthorized copying is difficult to control. The pocket-size cassette, requiring only an inexpensive tape player, is an even more elusive medium of private, uncensored communication. The home video recorder, still a relative newcomer, is expected to present the authorities with further problems, especially as Western television continues to penetrate the Eastern bloc countries. Still further in the future but inevitable is the spread of computers from office to home, along with the attendant problems of computer security and electronic mail bypassing the post office and telephone exchange. It would seem that the government's monopoly on communications and information will be progressively eroded by the contra-system.

De-Stalinization began in 1953 with the dictator's death and has been another major source of the contra-system—both for its further development in the USSR and its initial emergence in the new communist states of Eastern Europe. By eliminating terror as a means of governance throughout most of the Soviet bloc, de-Stalinization radically changed the cost-benefit ratio for individual risk-taking within and outside the official system. With the possibility of a death sentence or an indefinite term in the gulag archipelago gradually replaced by a deescalation of criminal sanctions and differentiated political justice, a citizen could now weigh the prospective benefits against the known "costs," if caught, of pilferage from the workplace, the private circulation of a *samizdat* manuscript, teaching a catechism to children in violation of the law, or making critical political comments. As the post-Stalin period wore on, these and other contra-activities grew bolder and more commonplace.

De-Stalinization also promised a better quality of life and the reform of various aspects of the existing system. Scientists hoped for greater access to the international scientific community, while humanists sought more "space" to experiment with modernist trends in the arts. Believers and minorities set more modest and realistic agendas.

Nearly every citizen, however, placed the highest priority on sorely needed improvement in consumption. It was widely understood that some type of reform of the inherited Stalinist command economy would be needed for improvement in the longer run.

Some of these hopes and expectations were realized, but many were not, especially after Khrushchev's ouster in 1964 and the slowing down of de-Stalinization by his successors. Everyday life improved and real gains in consumption occurred, but with no economic reform, except in Hungary, slippage began and scarcities increased. Scientists and artists achieved some of their objectives, but there was some regression and high expecations went unfulfilled. Of the minorities aspiring for more status, only the Slovaks in Czechoslovakia substantially improved their position, while among the believers, the Polish church made significant progress in its church construction program. Other aspirants for change settled for marginal concessions or none at all.

As a general rule, the greater the initial impact of de-Stalinization in a particular national society, the sharper the societal reaction when hopes and expectations were unrealized. Thus the reaction that gave impetus to contra-system development was sharpest in the USSR, Poland, and, after 1968, Czechoslovakia and less pronounced in Bulgaria and Romania. Intellectual disaffection led to the emergence of post-Stalin political dissent and the evolution of the parallel culture, while "middle class" consumer despair fueled the growth of the second economy.

The origins of the second economy can be traced to the advent of central planning. Managers who found rule breaking a necessary evil in order to attain planned targets had long sought refuge in the second economy. From the outset it was essential to informalize the overly organized economy to achieve growth and productivity. Extra-plan activity had long been accepted by the authorities as an indispensable lubricant for the overcentralized "first" economy. As a result of this tolerance and the general unwillingness of the Soviet and Eastern European leaders to undertake economic reform, the managerial branch of the second economy "matured" along with "mature socialism."

The real growth in second-economy activity, however, came from the participation of the masses of disappointed consumers. As certain regimes increasingly became unable to carry out their commitments under the social contract — material goods for political quiescence — the new "middle class" turned to the second economy to fulfill its needs. However, it was not without some initial moral reservations that ordinary law-abiding citizens found themselves slipping into the nether world of gray and black markets, or as one pundit put it, trolling in "the free ocean" stocked with "golden carp."[8] The transformative effect of this experience has generated a bilegal citizen — an honest and obedient person in nearly every way who, as a consequence of involvement in the subterranean economy, has learned to live by its unwritten rules as well.

The impact of détente — the third and final major source common to all contra-systems — during the early and mid-1970s was probably greatest on political dissent and the countercultural youth, with strong secondary effects on underground religion and ethnic activism. Although dissidence may have been the unwanted offspring of modernization midwifed by de-Stalinization, it was détente that nourished dissent and afforded it a margin of protection until it became self-sustaining. Soviet interest in the Strategic Arms Limitation Talks, the Soviet-American summits, the Helsinki Final Act of 1975, and the rise of Eurocommunism as a political force steadily diminished the benefits and raised the costs of full-scale repression of domestic dissidents.

The brief era of good feeling between the superpowers also provided some protective cover for the fledgling Soviet Jewish, ethnic German, and Armenian emigration movements, as well as the East German exodus beginning in 1975. Though emigration from the USSR in 1983 reached a low point for the post-détente period and officials intimate that "the last train has left the station," the Jewish and ethnic German movements appear to be sufficiently well integrated into the contra-system to survive the vicissitudes of East-West relations.

The balmier days of détente fostered the growth of other hardy religious and ethnic contra-groups whose roots have traditionally run deep in Soviet soil, including several "unregistered" or illegal denominations of evangelical Christians, Lithuanian Catholic activists, and Ukrainian ethnic advocates. Although détente no longer acts as a restraint on the authorities, it nurtured phenomena that have been well integrated into the contra-system.

Another consequence of détente was its indirect effect on the youth counter-cultures of the Warsaw Pact nations. Tourism to the region, less heavily jammed Western broadcasts, and scientific and cultural exchanges — all stimulated by détente — functioned as conduits for the dazzling but forbidden sounds and styles of Western youth. Along with the music, jeans, and T-shirts came the ir-reverance toward adult values and the now standard generational rebellion. It should come as no surprise that the countercultural youth of the Eastern bloc now see themselves as part of the international youth culture, transcending all boundaries and populated only by rock groups and their fans.

Two important sources of the contra-system are peculiar to Eastern Europe and worth mentioning, since the contra-system as a whole and many of its mis-cellaneous components are highly developed in that region. The Soviet Union may insist on leaving its Warsaw Pact partners in political-military undertak-ings, but Eastern Europe is clearly in the vanguard of contra-system innovation. The reason can be found in Stalin's death, which effectively interrupted the Stalinization process in large parts of the region, leaving intact certain "survivals of the past." Particularly in Hungary and Poland, the Communist parties never completely penetrated their societies. The consequence has been less effective control during crises (Hungary in 1956 and Poland in 1956, 1970–71, 1976, and 1980–81) and, not coincidentally, the development of the most avant-garde contra-systems in the region.

The second major Eastern European source of the contra-system is a kind of intraregional cross-fertilization between similar contra-phenomena. This process traces back to Stalin's expulsion of Yugoslavia from the Cominform for fear that Titoism, or the virus of "national communism," might infect the satellite states, which it eventually did in several instances. Since then, in addition to the inter-connections between contra-phenomena of a discrete contra-system, strong cross-border linkages have developed between the same components of different contra-systems. The evidence is circumstantial, but some regionalization of the second economy as well as cross-pollination among countercultural youth is perceptible. Scarce consumer goods seem to move through the region in the briefcases of official travelers, the luggage of intrabloc tourists, and the shopping bags of cross-border shoppers. The general rule appears to be that goods and foodstuffs move from the store shelves of the better stocked countries into the second economies of their less prosperous neighbors. In a similar unobtrusive fashion during the summers, Eastern European youth mingle in hostels, camping grounds, and on the beaches of the Balkans, where they barter pins, records, and tapes and thus interweave their native countercultures.

Finally, there is ample evidence of a strong intraregional linkage between the small dissident communities in several countries, with Czechoslovakia as the hub. When the dissident group "Charter 77" issued its manifesto in Prague in January 1977, an anonymous manifesto echoed it in usually silent Bulgaria, while an embryonic civil rights group emerged in Romania in emulation of the Czechoslovaks. Subsequently, representatives of Charter 77 and the Worker's Defense Committee (KOR) in Poland made direct contact in the border region of the two countries. Later, in 1979, when leading members of Charter 77 were put on trial, Hungarian dissidents petitioned their party leader Janos Kadar to intercede on behalf of the "Prague Six." And, in early 1984, Chapter 77 and Solidarity-KOR issued a joint statement, with which leading Hungarian dissidents associated themselves, calling for coordinated action on human rights by all three national dissident groups – an unprecedented suggestion.

Regional linkages are also evident in the religious and ethnic realms. Before the Polish crisis began in 1980, Czechoslovak novitiates training for the priesthood in underground seminaries would cross into Poland to be ordained by Polish bishops. In a similar vein, the cause of the persecuted Hungarian ethnic minorities in Romania and Czechoslovakia has been taken up by dissident intellectuals in Hungary who appeal for cultural autonomy on behalf of their ethnic brethren.

A discussion of the idiosyncratic features of individual countries as sources for their indigenous contra-systems would require a separate essay. Suffice it to say that certain idiosyncrasies account for the unusual strength of individual components or for national contra-systems as a whole. In Poland, for instance, such factors include the church, a predominantly independent peasantry, and a traditionally critical intelligentsia. As already mentioned, the East German regime must accommodate itself to the fact that 80 percent of the population can watch West German television, including news of the European peace movement. This influence, combined with that of an increasingly outspoken, officially approved Lutheran church, has led to an alliance between organized religion and mass political dissent, producing the largest and most active unofficial peace movement in the European communist community. A unique factor in Czechoslovakia is that a large cross-section of the population has been purged twice from public life in a single generation (1948 and 1968), thereby creating an enormous pariah class or a permanent, core contra-population.

Eastern Europe and the Soviet Contra-System

Soviet internal propaganda frequently cautions the public to be on guard against harmful Western influences, such as crass materialism, moral corruption, and political subversion. These are ideological code words for the second economy, the youth counterculture, and the dissident movement – all central components of the contra-system deeply entrenched in the USSR. Paradoxically, it is not the West but communist Eastern Europe that appears to be the principal source of contra-influences in the Soviet Union.

Soviet tourism to Eastern Europe, not to the West, arouses the greatest consumer envy when disparate living standards are compared. This phenomenon, compounded by a series of harvest failures and a food crisis since 1979, has encouraged large parts of the population to seek relief in the second economy.

Religious influences cross the Soviet borders from every direction, but once again Eastern Europe is the main source. The papal visits to Poland and the example of the Polish church itself have greatly stimulated religious activism in Soviet Lithuania and the Western Ukraine. In addition, Romanian evangelicals smuggle Bibles to their ethnic and religious brethren in Soviet Moldavia, while from the Near East militant Moslem fundamentalism is stirring up Soviet Moslems who speak of the coming of their own ayatollah to settle affairs with the Russians. Finally, the Hare Krishna sect arrived in the USSR not by caravan or in a smuggler's sack or via a papal cassette but through an international bookfair, where educated, middle-class Soviet citizens got their first glimpse of the latest addition to the archipelago of underground religion.

Similarly, ethnic unrest in the Soviet Union can frequently be traced to Eastern Europe. The Prague Spring of 1968 caused a stirring in Western Ukraine, always a hotbed of Ukrainian nationalism. And the Polish crisis of the 1980s has provoked a good deal of ethnic unrest in Soviet Estonia.

In fairness to Soviet propagandists, the West does seems to be the chief influence among rebellious youth. It all started with an international youth congress in Moscow in 1957 when Soviet youth first met their Western counterparts. A contemporary Soviet Jewish *refusenik* leader recalls meeting Israelis there for the first time. Later, via London and Paris, thousands of Third World students arrived in Moscow and other university cities to study, bringing with them the latest in Western styles. Then, in the 1960s, Soviet television began extensive coverage of American demonstrations protesting the Vietnam War, thereby unintentionally introducing the *hippi* look into Soviet youth culture. By the time the Olympic tourists arrived in 1980, the counterculture was in full swing.

Finally, political dissent has its own wellsprings in Soviet society, but at crucial intervals these have been fed by events in Eastern Europe. According to Vladimir Bukovsky, the Yugoslav Milovan Djilas's *New Class* was being secretly read in Moscow in the late 1950s and early 1960s. During the Prague Spring in 1968, Soviet dissidents monitored developments, pinning their hopes for a Soviet reform process on a Czechoslovak precedent. Later that year, the Soviet invasion of Czechoslovakia served to politicize many at the periphery of the dissident movement and to radicalize some in the center, the latter development leading to a remarkable, brief peaceful protest in Red Square. Most recently, the rise of Solidarity in Poland in 1980–81 briefly raised the hopes of Soviet labor activists, although of course to no avail.

Possibly in recognition of the special place of "backchannel" influences from Eastern Europe on the Soviet contra-system, a prominent Marxist philosopher in the USSR lashed out a few years ago at "private ownership habits, nationalism, religious fanaticism and Philistine mentality" in the Soviet Union.[9] Martial law had just been declared in Warsaw, and the philosopher was drawing the lesson of the Polish experience.

Conclusion

As the official system's alter ego, the contra-system has become a prominent part of Soviet reality. What options lie open to the Soviet leadership? Moscow need only look to Eastern Europe for an array of policy choices for dealing with the contra-system. These include the policies of correction, co-optation, coexistence, and containment.

In Yugoslavia, where privatism has been raised to a public virtue, the authorities frequently correct a contra-problem by responding to the need it represents. Over time, the Soviet leadership appears to be doing the same with regard to the parallel culture by gradually and perhaps grudgingly yielding ground to modernist art forms. In Hungary, where large parts of the second economy have been drawn into the planning process, the solution tends toward decriminalization and co-optation. Similarly, in the USSR where it is now ordained that "Developed Socialism" is not incompatible with blue jeans, long hair, electric guitars, and pop music, co-optation is apparently the current approach to the countercultural youth.

By contrast, in Poland, where the church is rooted in the national consciousness and fulfills vital spiritual needs, the changing regimes have little choice but to practice coexistence. This would also seem to be the prevailing situation of the second economy in the Soviet Union. In its way, the second economy fills essential material needs and has come to be politically condoned by the party as "an informal alternative to institutional reform."[10] Finally, in Czechoslovakia, containment of contra-phenomena tends to be the norm. Regarding this policy option, Soviet authorities need little guidance, since they continue to hold the line against all kinds of dissidence – political, religious, and ethnic – through an elaborate system of repression.

Thus the Soviet party-state copes with its formidable contra-system through an eclectic combination of policies – giving ground here, holding it there. For the post-Stalin leadership, the challenges of the contra-system have provided an on-going lesson in the limits of power.

Notes

1. Alexander Kazhdan, "An Unsentimental Journey Across Russia," *Problems of Communism* 31 (July–August 1982):69.

2. Andrzej Korbonski, "The 'Second Economy' in Poland," *Journal of International Affairs* 35 (Spring/Summer 1981):9.

3. Mark Brandenburg, "Under the Ice," *New Republic*, 23 Apr. 1984, 15.

4. Janos Bak and Lyman H. Legters, "The Outlook for Reform in Eastern Europe," *Praxis* 3 (April 1983):67–68.

5. Robert Sharlet, "Varieties of Dissent and Regularities of Repression in the European Communist States, in *Dissent in Eastern Europe*, ed. Jane Leftwich Curry (New York: Praeger, 1983), 8-10.

6. Gregory Grossman, "The 'Second Economy' in the USSR," *Problems of Communism* 26 (September–October 1977):25; and Konstantin Simis, *USSR: The Corrupt Society* (New York: Simon & Schuster, 1982), chaps. 5 and 6.

7. Inga Markovits, "Law or Order: Constitutionalism and Legality in Eastern Europe," *Stanford Law Review* 34 (February 1982):600.

8. Yuri Brokhin, "Under Soviet Communism, All Pickpockets Are Equal," *New York Times* 10 Sept. 1975, p. 45.

9. "A Birthday for Brezhnev," *Newsweek*, 28 Dec. 1981, 45.

10. Charles A. Schwartz, "Corruption and Political Development in the USSR," *Comparative Politics* 11 (July 1979):441.

The Soviet Union: World Power of a New Type

This essay will examine the distinctive nature of the Soviet Union as a world power and assess the special character of the Soviet challenge to the international system. The basic theses of my analysis can be stated briefly at the very outset:

1. That the expansionism of the Soviet imperial system is a unique organic imperative produced by the sense of territorial insecurity on the part of the system's Great Russian national core.

2. That as a result of the Great Russian stake in the imperial system a genuine evolution of the Soviet system into more pluralistic forms is not likely in the foreseeable future.

3. That the political priorities and bureaucratic distortions of the communist system confine the Soviet Union to the role of a one-dimensional military world power.

4. That the Soviets — who now have military global reach but who lack political global grasp — feel themselves both too strong internationally to accommodate to the status quo and too weak domestically not to fear it.

5. That as an organically expansionist but one-dimensional military world power lacking the capacity to effect a genuine revolution in the world system, the Soviet Union is confined to the essentially negative role of disrupter of wider and more cooperative international arrangements.

6. That a major disruption of the international political system could occur as a consequence of the Western failure to offset Soviet military power while not coping effectively with the mushrooming crises in the strategically and geopolitically center zones of the Middle East and Central America.

Address presented at the International Institute of Stratgeic Studies, Silver Jubilee Annual Conference, Ottawa, Canada, 8–11 September 1983. The collected papers from this conference will appear in 1984 in the IISS's Adelphi series.

Theses 1 and 2: A Uniquely Organic Imperialism

The Soviet Union is the political expression of Russian nationalism. The Great Russians dominate the multinational Soviet Union, populated by some 270 million people. Through the power and resources of that Union, they dominate in turn a cluster of geographically contiguous states numbering approximately an additional 115 million people. In effect, about 135 million Great Russians exercise political control over a political framework that cumulatively encompasses some 385 million people spread over much of the Eurasian continent.

This is not to say that the system is one of simple national oppression. The Great Russians rule as much by co-optation as by suppression. The historical record of Russian imperial preponderance is replete with examples of successful co-optation, corruption, and integration of foreign elites, of the gradual absorption politically and even culturally of ethnically related peoples, of the creation of a sense of a larger community. Nonetheless, in the background of this process is the reality of Moscow's power, which is applied ruthlessly whenever a given nation chooses to resist domination and especially if it seeks to detach itself from the Russian-dominated larger whole.

The distinctive character of the Russian imperial drive is derived from the interconnection between the militaristic organization of the Russian society and the territorial imperative that defines its instinct of survival. As often noted by both Russian and non-Russian historians, from time immemorial Russian society expressed itself politically through a state that was mobilized and regimented along military lines, with the security dimension serving as the central organizing impulse. The absence of any clearly definable national boundary made territorial expansion the obvious way of ensuring security. Such expansion then bred new conflicts, new threats, and a further expansionary drive. A relentless historical cycle was thus set in motion: insecurity generated expansionism; expansionism bred insecurity; and this insecurity, in turn, fueled further expansionism.

Russian history is consequently a history of sustained territorial expansionism. This sustained expansion from the northeast plains and forests of Muscovy has lasted — almost on a continuous basis — for more than 300 years. It has involved a push westward against major power rivals, resulting in the eventual expulsion of Sweden from east of the Baltic and in the partition of the Polish-Lithuanian Republic. It has involved the persistent drive southward, culminating — in the wake of defeats inflicted on the Ottoman Empire — in the subordination of the Ukrainian Cossacks and the Crimean Tatars and in the absorption of several Caucasian nations and of Moslem Central Asia. It has involved a steady stream of settlers, penal colonists, and military explorers eastward, along the brim of the Chinese empire, all the way to Kamchatka. Such territorial expansion is doubtless — both in scale and in duration — one of the most ambitious examples of a relentless imperial drive in known history.

The Russians have come in this manner to control the world's largest real estate. They do so by inhabiting relatively densely its inner core – the large area known as European Russia – and by settling in smaller but still politically significant numbers in strategically significant colonial outposts in the Baltic region (including Kaliningrad), parts of Byelorussia, Eastern Ukraine, the northeast shore of the Black Sea, large parts of Kazakhstan, and along a long security belt spanning the trans-Siberian Railroad all the way to the Soviet Far East. The empty vastness of Siberia has thus been effectively sealed off and remains available for gradual colonization.

In the process, the Russians have come to dominate the weaker peoples inhabiting some of these territories, by subordinating them politically, co-opting them culturally, and sometimes decimating them biologically. The non-Russian nations are controlled from the center and prevented from coalescing against the politically dominant Great Russians, who populate the strategically located central inner core of the multinational state.

The Russian imperial system – with its mixture of co-optation, subordination, and strategic settlement – thus emerged in a manner that differs profoundly from the experience of other recent empires. Naval expansion to remote lands, followed by limited settling, was not the method. It was much more organic – a process of steady seepage into contiguous territory, with the atavistic instinct of survival dictating the felt need to acquire more land, with "insecurity" being translated into persistent expansion. As a result, and contrary to many journalistic clichés, Russia historically was not so much a victim of frequent aggression but rather the persistent aggressor itself, pressing from the center in any direction, whenever opportunity beckoned. A list of aggressions committed in the last two centuries against Russia would be dwarfed by a parallel list of Russian expansionist moves against its neighbors. The vaunted Russian sense of insecurity exists – but not because Russia was so frequently aggressed against but because its organic expansion has prompted, and was prompted by, territorial acquisitiveness, with its inevitably antagonistic ripple effects.

An additional, and enduring, consequence of such sustained territorial expansion has been the emergence of an imperial consciousness among the Great Russian people. Such a notion of "imperial consciousness" is difficult to define, but difficulty of definition is not a negation of the phenomenon. There is something strikingly imperial in the insistence of the Russians on describing themselves as the "Big Brother" of the dominated peoples, in their spontaneous determination to build huge Russian orthodox cathedrals in the very centers of dominated capitals (as in Helsinki and Warsaw – and even to replace the Warsaw "Sobor," which the newly emancipated Poles blew up in 1919, thirty years later with the monumental Stalin Palace of Culture), and in the deeply rooted feeling that somehow the non-Russian nations of the Soviet Union and of Eastern Europe must be retained as part of Mother Russia's special domain. Anyone who has seen, or read reports of, how the Soviet ambassadors stationed abroad handle their periodic joint sessions with fellow ambassadors from the Warsaw Pact obtains an insight into imperial and hierarchical relations.

Great Russian imperial consciousness is a complex web of religious messianism, which has long associated Moscow with the Third Rome, of nationalistic instincts of survival and of power, and of the more recent universalistic ideological zeal. In addition, territorially expansive insecurity has been reinforced by the communist obsession with internal and external enemies, reinforcing an already existing paranoiac attitude toward the outside world. This complex web of motivations has helped to generate and sustain a world outlook in which the drive to global preeminence, for decades measured by competition with the United States, has become the central energizing impulse. That impulse sustains the predatory character of Great Russian imperialism.

It is this drive toward global preeminence as well as the vested interest in the imperial system that inhibits the prospects of a qualitatively significant evolutionary change in the character of the Soviet system. Without Soviet intervention, Czechoslovakia under Dubcek or Poland under Walesa would probably have become social democratic republics, with communist totalitarianism effectively dismantled.

But Soviet intervention occurred for the very same reason that internal evolution toward greater political pluralism within the Soviet Union will be intensely, and probably even more successfully, resisted for a very long time to come. The reaction against peaceful change in Eastern Europe stemmed from the same impulses that make Great Russians fear any significant relaxation of central Moscow control. A genuinely far-reaching decentralization of the Soviet system, even if only economic, would pose a mortal danger to Great Russian imperial control and thus, in the Russian psyche, eventually to the security of the Great Russian people. After all, what does "only economic" decentralization mean in political terms insofar as the Soviet Union is concerned? Inevitably, it would have to mean a greater degree of autonomy for the non-Russians who would then be in a position to translate greater economic self-determination into growing political self-determination.

To the majority of the Great Russians, that is a highly threatening prospect. Any significant national self-assertion on the part of the non-Russians constitutes also a challenge to Russian territorial preeminence and could possibly even pose a biological threat to Great Russian national survival. Where would genuine decentralization, the acceptance of more democratic norms, and the institutionalization of pluralism eventually lead? Where, indeed, could one even draw proper lines between the Great Russians and the others, given the demographic intermingling of the recent decades? There would be escalating tensions and eventually head-on conflicts in a variety of areas: in some of the Baltic republics heavily settled by unwelcome Great Russians; in the culturally comingled areas of Byelorussia and the Ukraine; and certainly on the fringes of the Caucasian and Central Asian republics.

The dismantling of the overseas British and French empires did not mean the end of either Britain or France. But the dismantling of the territorially contiguous Russian empire could even threaten Russia itself, given the absence of natural frontiers. The difficulties France faced in Algeria would be dwarfed on the peripheries of the purely Great Russian lands. Any attempted disentangling along national lines would be messy and bloody, and awareness of that prospect makes almost every Great Russian instinctively wary of tolerating any significant devolution of Moscow's central control. The instinct for survival gives the autocratic, highly centralized, and imperial Soviet system unusual staying power, neutralizing the kind of inner self-doubt and imperial fatigue that induced Britain and France to accede to the dismantling of their empires.

Theses 3 and 4: A One-Dimensional World Power of a New Type

Western observers of the Soviet system have been loath to concede that its political centralism has staying power and that the Russian imperial impulse is vitally inherent to that system. It is certainly more reassuring to believe that both conditions are evanescent: that the system will mellow because of either containment or economic development (or a combination of both) and that its imperial drive will wane with the allegedly inevitable fading of Marxist zeal. The transformation of the system and the waning of its imperial ambitions will thus relieve the West of the obligation of having to face up to the much more difficult problem of determining how to coexist historically in the nuclear age with a powerful and closed political system motivated by vague but highly unsettling global goals.

But what will happen if the Soviet system does not mellow and its military power continues to grow? Rarely if ever do Western observers address themselves to the international implications of this issue, except occasionally from the extreme-right perspective cast usually in highly Manichaean and moralistic terms. Yet the issue demands attention and, above all, sober realization that for many decades to come an uneasy historical—but not entirely peaceful—coexistence with a militarily powerful Soviet Union may continue to teeter on the edge of the nuclear abyss.

The point of departure for a realistic appraisal of the relationship must be recognition of the special character of the Soviet system as a world power. The Soviet Union is a new type of world power in that its might is one-dimensional; thus it is essentially incapable of sustaining effective global dominance. The fact of the matter is that the Soviet Union is a global power only in the military dimension. It is neither a genuine economic rival to the United States nor—as once was the case—a source of a globally interesting ideological experiment. This condition imposes a decisive limitation on the Soviet capability to act in a manner traditional to world powers or claimants to the status of world power.

Traditionally, both the dominant world military power and its principal rival possessed similar political and socioeconomic systems, each with the capability for sustained and comprehensive preeminence. Since the late Middle Ages, naval power has been the central instrument for exercising global military reach. To the extent that such global reach can be said to have existed in the age of slow communications and limited weaponry, the powers exercising it and their principal rivals were — broadly speaking — Portugal versus Spain during much of the sixteenth century; the Netherlands versus France during the seventeenth century; Britain, then France, and later Germany, respectively, during the eighteenth and nineteenth, and part of the twentieth centuries; and, finally, the United States versus the Soviet Union during the second half of the twentieth century. In all cases until the most recent, the contest was between powers at a comparable level of development, with the rival quite capable of also providing wider commercial and political leadership as a supplement to its military preeminence. In effect, the rival, in displacing the preeminent global power, could both provide and sustain equally comprehensive leadership.

The unusual quality of the Soviet global challenge is that the Soviet Union is manifestly unequipped to provide constructive and sustained leadership in the event that it unseats the United States as the number one world power. The Soviet Union could not provide global financial leadership. Its economy could not act as the locomotive for global development and technological innovation. Its mass culture lacks wide appeal, and its leading intellectuals and artists have been steadily fleeing the Soviet Union. In brief, American displacement could not be followed by a Soviet replacement.

The main reason for this condition is to be found in the Russian communist system itself. Its bureaucratization, centralization, and dogmatization of decision making have stifled socioeconomic initiative to an unprecedented degree. As a result, the Soviet record in all nonmilitary dimensions of systemic performance ranges from the average to the mediocre. It still takes a *political* decision at the highest level for the Soviet economic system to produce an item that is generally competitive worldwide. Soviet economic performance over the years has required social sacrifice altogether disproportionate to the actual output. Perhaps never before in history have such a gifted people, in control of such abundant resources, labored so hard for so long to produce relatively so little.

Comparative studies of socioeconomic development, such as those by Cyril Black of Princeton, show that today the Soviet Union occupies in world rankings of social and economic indices a place roughly comparable to that it held at the beginning of this century. Black concluded: "In the perspective of fifty years, the comparative ranking of the USSR in composite economic and social indices per capita has probably not changed significantly. So far as the rather limited available evidence permits a judgment, the USSR has not overtaken or surpassed any country on a per capita basis since 1917 with the possible exception of Italy, and the nineteen or twenty countries that rank higher than Russia today in this regard also ranked higher in 1900 and 1919. The per capita gross national product of Italy, which is just below that of the USSR today, was probably somewhat higher fifty years ago."[1]

In other words, the extraordinary sacrifices, the unprecedented loss of life, and the sustained social deprivation that every Soviet citizen has felt have yielded results comparable to those achieved by other societies at a much smaller social cost. Moreover, the pace of Soviet economic development since World War II has been only average, despite the fact that initially the Soviet Union had the statistical advantage of recovering from an artificially low plateau generated by wartime devastation. In 1950, the Soviet GNP accounted for about 11 percent of the global product; more than three decades later it is still 11 percent. No wonder that Soviet propagandists now prefer not to recall Khrushchev's challenge of 1960 to surpass the United States in absolute production by 1970 and in relative per capita production by 1980.

The picture is just as bleak in the social and cultural dimensions of Soviet life. Recent studies point to a decline in male longevity, to the poor state of Soviet health care, to increasing infant mortality, and to the spread of alcoholism. Intellectual and artistic life has become stifled; social innovation has been shackled by bureaucratic inertia. In brief, the Soviet Union is not a society capable of projecting an appealing image to the world, a condition essential to the exercise of global leadership.

The main effect of this poor performance is twofold. First of all, it magnifies the traditional Russian and the doctrinaire communist suspicions regarding the outside world. That world is perceived as bent on dismantling Moscow's empire and on promoting an anticommunist counter-revolution. The outside thus continues to look threatening to the Soviet Union despite its attainment of the status of a global military superpower. Though the Soviets take great pride in their new military prowess and have used it to claim coequal status with the United States, in the Soviet perception of the world the United States looms as a giant, with its finances, communications, and mass media enveloping the world with many tentacles. American technology (currently microelectronics, for instance) keeps on providing the American military establishment with new capabilities that the Soviets take more than seriously. In the Far East, the potential looms for a Chinese-Japanese constellation, while in the West there is always the magnetic pull on Eastern Europe of a Europe that has not fully resigned itself to an indefinite post-Yalta division.

All of this enhances Soviet paranoia and contributes directly to the second major effect of the one-dimensional character of Soviet global power. It generates an erratic pattern of accommodation and competition with the United States in which the Soviet seek to attain a condominium with Washington and yet fear becoming locked into the role of the junior partner, in effect committed to the maintenance of the global status quo. Moscow rejects that status quo, for it would not only perpetuate American preponderance but — in Soviet eyes — would also serve as the point of departure for policies designed to promote "peaceful evolution" of a contained Soviet Union, i.e., its political subversion.

As a result, the promotion of regional conflicts, the inhibition of wider and more genuinely supernational international cooperation, and the opposition to what is called "world order" are strategies that the Kremlin finds compatible with its own one-dimensional global military power. That military power permits Moscow to play a wider role in keeping with the Soviet imperial consciousness, reduces the fear that regional conflicts could precipitate a direct conflict with the United States, and enables the Soviet Union to use military leverage to undermine American preeminence in areas hitherto considered as safe United States havens. Particularly important and effective in this respect is the Soviet ability (in excess of the American) to deliver promptly from its large inventories huge amounts of military equipment to Soviet clients and would-be friends. In effect, a policy of gradual undermining American global preeminence is a key aspect of the historical self-definition of the Soviet Union as a global power.

And this leads to a broader conclusion still: the real danger to the West is not that the Soviet Union will someday succeed in imposing a *Pax Sovietica* on the world. Rather, it is that the Soviet Union, as a one-dimensional world power committed to the disruption of the existing arrangements and therefore to the displacement of the United States, will contribute decisively not to a world revolution in existing international arrangements but to greater global anarchy from which all will suffer.

Theses 5 and 6: A Partially Revised Perspective on the Soviet Challenge

Implicit in the foregoing conclusion are some revisions of the prevailing Western view regarding the nature of the Soviet threat. In the immediate post-World War II era, the West was preoccupied with the fear that vast Soviet armies would pour westward, swamping Western Europe. Internal high-level American discussions — as recent studies by D. A. Rosenberg show — focused heavily on the question of how the United States should respond, given its limited but monopolistic nuclear arsenal. Berlin became the symbolic linchpin of Western resolve, with the blockade providing a test of American-Soviet wills.

Western, and notably American, anxiety mounted further after the communist invasion of Korea, leading for the first time to comprehensive nuclear war planning by the United States and to the creation of the Strategic Air Command (SAC) as the principal means of massive retaliation. In the late 1950s, Khrushchev's boasting about missiles precipitated more intensified American efforts to offset the allegedly emerging Soviet advantage, which resulted in a considerable American strategic superiority by the early 1960s. However, by the late 1970s and early 1980s, with the United States homeland fully vulnerable to a Soviet attack, the Soviet Union was again perceived as on the verge of obtaining a politically significant military edge. President Reagan even explicitly proclaimed that the Soviet Union is already strategically superior to the United States.

In fact, during much of the postwar era, the Soviet challenge to the West — contrary to prevailing perceptions — was not primarily military, and even now the much more important military dimension of the Soviet threat needs to be seen in a broader political framework. During the immediate postwar years,

Stalin did engage in some peripheral probes designed to establish the resilience of the new geopolitical realities, but his challenge was not primarily a military one. Indeed, the West greatly overestimated the existing Soviet military capabilities, in apparent ignorance of the large-scale demobilization of the Red Army. To be sure, the West and especially the United States disarmed most hastily, but the West confronted an East that was socially exhausted and militarily also readjusting to a peacetime status.

The primary challenge in those years was in fact ideological-political. The Soviet Union emerged from World War II with unprecedented prestige. It was hailed and idealized in the West, and not only by fellow travelers. Many in the West so desperately wanted to believe that the USSR would remain a postwar ally that they bent over backward to see the Soviet point of view on contentious international issues. Moreover, to the populations of war-devastated countries, the Soviet Union projected the image not only of a victor but also of an apparently successful socioeconomic system. That image generated ideological support and invited political imitation. An enormous American effort, above all the Marshall Plan, was required to neutralize that appeal — and it was on this front, and not purely on the military level, that the initial historical confrontation occurred. This is not to deny the importance of NATO or of the Korean War in the containment of the Soviet Union, but rather it is to postulate that the political-ideological dimension was critical in the rivalry.

The next crucial phase in the Soviet challenge occurred during the late 1950s and early 1960s. Khrushchev's policy of premature globalism, based on deliberately falsified claims of missile superiority, collapsed during the Cuban missile crisis of 1962. Khrushchev's challenge was also predicated, however, on a more generalized historical vision in which economic optimism was the decisive element. The Soviet leader's vulgar "We will bury you" was not — as it was widely perceived at the time — a physical threat but a historic gauntlet, derived from misplaced confidence that American economic stagnation and Soviet economic dynamism would result in the emergence by the 1970s of the Soviet Union as the world's number one economic power.

That did not happen. In 1980 the Soviet Union was as behind the United States as it had been a quarter of a century before. It is now behind Japan as well. The vaunted technological race ended with the American flag on the moon. Today the Soviet economy is widely perceived as being, if not in crisis, then at least noninnovative and confronting increasingly difficult trade-offs. Soviet agriculture is an undisputed failure. The Soviet system generally has lost its ideological appeal, and that, too, detracts from Soviet global influence.

By the 1980s, however, Soviet military power had acquired, for the first time, genuine global reach, thus compensating for the lack of systemic appeal. This new condition was clearly gratifying to the Soviet leaders, and anyone who has dealt with them can testify to their pride in the Soviet Union's new status as a global superpower.

But global reach is not the same thing as global grasp. The Soviet challenge today, as already noted, is one-dimensional; therefore, it cannot be the point of departure either for comprehensive global leadership or for an enduring global partnership with the United States. The ambivalent condition of one-dimensional power induces a world outlook that is a combination of possessive defensiveness and disruptive offensiveness.

To be sure, it is quite doubtful that the Soviet leaders operate on the basis of some broad revolutionary blueprint or that they even have a systematic long-term strategy. In real life, most decision makers are compelled to respond to circumstances and to cope with a myriad of specific issues, and they hence lack the time and the intellectual inclination to engage in any systematic long-term definition of policy goals. The Soviet leaders doubtless are no exception. But the Soviet leaders do operate in the context of an orientation in which the retention of what Moscow controls and the disruption of what Washington seeks to organize provide lodestars for more specific tactics and strategies.

It is important to recall here that there is a basic difference between a genuinely revolutionary world power and a disruptive world power. Napoleonic France threatened not only the status quo; France's socioeconomic development was such that the country could serve as the center of a new international order that would have emerged if Napoleon had prevailed over Britain and Russia. In that sense, France was a genuinely revolutionary power. To an ominous degree, both Hitler's Germany and Tojo's Japan also had the revolutionary potential for creating a new international system, if German and Japanese arms had won the war.

In contrast, the Soviet Union pursues a disruptive, rather than a truly revolutionary, role. It is confined to that limited role by the nature of its one-dimensional power and also by the character of nuclear weapons. Nuclear weapons eliminate the possibility of a central war serving as the revolutionary cataclysm. Until the advent of the nuclear age, a world power could be displaced by its rival through a direct military confrontation. A nation could then translate a military victory into premier status by exercising the other attributes of national power, such as the economy, finances, science, and national culture. The nuclear age has had the effect of making these other means of exercising world domination the more critical instruments for *achieving* world domination.

Yet the Soviet Union is most deficient in these other attributes of power. Moreover, there is no reason to believe, given the inherent limitations of the Soviet system, that this situation will soon alter to the Soviet Union's benefit. The Soviet Union is thus condemned to seeking global status neither by direct nuclear collision nor by peaceful socioeconomic competition. The only way open to global status is that of attrition and gradual disruption of stable international arrangements so that the United States suffers directly and indirectly.

The most effective way of pursuing such a strategy of disruption is to achieve and maintain sufficient military power to deter the United States's reactions and to intimidate the United States's allies while encouraging trends hostile to the

United States's interests in strategically vital areas that possess the greatest potential for a dynamic shift in the global political-economic balance. Today, these areas are, above all, the Middle East and Central America.

Accordingly, what happens in these two strategically and geopolitically sensitive zones will determine the longer-range pattern of the American-Soviet relationship and define the Soviet global role. A progressive deterioration of the political stability of the Middle East, combined with the gradual political reentry of the Soviet Union into a region from which it has been excluded since 1973, could have far-reaching implications for American relations with both Europe and the Far East. The strategic salience of this region is such that any qualitatively important decline in American influence, especially if matched by a corresponding rise in Soviet political presence, is bound to have far-reaching and worldwide strategic consequences for the nature of the American-Soviet global equation.

Similarly, how the United States handles its new dilemmas in Central America, and in the longer run also the United States-Mexican relationship, is bound to affect the global balance and therefore the Soviet world role as well. As in the Middle East, it is again not so much a matter of what the Soviets may be doing as of how the United States conducts itself, either by commission or by omission. If American policy results in the Americanization of sociopolitical conflicts to such an extent that the Western Hemisphere is increasingly turned against the United States, and the American-Mexican problems become consequently so complicated that the United States loses its capacity for helping in the resolution of Mexico's internal problems, the result will be a far-reaching decline in American global standing.

That, in turn, would reinforce the Soviet imperial consciousness and the expansionary impulse, while further strengthening the existing structure of Soviet power and the basic character of the system. Indeed, it is appropriate to recall in this connection that insofar as Russian historical experience is concerned, internal political change of a truly significant character has tended to occur only in the wake of external defeats, whereas external successes have tended to reinforce centralism and ideological control. Moreover, as Arnold Horelick has shown in a recent Rand study, an improved Soviet domestic performance also tends to encourage more assertive external behavior and the surfacing of greater external ambitions.

In contrast, external setbacks have induced profound reassessments of Russian internal policies and have occasionally produced even significant systemic changes. Despite the internal weakness of the tsarist regime, its pervasive corruption, and its mindless bureaucracy, the basic structure of its power endured for a long time — and collapsed finally only because of its massive military defeat during the three devastating years of World War I. Moreover, the occasional periods of internal reform that occurred during the 1860s and in the first decade of the twentieth century were followed immediately by external defeats in the Crimean War and in the Russo-Japanese War. The great Russian historian

V. O. Kluchevsky noted that "a Russian war carried to a successful [end] has always helped to strengthen the [existing] order," but "progress in Russia's political life at home has always been gained at the price of Russia's political misfortune abroad."

By having become a global military power, the Soviet Union has broken through the United States policy of geographic containment. At the same time, by expanding its exposure when its own capacities are still very one-dimensional, the Soviet Union is exposing itself to the possibility of overextension and eventually to a major external misfortune, because of some protracted military-political misadventure. And in that respect Moscow's strategy of deliberate exploitation of global turbulence could turn out to be historically disastrous.

Policy Implications

The policy implications that follow from the foregoing analysis can be posited briefly:

1. The military dimension of the East-West competition—notably of the United States-Soviet rivalry—is of critical importance in a negative sense. Although the rivalry is not likely to be finally resolved by a clash of arms, the West must exercise every effort to make certain that the Soviet Union does not gain a military edge that would enable it to attempt political intimidation.

2. Arms-control arrangements should be assessed primarily in terms of their contribution to the maintenance of a stable East-West military balance. That is their central role. Arms control, moreover, should be pursued without historical illusions regarding the impact of any agreement on the character of the Soviet system and its relationship with the West, for the long-term political rivalry will not be ended even through a comprehensive arms-control arrangement.

3. A major Soviet external misfortune is likely to have the most immediate impact on Eastern Europe. This region is manifestly restless and resentful of Soviet control. Any sign of Soviet weakness and any prolonged, debilitating Soviet foreign entanglement will be exploited to break the weakest link in the Soviet imperial chain. Moreover, the region is most susceptible to Western ideas and culturally attracted to Western Europe. It offers, therefore, a topical focus for Western policies designed to dilute the Soviet imperial impulse.

4. Western—and especially American—efforts to maintain and promote regional stability, notably in such vital areas as Central America and the Middle East, will be decisive in determining whether Soviet global influence expands to the detriment of international stability. American passivity in the Middle East and American overengagement in Central America are the most immediate geopolitical dangers.

5. The positive task of shaping a wider international system that genuinely embraces the newly emancipated Third World, and thus replaces the narrower

European world order that collapsed during the course of World War II, will have to be pursued for some time without constructive Soviet involvement. The Soviet Union — too strong not to be a rival, yet feeling itself too weak to be a partner — cannot be counted on to become a true participant in the constructive global process, since its systemic interests are diametrically opposed to the preservation of the status quo in a world that Moscow can disrupt but not dominate.

6. Historical coexistence with the Soviet Union will remain dominated by the largely negative task of avoiding a nuclear catastrophe. Western acts of commission or omission will ultimately determine whether that historical coexistence — a precariously peaceful coexistence at best for a long time to come — will eventually produce a more harmonious relationship or deteriorate into wider global anarchy.

NOTE

1. Cyril Black, "Soviet Society: A Comparative View," in *Prospects for Soviet Society*, ed. Allen Kassof (New York: Praeger, 1968), 42–43.

Socialist Stagnation and Communist Encirclement

SEWERYN BIALER

The Soviet Union will encounter formidable obstacles in its efforts to sustain and advance its world power during the 1980s. Much of its success will depend on circumstances beyond Soviet control—not the least of them being the changing international environment and the capacity of the United States to mobilize, expand, and effectively utilize its own vast resources. The growth of Soviet power will also depend on how successfully the new leadership in Moscow responds to the more predictable, well-defined, and immediate problems under its direct authority.

Soviet power cannot grow unless the Soviet leaders arrest the adverse trends in their domestic economic, social, and political environment; unless they manage, despite these trends, to sustain their military buildup; unless they contain and minimize the repercussions of the disaffection within their "internal" and "external" empires; unless they stabilize their periodically explosive relations with China; and unless they evolve a coherent, imaginative, and active foreign policy to replace the failed détente with the United States. Moreover, these sources of instability must be confronted at a highly vulnerable time, when a new leader is attempting to consolidate his authority and the governing hierarchies are replacing the current leading elites.

Socialist Stagnation

The profound economic, social, and political problems that Brezhnev bequeathed to Andropov and Chernenko represent the cumulative effects of the inherent weaknesses in the basic Soviet structures. The most immediate prob-

Adapted from an address presented at the International Institute of Strategic Studies, Silver Jubilee Annual Conference, Ottawa, Canada, 8–11 September 1983. The collected papers from this conference will appear in 1984 in the IISS's Adelphi series.

lems facing the Soviet Union are in its economic structure. Without decisive action by Chernenko, the situation promises to become even more acute as the 1980s progress. If the economic situation is not as catastrophic as some analysts in Washington believe, it is far from being as routine as Soviet leaders say it is. For many decades the political "superstructure" has shaped the socioeconomic "base" in the Soviet Union. Now the time has come for the "base" to take its revenge on the "superstructure."

Soviet economic problems are well known to specialists. Some have their sources in the economy's maturity, some are directly connected to the archaic and cumbersome economic system, some are the consequence of specific policies and their inertial continuation, and some are exogenous. Among the problems facing the Soviet economy is that its planning system is geared to one indicator, the size of output. Prices, costs, and profits provide no true measure of performance, and managerial and incentive systems primarily reward quantity, not quality, of production. The list of economic problems also includes the scarcity of investment capital; the limited ability to pay for technological imports; unfavorble demographic trends that bring fewer newcomers annually to the labor force; the inability of agriculture to keep pace with population growth; the lack of a satisfactory infrastructure; the exhaustion of cheap, abundant raw materials; the slow and uneven growth of energy resources; and the backwardness of the machine-building industry. Given all these problems, in the 1980s the Soviet gross national product will grow at the rate of 2 to 3 percent annually, according to optimistic estimates. Even more significant is the low quality of both the inputs and the outputs of that growth.

Although there are not more economic problems now than at many other troubled times in the past, the problems are qualitatively different in two important respects. First, the economic problems of today are associated with stagnation; those of the past were associated with growth. Second, the Soviet leaders can no longer use the only means that the system provides to combat problems — crash mobilizations of people, capital, and resources. In place of *extensive* sources of growth, *intensive* sources are needed — high technology, high quality, and high labor productivity. To mobilize these new sources of growth would require major reforms. The alternative is a faltering economic performance.

Until now, the Soviet Union has not experienced economic stagnation. In this sense, the 1980s will be very different from the past, and therefore it is unknown to what extent economic stagnation will encourage social instability. Stalin ended the threat from the countryside by crushing the independent peasantry and establishing a coercive agricultural system. After Stalin, the threat to social stability came from the "intelligentsia," the youth, and the open dissenters. But the new "intelligentsia" remains clearly within the system — career-oriented and materialistic. The youth, unlike that of any other industrial country, has not made its "revolution," and the dissenters have been successfully isolated.

In the 1980s social instability may come primarily from a more critical stratum, the industrial workers. The factors that have ensured labor peace in the past will be considerably weakened in this decade. The repressive police state will most probably become even stronger and more active. Yet it is difficult to predict how urban workers will react to the stagnation or decline in their standard of living, which has been steadily rising for two decades. Their plight could be further exacerbated by any serious industrial reform that would bring a combination of economic austerity and state pressure for improved performance. Finally, the intergenerational mobility of workers into the middle and professional classes is declining and will continue to decline as a result of competition from the extensive middle class, stagnation or even a decrease in educational expenditures, and reduced economic growth.

Another potential source of social instability emanates from the non-Russian nations of the federation. The many factors that have ensured social peace in these nations will be considerably weakened in the 1980s as the economic base erodes. The nationality problem, however, is unlikely to constitute a main source of social instability in this decade — even if it remains potentially the most resistant to an enduring resolution and the most destructive to the existing system.

Economic and social problems will most likely exacerbate the political problems generated by the irrefragable legacy of political Stalinism and the complex succession process. The new leadership must contend with age-old (tsarist and Soviet) problems of social discipline and bureaucratic inertia and corruption. Social discipline has recently deteriorated remarkably, even by Soviet standards. One finds surging absenteeism, unacceptably high worker turnover, substandard quality of production, rampant alcoholism, and so much theft that it amounts to a secondary redistribution of national income. Some Soviet sociologists and economists question whether official attempts to stimulate a greater sense of responsibility and improved work habits can impress the present generation of workers at all.

The recent bureaucratic stagnation has no close parallel in past Soviet history, except perhaps that of the last years of Stalin's rule. The already cumbersome process of decision making became even more intractable during Brezhnev's decline. Bureaucratic routine prevailed at every level. At the center, crucial decisions were delayed too long. Costly investment policies were pursued without alteration, even though they yielded few of the expected results. The stability of cadres was higher than at any previous period as the older elite barred advancement to an entire generation of middle-aged officials in middle-level positions. Meanwhile, clientalism, patronage, and corruption pervaded the entire party-state apparatus from Moscow to the smallest district.

Another potential source of political instability lies in the relations among the various elites and bureaucracies. Here, too, the factors that have ensured political peace will be considerably weakened by declining economic growth. Inevitable scarcities and austerity will undermine the enduring equilibrium of the Brezhnev years as competition for growth resources divides spokesmen for the military and civilian sectors, for agriculture and industry, and for the territories of European Russia, Ukraine, Siberia, and Central Asia.

Decisions on economic reform will have to be made in the 1980s. Only when survival is at issue will Soviet leaders accept the high political cost of radical reform. Economic reforms require a withdrawal of subsidies from the basic commodities and would draw strong opposition from middle-rank officials and managers who have learned to take advantage of the existing system. The repercussions of limited reform—not to speak of radical reform—are perhaps the major domestic political problems of the 1980s.

The extent to which Soviet domestic problems will affect the growth of Soviet power in the 1980s remains to be seen. Both economic and military power will probably advance at lower rates than during Brezhnev's first decade. The drop in the annual growth rate to about 2.5 percent will complicate decisions concerning military appropriations. The choice is not between guns and butter but between an increase in the current direct expenditures on arms and maintenance of the military forces and an increase in the large-scale investment in the military-industrial plant to support future military growth. To maintain both at their 1970s levels is economically and politically impossible.

Major impediments to sustained, high-quality military development will originate either on the demand side, from cuts in military spending, or on the supply side, from the inability of the economy to deliver the necessary resources. The continued separation of the military and civilian sectors also inhibits technologically advanced military growth. The technological base of the Soviet economy is too small and narrow to support large-scale military progress at a reasonable cost. The traditional route to success in the military area—concentration on a very few priorities regardless of cost—is no longer open. The number of priorities is growing, the strength of competing claimants is increasing, and the width of the technological gap between the military and civilian sectors makes the transfer of resources very difficult. Finally, the quality of the Soviet armed forces may be seriously impaired by the combined effects of long-neglected health services, low educational levels, and a shift in the ethnic mix of Soviet recruits toward non-Slavic minorities. Political tensions may result from the association of Slavic officers and non-Slavic draftees, while the armed forces in general may become less reliable as a major socializing agency in the party-state.

This assessment does not imply that Soviet leaders will fail to match American efforts in a continuing or accelerating arms race. It demonstrates, however, that the economic, social, and political costs of the arms race to the Soviet Union will be much higher than in the past. It suggests that the Soviet leaders may prove more responsive to serious proposals on decelerating the pace of arms production. For the immediate future, the Soviet leaders will be preoccupied with major domestic problems. This situation reinforces the basic mode of retrenchment that has been characteristic of Soviet foreign policy in recent years. This retrenchment, however, does not depend on internal sources alone. It also reflects the failure to conceive an alternative to the coherent foreign policy structured around détente with the United States, the need to perpetuate détente with Western Europe, the reluctance to test Reagan's hard line, and, not least, the consequences of "communist encirclement."

Stalin's successors inherited the concept of the dread *"capitalist* encirclement," which energized Soviet military and foreign policy. To the degree that fears of the consequences of capitalist encirclement have receded with the growth of Soviet power since Stalin's death, another set of problems that may be termed *"communist* encirclement" has become more central in policy formulation.

This second type of encirclement may be seen as four concentric arcs at different spatial and political distances from vital Soviet interests, each of which over time generates problems of varying intensity and danger. The first arc, nearest to the center both physically and politically, encompasses the Soviet "internal empire," the belt of non-Russian nations dominating the periphery of the USSR. The second arc includes the Soviet "external empire," the phalanx of Eastern European nations that owe their existence and survival as communist states to Soviet force, threatened and actual. (Cuba and Vietnam should be regarded as separate cases.) The third arc, farther yet from the center, consists of China, the colossus risen from an authentic revolution and transformed into a long-range threat on the Soviet eastern border. The fourth arc, farthest from the center, collects those remains of a once cohesive international movement dominated by Moscow, the many communist parties that now exhibit a troublesome autonomy. This essay will focus on the second and third arcs.

The Second Arc: The Eastern European Empire

Soviet leaders from Stalin to Chernenko have remained determined to preserve and dominate the "external empire." It is a commitment that differs little from the commitment to protect the integrity of the "internal empire." But security interests alone cannot explain the depth of the Soviet determination to maintain the Eastern European empire regardless of the cost. Soviet leaders, of course, see the retention of this extensive buffer zone between the USSR and Western Europe and the ability to mobilize the military and economic potential of Warsaw Pact members as a necessary counterbalance to NATO. These security considerations, however, do not require a high level of Soviet control over the social and political developments in the Eastern European countries. If security interests do not account for the depth of commitment, neither does the utility of Eastern Europe in advancing Soviet global ambitions—for example, the dispatch of Eastern European security and military forces to the Third World.

The explanation goes well beyond pragmatism. Victory in World War II was the key legitimizing experience of Soviet rule at home, and control over Eastern Europe was the major spoil of war. A determination to retain the Eastern European empire creates a fundamental bond between the Soviet government and its Great Russian and other Slavic populations. It also constitutes a key justification for the preeminent role of the political leadership and party elite within the complex elite structure.

Loss of control over Eastern Europe, not to mention the disintegration of the "external empire," would probably strengthen centrifugal tendencies within the "internal empire." Therefore, the key question concerning Soviet policy in this area is not whether the Soviets will relinquish their hold but what means they will choose to preserve their domination and how successful they are likely to be.

Since 1953 the Soviet Union's position has been intransigent with regard to maintaining the Communist parties' monopoly of power, the highly monolithic and orthodox character of these parties, and their organization in accordance with Leninist principles. The Soviet leaders have insisted that the security and armed forces of the satellite nations be subordinated to a dual system of native party supervision and direct control by the Soviet security and military command. They have unswervingly placed the communications media under strict party control and have carefully monitored breaches in censorship and criticism of the Soviet Union. They have not permitted any autonomous political organizations to exist, let alone to challenge the party's monopoly.

Soviet controls, however, have been relaxed in some areas, particularly in economic organization and reform. The Soviet leaders have reluctantly tolerated economic experimentation, leaving initiatives to native party leaders. They have limited their efforts to harness satellite economies to the service of Soviet goals. There has been little economic integration of Eastern European economies with the Soviet economy. The Soviets have also tolerated a relaxation of restraints on private if not political freedoms, again leaving the decisions to local party leaders. And, until the recent events in Poland, direct daily supervision of satellite party activities had been less stringent than under Stalin.

After three decades of Soviet domination, one must conclude that the Soviet "external empire" has peaked; its decline has commenced. However Soviet leaders evaluate the trends, evidence of decline may be found in economic, military, political, and ideological areas.

Economically, the Eastern European countries have become a burden for the Soviet Union. Not only would the Soviet Union receive higher prices in world markets for the raw materials it now sells to its economically dependent satellites, but it would also earn enough to purchase highly essential advanced technology. Instead, in exchange for its raw materials, the Soviet Union routinely accepts Eastern Europe's inferior goods, which are unsuitable for sale in world markets. Furthermore, Eastern European countries apparently do not bear their proportional share of military expenditures as members of the Warsaw Pact.

Militarily, the potential contribution of Eastern European countries to Soviet conventional war capabilities is severely limited; it is probably even a minus factor. In case of war, the Soviets could rely only on select Eastern European elite units to supplement Soviet forces. In case of protracted war, the Soviet Union would most likely have to provide more troops to ensure Eastern Europe's political reliability than Eastern Europe would provide for the front line. This assessment, however, does not apply to the potential value of deploying select Eastern European military units in Third World countries to enhance Soviet influence and expansion, as has been done with Cuban troops.

Politically, the "external empire" has probably become an embarrassment and a handicap to the Soviet Union in its pursuit of foreign political objectives. Soviet domination of Eastern Europe seriously inhibits a renewal of détente with the United States. It cements the defensive military and political alliance of Western Europeans who daily witness its military-colonial dimension. It stands as the most significant obstacle to a cohesive international communist movement under Soviet direction and accounts for the spread of Eurocommunism. The United States cannot accept détente with a power that intervenes dramatically in Eastern Europe. As Europeans, America's NATO allies are especially sensitive to this blatant expression of Soviet imperial appetites. Furthermore, there is little difference between the European right and left in condemning repressive communist measures that are directed not only against dissidents and intellectuals but also against workers and free trade unions. Indeed, an enduring Soviet détente with Western Europe will lapse only on the day that Soviet troops invade an Eastern European country.

The Eastern European countries are also a prime example of the failure of Soviet ideology and the Soviet model of "socialism." For decades, Soviet leaders and ideologues have accounted for political repression, intellectual intolerance, economic backwardness, and social inequality in their country by referring to tsarist underdevelopment, to the isolation of Russia's revolution, and to capitalist encirclement. Yet these basic features of Soviet power have not essentially altered, despite the added security of westward expansion. And now they characterize some countries that enjoyed more democratic traditions and others that had higher levels of industrialization before the Soviet takeover.

The Eastern European empire will decline because almost all of the component states lack internal legitimacy. Soviet and satellite leaders had expected that the governments imposed on the area in 1944–48 by Soviet force behind narrow native communist bridgeheads would, over time, erase the popular memory of their violent origins. Almost forty years later, these governments have failed to do so.

The legitimacy of regimes spawned by revolution, whether "authentic" or "inauthentic," may derive from popular support expressed in traditional or legal forms, from elite support reflecting the cohesion and interlocking strength of key power centers, and from performance. Legitimacy grounded in popular support did not obtain, because patent Soviet controls and interventionism denied native governments its traditional source, nationalism, and its legal source, free elections at all levels. Legitimacy grounded in elite support did obtain under ordinary circumstances, but the cohesiveness of the power structure and the reliability of support from other power centers (the security and armed forces, the communications networks, the official trade unions, and so forth) weakened in times of crisis (1953, 1956, 1968, 1980, and 1981). This form of legitimacy ultimately depends less on internal structures than on external coercion. It is only through performance that East Germany and Hungary gained a limited and grudging acceptance among the population. Yet legitimacy grounded in performance is the most fragile and least dependable form of all.

The real test of a regime's legitimacy occurs during crises when rulers attempt to mobilize reserves of support. The paucity of such reserves in Eastern Europe demonstrates that satellite governments rely on Soviet power and determination to sustain them and on popular fears of the danger from the East. Especially disquieting for the Soviet leaders is the report that the younger generations of Eastern European countries exhibit a level of dissatisfaction with communist regimes equal to or higher than that of the older generations.

The native power elites' dilemma is insoluble. On the one hand, they can gain strong popular support only by advocating the anti-Soviet cause of national independence with the accompanying risks of Soviet military intervention. On the other hand, they can retain power only by ensuring unqualified Soviet support and, if necessary, Soviet military intervention. Communism was victorious in the twentieth century primarily because the regimes that were forged in "authentic" communist revolutions identified themselves with national interests, nationalism, and independence. It is the crucial flaw of communist regimes in Soviet-controlled Eastern Europe that they cannot do so.

Yet other circumstances work to thwart an acceptance of these regimes as legitimate. First, in contrast to the Soviet Union, Eastern Europe has failed to produce professional classes that identify more than superficially with the regime. While persons with a higher education in the Soviet Union do not exhibit the hallmark of an "intelligentsia," that is, a critical political attitude, Eastern Europe boasts a genuine intelligentsia, created under communist rule, that is potentially or actually hostile to communist leadership. Second, Eastern Europe remains immune to Soviet Russian cultural influence. The contempt for Soviet Russian culture, the shallow acceptance of dogmatic Marxism-Leninism even in the party, the deep attachment to religion and church, and the attraction to Western values and traditions – all combine to reduce the communist leadership to an alien and superficial stratum markedly different in stability and effectiveness from its counterpart in the Soviet Union. Third, almost unique among historical empires, the Soviet dominator surpasses the dominated in only one attribute – absolute military power. It lags behind in standard of living, economic development, educational levels, and cultural richness.

Absolute military power, however, has so far sufficed and will most likely continue to forestall defection, not to say disintegration. After all, historically, empires do not disintegrate when the metropolitan power is at the peak of its military strength. But if apocalypse does not threaten the Eastern European empire in the next decade, serious instability surely will.

In the 1980s, legitimacy grounded in performance may wreck on the shoals of economic distress. Because the Eastern European regimes base their legitimacy on economic performance, a pattern has emerged, according to which economic discontent translates into social and political instability. Virtually the same serious economic problems confront Soviet and Eastern European leaders. Much-needed improvements in economic performance for both will depend essentially on a successful shift from extensive to intensive sources of growth. But the difficulties in Eastern Europe are more serious economically, more dangerous politically, and more unpredictable in their likely outcome.

Eight circumstances aggravate the situation for Eastern Europeans and herald an even greater general destabilization there in this decade than in the Soviet Union:

1. Eastern European economies have already utilized intensive sources of growth to a much greater extent than the Soviet Union. Fewer reserves exist for correcting the irrational organization of production, incentives, and diffusion of high technology than in the Soviet Union.

2. In the Eastern European economies, the growth of military expenditures is even more burdensome than in the Soviet Union.

3. Economic difficulties will probably force the Soviets to reduce or eliminate their subsidies that take the form of selling energy and other raw materials below world prices and of buying inferior goods that would not find other markets.

4. Eastern Europeans will find it increasingly difficult to compete in Third World markets and to enter Western markets, where near-term recovery will proceed mainly from utilizing existing industrial capacity.

5. All Eastern European countries must service foreign debts that are sizeable and, in the case of Poland, catastrophic, while pressing for export production that will further constrict domestic consumption.

6. Poland's insolvency sorely disturbs regional economic development; not only has Poland failed to deliver goods and credit repayments to its eastern neighbors, but these last must also commit substantial resources to alleviate Poland's difficulties.

7. All Eastern European countries have undertaken and will have to sustain well into the 1980s austerity programs that strike the working class and undermine efforts to raise labor productivity.

8. In the 1980s Eastern European leaders will find it difficult to alleviate their economic difficulties by accelerating the implementation of existing reforms or initiating new ones.

The Soviet bloc's economic dilemmas of the 1980s will in all probability have a greater destabilizing impact on Eastern Europe than on the USSR. The expectations of Eastern European populations far exceed those of the Soviet working class, and the gap between what is and what they think should be will certainly increase their dissatisfaction. Moreover, should the austerity programs disproportionately burden the Eastern European working classes, as seems probable, the disparity in living standards among diverse groups will reinforce the sense of injustice that was the single most important impulse in the Polish eruption of 1980. This cause of discontent may erupt more dramatically in Hungary, where the differentiation of personal income and the standard of living is more visible if not much greater than in neighboring eastern states. The Eastern European working classes' dissatisfaction will also feed on the consequences of reduced educational expenditures in a time of budgetary constraints. Education has been the most important avenue of intergenerational mobility and a major guarantor of relative stability.

Only the prolonged Polish crisis indicated to the Soviet political elite and their advisers the systemic nature of the crisis in Eastern Europe, with its threat of imperial decline. The Polish case demonstrates the disruptive potential of these complex underlying problems common to all Eastern Europe and the Soviet determination to secure its dominion at any cost.

The Polish case is unique in several respects. Major groups of the working class initiated, sustained, participated in, and provided leaders for the organized defense of their rights. The workers' movement merged with a majority of the intelligentsia and later with part of the peasantry to express a unified Polish national stance against communism. Security and elite military forces neither disintegrated nor betrayed the formal government in Poland as they did in Russia's revolutionary year of 1917. If in both historic situations the minority emerged victorious over the majority, Poland's fate, unlike Russia's, was decided by an overwhelming external force.

Other examples of uniqueness can be cited. The proposed economic and political socialist alternative to orthodox communism exhibited depth and coherence. The disintegration in the party and state apparatus ceased only with the forced installation of a military-security government. And even after the imposition of martial law and the crushing of Solidarity, the Polish nation's nonviolent active resistance to military rule and Soviet communism persisted. Finally, Poland's military contribution to the Warsaw Pact was eliminated, an alarming turn obliging the Soviets to redesign contingency plans for a war in Europe.

The installation of a military-security government represented an act of desperation for Polish communists and their Soviet mentors — not an act of long-range planning. It avoided the more costly and unpredictable alternative of direct Soviet armed intervention; but from the Soviet perspective, nothing has been solved. The pope's visit in June 1983 exposed the vast gulf between a hybrid government without subjects and a disaffected population without influence. Solidarity was defeated as an organization and the representative of dual power, but the other power, the Catholic church, emerged even stronger in authority and more radical in aspirations. At the same time, the communist establishment has been divided dangerously along two axes — the party versus the military and the moderates versus the hardliners. Since its very inception, military rule with the attendant military infiltration of the weakened party apparatus at all levels has appeared to be the only alternative to greater chaos.

Tsarist and Soviet tradition firmly upholds the principle and practice of civilian and party ascendancy over the military. Today Soviet leaders are paralyzed on the one hand by the fear of prolonging a military regime in Poland and the fear of abolishing it in favor of civilian party rule on the other. To avert a popular explosion, to prevent a resurgence of Solidarity, and to ensure a minimum of political instability in Poland are the immediate Soviet objectives. Only a military-security government would appear capable of achieving them.

Neither Polish citizens, Polish communists, nor Soviet leaders can find comfort in the prospects for the future. A violent outbreak remains possible, with its inevitable armed response from the East. If such developments do not occur, the restoration of an orthodox communist regime will be impossible for the next three to five years because it could provoke civil war. Also, a competing political organization modeled on Solidarity cannot be restored, because it would provoke Soviet invasion.

The sole feasible short-term solution would involve a political compromise mediated by the church that would gradually reorganize the communist regime and return its overall political monopoly and at the same time grant certain demands of the defunct Solidarity to officially sanctioned trade unions. The restored regime would recognize the church's place in Poland's spiritual and, to some extent, secular life. It would redirect its economic planning to satisfy modest goals of the consumer. A number of years will be required to stabilize the economic and political situation, to achieve pre-Solidarity levels of production, and to plan for major changes in the Polish economic system. The level of political, social, and economic stability in Poland will likely remain low through the 1980s, and changes in policies and structures will be introduced gradually and with only partial effect.

The Soviet leaders are now persuaded that they committed a number of mistakes in Poland. Impressed in the early and mid-1970s by the satellite's drive to build a "second industrial Poland," fueled largely by Western credits, the Soviets failed to press for alterations in goals and means. Surprised by the extent of labor unrest in the summer of 1980, the Soviets failed to intervene decisively in internal Polish party matters or in relations between the party and Solidarity. The Polish case illustrates the independence of the native communist leadership in Eastern Europe with regard to domestic and especially economic questions, the USSR's slack monitoring of internal developments, and the unsatisfactory initial Soviet response to the Polish turbulence.

Soviet economic difficulties in the 1980s, which have been exacerbated by the state of the international money and commodity markets, have seriously impaired the Soviet Union's ability to bear the burden of substantial subsidies to Eastern Europe (as well as to Cuba and Vietnam). This burden now absorbs between a quarter and a third of the increments of Soviet investment growth. At the same time the party leadership is becoming increasingly impatient with the modest level of Eastern European participation in Soviet economic development.

Eastern Europe's vulnerability to social unrest significantly complicates Soviet relations with the West and presents irreconcilable contradictions to Soviet policymakers. Soviet officials fear Eastern European economic dependence on the West (what the Soviet press calls "the imperialist trap"), while acknowledging that Western European support of Eastern European economic development might ease pressure on Soviet resources. Social peace and a degree of cultural liberalism in Eastern Europe cements the Soviet détente with Western Europe and underpins any hope for restoration of détente with the United States. Improved relations with the West, and especially with the United States, however, encourage liberal forces in Eastern Europe and impede Soviet efforts to contain them.

It has often been stated in the specialized and general Soviet press that the USSR should learn from the experience of Eastern Europe, especially that of Hungary and East Germany. In Eastern Europe, however, the Soviet leaders are not pressing to introduce economic reforms where they do not already exist—in Czechoslovakia, for example. Nor, on the other hand, are they pressing for a return to orthodoxy in countries where reforms are well advanced. The primacy of political over economic considerations lies at the root of the inconsistency. The Soviets apparently accept established reforms and their economic consequences while fearing the political consequences of new or bolder reforms. Thus the major influence on Soviet attitudes comes from Poland, not Hungary.

Soviet policy in Eastern Europe during the 1980s will stress political stability over economic development. That stability ultimately depends on improved economic performance, which in turn depends on potentially destabilizing economic reform. This predicament mirrors the contradiction between the two key Soviet goals in Eastern Europe—preserving Soviet dominion and ensuring domestic stability. The first requires orthodoxy. The second requires innovation.

No survey of the Soviet Union's "second arc" would be complete without exploring its significance for the domestic and foreign policies of the imperial power itself. Eastern Europe is a bridge between Western countries and the Soviet Union, at least for technological transfer and economic experimentation. The far greater significance of the Eastern European empire, however, is its very existence and its endemic instability. Eastern Europe inhibits political and economic liberalization in the USSR. The Soviet leaders fear the consequences across borders in either direction of any departure from a sterile orthodoxy.

The effect on Soviet foreign policy is even more complex and contradictory. First, the commitment to hold the Eastern European empire is far more important to Soviet leaders than the commitment either to secure a durable rapprochement with the West or to expand their power in the Third World. Second, Eastern Europe (especially East Germany and Czechoslovakia), significantly contributes to the extension of Soviet influence in the Third World—through military and security advice and through training, weapons delivery, and economic exchange and aid. Third, given that priorities in Soviet policy are directly correlated with distance from Moscow, difficulties in Eastern Europe tend to reinforce retrenchment in foreign policy, as the Polish case shows. Fourth, the situation in Eastern Europe bears heavily on the policy of détente with Western Europe and the United States.

Because of the importance of the European détente to Soviet interests, Western

Europe has the leverage to moderate Soviet policies in Eastern Europe. Less discussed but more important is the leverage that dominion over Eastern Europe affords the Soviet leadership vis-à-vis Western Europe. Twenty-two million East German hostages serve as a powerful restraint on West German policy toward the Soviet Union and on West German willingness to support American post-détente policy toward the Soviet Union. Moreover, the rebirth of strong German nationalism, this time on the left of German politics, has again raised the question of German reunification, not as a long-range historical prospect but as a question to be resolved in this century. Such considerations give the Soviet Union room for manipulation in German politics. As for the United States, the Soviet leaders must decide whether the advantages of a renewed détente — so far the central and seemingly irreplaceable focus of Soviet foreign policy — outweigh the disadvantages in the form of inevitable pressures for liberalization and independence in Eastern Europe.

If successive explosions fail to rock Eastern Europe during the remainder of the 1980s, serious tensions will persist within client states and between them and the imperial center. For years to come Poland will remain the focus of Soviet attention and fear in the area. It remains to be seen whether Western Europe will exercise its virtually unused leverage to affect the Soviet imperial policy and the direction of Eastern European development. (Without some semblance of détente with the Soviet Union, the United States holds practically no such leverage.) The situation in the second arc during the 1980s will act as a restraint on vigorous Soviet policies toward the outside world, but it is futile to hope that Soviet foreign policy will abandon global objectives to concentrate on either imperial or domestic problems.

For forty years the Soviet Union has had the good luck to confront crises in only one Eastern European country at a time. Even if this luck holds in the 1980s, Eastern Europe will spotlight Soviet weaknesses and failures. Even more important, it may generate the sparks that could ignite a large-scale military conflict. Soviet-Eastern European relations will impede East-West cooperation, especially in the area that affects all mankind — the control and reduction of nuclear weapons.

The Third Arc: China

Ever since Khrushchev discredited Stalin's legacy in 1956, Soviet leaders have encountered the greatest risks and costs of communist encirclement in its relations with China. Along thousands of miles of eastern and southeastern borders, vast quantities of men and matériel were fixed in varying degrees of readiness against this once-loyal communist ally, while military planners were obliged to make complex preparations for war on two fronts. Since 1979, however, the conflict between the Soviet Union and China has moderated. Both sides have cautiously and slowly moved toward a normalization of state relations. They will probably soon achieve a degree of rapprochement that would have appeared highly unlikely to most informed observers just a few years ago.

Most important, China has gradually modified its position on the three pre-conditions essential for serious negotiations and improved relations. For some time, China had insisted on Vietnamese withdrawal from Kampuchea, Soviet withdrawal from Afghanistan, and Soviet reduction of forces on the Chinese border, together with total withdrawal from Mongolia. Following two years of cautious modification, China now appears ready to negotiate if the Soviet Union is willing to begin a partial fulfillment of any one of the preconditions.

Why has China shifted its policy to this extent, especially in the last three years? The answers lie in its evaluation of the Chinese domestic situation, the balance within the Sino-Soviet-American triangle, and the changing international environment. President Reagan's policy toward China has clearly damaged Sino-American relations and accelerated the process of Sino-Soviet rapprochement. Ironically, the United States's consistent hard line toward the Soviet Union — a posture that China urged in the past — now works to distance China from the United States. Reassured by Reagan's strong stance against the Soviet Union, China can relax its vigilant warnings about Soviet hegemonism. Indeed, one can argue that poor Soviet-American relations draw China toward the Soviet Union while good Soviet-American relations draw China closer to the United States.

The softening Chinese position on the preconditions for normalization with the Soviet Union stems less from specific American policies, however, than from the need for stabilized relations with a less threatening neighbor in order to pursue internal modernization. The Chinese leaders perceive less danger from a Soviet Union beset by domestic and especially economic difficulties, and they expect the phase of retrenchment to persist in Soviet foreign policy. All of these considerations strengthen the position of those in the Chinese elite, especially the Chinese armed forces, which favor more independence in China's position within the strategic triangle and criticize excessive leaning toward the United States.

Difficulties encountered in implementing the ambitious program of reforms in China demand a greater concentration on domestic affairs and a greater need to minimize the danger from the Soviet Union. Of the "four modernizations," China places military modernization last. Abandonment of old slogans, devolution of economic power, reevaluation of the past, and uncertain plans for the future — all heighten the anxiety among the leaders and bureaucracies that control over the population, particularly the youth and the intelligentisia, will be lost. They strenuously seek a new ideological compass by which to guide the population and strengthen authoritarian control. In this regard the West constitutes a greater danger than the Soviet Union, as the leadership acknowledged by terminating the short-lived "democracy" campaign. As a matter of fact, China is becoming more interested in certain phases of Soviet historical development. The process of post-Mao evolution has many elements in common with both the New Economic Policy (NEP) and with the post-Stalin experience.

Several years ago, Western policymakers and analysts tended to exaggerate the unalterability of Sino-Soviet tensions. Now they tend to exaggerate the likely consequences of reconciliation and its susceptibility to Western, especially

American, influence. Although it is impossible to predict the detailed progression of the Sino-Soviet rapprochement, it is possible to be quite certain about its limits. Normalization would end the reciprocal vilification in the press; stimulate scientific, educational, cultural, and athletic exchange; increase the communication of unclassified materials and facilitate the visits of journalists and economic experts; reduce the isolation of accredited diplomats; reinstate Chinese relations with pro-Moscow communist parties; and, more important, expand trade, perhaps even substantially. Quite possibly, the Sino-Soviet border dispute will be resolved by compromise. Eventually, a Sino-Soviet agreement could produce mutual troop reductions along the border, and a nonaggression treaty might be signed.

Normalization, however, will bring no Sino-Soviet political or military alliance — not even détente. Nor will it restore friendly relations between the two communist parties. Normalization will reduce tensions, but it will not erase China's suspicions of Soviet hostility to Chinese ambitions. It will not deter Chinese efforts to reach agreement with Japan on issues of defense and trade. Finally, China will perpetuate Sino-Soviet tensions in the Third World by opposing Soviet "hegemonist" expansion there.

Normalization of Sino-Soviet relations will leave certain cardinal facts of the Sino-Soviet-American triangle unaltered. The Soviet Union and China remain potential enemies whose security is measured only in relation to each other's weaknesses. The Soviet Union remains a present and future danger to China, while China will continue to fear little and gain much from the United States while it is hostile to the Soviet Union. Regardless of normalization, the Soviet Union aims to prevent or delay China's attainment of genuine great-power status. Prejudice and fear govern Soviet relations with a country with which it shares a border of 6,000 kilometers, contains the largest population in the world, and possesses the will and resources to reclaim its historic greatness. As long as the Soviet threat persists, the United States has no reason to oppose the growth of Chinese power and international stature, even if it has no enthusiasm for underwriting the Chinese process of modernization.

Normalization will not obviate the need to keep one-third of the Soviet armed forces and one-quarter of the Soviet rocket forces opposite China. Nor will it relieve Soviet military planners of the necessity to plan for a two-front war and economic planners of the necessity to finance it. Nor will normalization facilitate the more central Soviet goals of destroying the Western alliance or restoring a semblance of détente with the United States.

Normalization will strengthen China's position in the strategic triangle, but it will not secure China a place equidistant from both partners. Given Chinese fears, needs, and interests, its position in the triangle will remain skewed in favor of the United States. Sino-American relations will remain closer than either Sino-Soviet or Soviet-American relations. The United States remains the pivotal country in the strategic triangle and derives more advantage from it than either of the other two powers.

Current Soviet policy exhibits a new urgency and flexibility that is rooted in the disintegration of the Soviet-American détente, the threatening American military buildup, and the potentially greater Japanese military presence. If Soviet fears of encirclement subsided during the early 1970s, they surfaced again by the end of the decade. The Soviet Union not only began to see itself as the object of an unfriendly encirclement, both "capitalist" and "communist," but it also began to exaggerate the growth of both Western and Eastern components of the encirclement.

Conclusion

Since the mid-1970s, the Soviet Union has been expanding externally while declining internally, and now contradictory pressures vastly complicate the policy choices of the Soviet leaders. On the one hand, the magnitude of domestic difficulties demands urgent and concentrated attention. On the other hand, the international environment offers considerable opportunities to expand Soviet power and influence, especially in the Third World. Internal decline will surely continue or even accelerate during the remainder of the 1980s. The desire to translate newly achieved Soviet global military power into international influence will perhaps heighten the risk of active Soviet intervention in the world's most troubled regions. The key question is whether the Soviet leadership will alleviate and resolve problems within the Soviet Union and its empire or pursue external advantages.

As for China, the pursuit of a new direction in foreign policy represents merely another, though significant, expression of how its leaders regard their national interests. The process of normalization has an internal and profound dynamic, which is neither sparked nor guided by the conduct of the United States. If President Reagan's policies toward China have had an impact on the direction of Sino-Soviet rapprochement, they certainly do not explain it. Former officials of the Carter administration accuse Reagan of losing "our China card," thereby perpetuating vain illusions and a shortsighted manipulative approach to relations with China. The United States would be well advised to forget the "China card" and be satisfied with the existence of an independent China. Its geographical location, its historical attitude toward Russia, its military power, and its experience with Soviet leadership provide an important obstacle to the expansionism of the Soviet Union.

The United States and its Western allies have greater opportunities now than they had in the 1970s to influence Soviet international behavior. The combination of circumstances within and outside the Soviet Union encourages prospects for moderating the inevitable conflict between East and West by devising acceptable rules of international conduct on both sides and by achieving agreements on limiting, reducing, and stabilizing the arms race. The Soviet Union will be more amenable to serious negotiations while it is preoccupied with domestic and imperial problems, while it contemplates the escalating costs of a new arms race, while the Kremlin successions have interrupted the inertial drift of Soviet policies, and while Soviet leaders are learning that there is no substitute for better relations with the United States and for a controlled management of the East-West conflict. The principal question of the 1980s is not what Chernenko will do. Rather, it is what the United States and the Western alliance will do, for the policies of Moscow's new leader will largely depend on their actions.

Tell Me, Daddy, Who's the Baddy?

MARSHALL D. SHULMAN

The title I have given to this essay may seem irreverent, but it is not frivolous. Translated into ivy language, it suggests an authority figure identifying the hostile out-group, thereby giving us — the in-group — comfort, identity, stability, orientation, and relief from complexity. That is the heart of the matter. It is a universal psychological mechanism having no clearer application than in relations between the United States and the Soviet Union. For those who like their academic communications to sound serious, I supply the following subtitle: An agenda for the study of psychological factors in Soviet-American relations.

The main thrust of what I have to say is not novel, though it is not yet well understood. It is that psychological factors distort perceptions held by each country of the other and that these distortions lead to irrational responses in both directions.

It is important at the outset to underline an essential caveat: I do not wish to be understood as saying that the differences between the two countries are only matters of perceptual distortions; they are real, and they are serious. But familiar psychological mechanisms, most often operating below the conscious level, tend to make these differences appear absolute and therefore intractable. As a consequence they tend to make the responses of each country toward the other, and their interactions, less proportionate and less rational. The more aware we become of the influence of these psychological factors, the better we will be able to approach objectivity in our perceptions, to distinguish what is real from what is distorted among our differences, and to act with greater rationality.

Although most of my illustrations will be drawn from the American side of the relationship, I believe these psychological mechanisms work with equal force in both directions. From the United States perspective, Russia is remote, un-

Talk given at the Symposium on Political and Psychological Aspects of Soviet-American Relations, under the auspices of the International Society of Political Psychology, in collaboration with the Research Institute on International Change, Columbia University, New York, New York, 6 May 1983.

familiar, and enigmatic. Much about it is unknown, and some is unknowable. According to our temperaments, we project our preconceptions into these dark areas, some from our hopes and some from our fears. Once I sought to express this phenomenon by subtitling a talk on the subject "From Rorschach to Rashomon to Bumper Stickers." The idea, of course, was that we went from the interpretation of ink blots to egocentric perceptions of events to simplistic slogans. But Walter Lippmann put it more elegantly some sixty years ago. In dealing with foreign-policy problems, he said, we tend to act on the basis of "pictures in our heads."

What are the "pictures in our heads" of the Soviet Union, and where do they come from? They come from many different sources, some from preconceptions whose source may be long forgotten and some from our particular experiences. Take, for example, the experiences of an émigré from the Soviet Union, who may have spent years either working in a labor camp or waiting for an exit visa. When he thinks of the Soviet Union, he may think primarily of the police and party bureaucrats with whom he had to deal, and the vision that comes to his mind is of a bunch of thugs with whom one cannot and should not do business. A professional diplomat who has spent frustrating hours dealing with the UPDK (Diplomatic Corps Administration) may come to think of the Soviet Union as a country of surly bureaucrats. A businessman who has dealt mostly with economic managers may visualize the Soviet Union as a country of hard-bargaining but hard-working managers and, if he has been the beneficiary of warm hospitality, as a congenial country. To the professional military planner, the Soviets are the "Reds"—the ruthless and omnicompetent enemy poised to attack. Some think of *the* Soviet citizen as a unified stereotype; others, with broader experience, think of diversified and differentiated groups within the population. These are among the "pictures in our heads" that tend to determine how we fill in the blanks in our knowledge.

Some Familiar Psychological Processes

Some of the psychological concepts developed to deal with interpersonal relations may have suggestive applications to international relations generally and Soviet-American relations in particular. A few such concepts will illustrate the possibilities for joint exploration by psychologists and political scientists. I should point out, however, that not all of these psychological concepts are universally accepted or interpreted in the same way by the various schools of psychological thought.

There are, for example, a range of theories that concern *anxiety* and the various *defense mechanisms* by which individuals cope with anxiety and which seem relevant to perceptions, attitudes, and responses to the Soviet Union. One textbook defines anxiety as "the experience of tension that results from real or imaginary threats to one's security."[1]

Freud distinguished between "reality anxiety" and "neurotic anxiety." It seems evident that "reality anxiety"— the sense of personal and economic insecurity — has intensified in the face of complex and little understood forces that have transformed the way we live and widened the gap between the experience of one generation and the next. The resultant disorientation has weakened the traditional sources of authority — the state, the church, and the family. Disorientation is manifest to some degree in every industrial society in the world (and in some developing societies as well), and one of its effects has been the resurgence of nationalism and of political and religious fundamentalism as part of an effort to return to earlier touchstones of reality.

Can one doubt that these sources of anxiety, further intensified by the inescapable vulnerability to nuclear destruction felt by people everywhere, profoundly affects the perceptions, attitudes, and responses observed in the Soviet-American relationship?

Confronted with anxieties, the individual who cannot cope falls back on some familiar defense mechanisms. One of them, known as *displacement*, is obviously manifested in Soviet-American relations. Fears, failures, and anxieties generated from other sources are commonly attributed to the Soviet Union as the source of our troubles. We have seen this in the attribution to the Soviet Union of responsibility for all unheavals in the Third World. The revolutions in Iran and in the former Portuguese colonies in Africa, and the upheavals in Central America, have been explained as the result of Soviet machinations, as has the antinuclear-war movement in Europe and the United States.

Denial (a defense mechanism related to the political-science concept of cognitive dissonance) protects the individual against unpleasant realities, complexities that exceed the capacity to absorb, or elements that do not conform to comfortable preconceptions. Perhaps the most striking illustration of denial is the "unthinkability" of nuclear war.

Projection is seen in the widespread tendency to validate American feelings of hostility toward the Russians as a legitimate response to feelings of hostility attributed to them. Projection is also manifested in the "we-they" phenomenon, that is, the tendency to apply separate standards to the good "in-group" and the bad "out-group"— to look with indulgence on our actions and with harsh severity on theirs. This phenomenon, which may be observed between any paired grouping, whether black versus white, men versus women, or workers versus management, has been applied with special force to the observable tendency of both Russians and Americans to see themselves as the "good in-group," and the others as the "bad out-group," leading in its extreme manifestation to a Manichaean struggle between God and Demon, between absolute good and evil.[2]

A further development of this psychological phenomenon, described as "paired differential bonding," may have particular application to the Soviet-American relationship. The work of the psychiatrist Charles Pinderhughes finds psychological roots for the tendency, noted in animals and in infants from the age of eight months, to create a sense of identity through paired dichotomous concepts.[3] "All unambivalently constant relations," he says, "are basically paranoid, as objects of affiliative-affectionate bonds are aggrandized and objects of differentiative-aggressive bonds are denigrated." By this biologically rooted mechanism, which Freud saw as instinctual, children learn to show religious, social, class, caste, and ethnic group preferences, and to apply sterotypes to the out-groups, which Gordon W. Allport defined as "exaggerated beliefs associated with a category." This stereotyping, which makes it possible to handle countless stimuli, offers stability and certainty at the expense of objectivity and validity.

The concept of "paired differential bonding" is suggestive of many insights into the Soviet-American relationship, not only because it offers a theoretical explanation for the tendency to focus hostile and aggressive feelings upon the Soviets as the "out-group" but also because it implies a bond of a common fate that ties the adversary groups to each other.

Further, this mechanism that leads to the idealization of one's own group and to the harsh denigration of the opponent group suggests a psychological basis for the double standard characterizing much of the writing about the Soviet Union and the United States. The Soviet military programs are assumed to reflect hostile intentions; American military programs are by definition defensive. The expansion of tsarist Russia and the Soviet Union to the Pacific is proof of inherent Russian and Soviet tendencies to expand for the purpose of conquering the world; the continental expansion of the United States was a matter of right. Soviet activities in the Third World are manifestations of aggression; United States activities in the Third World are altruistic. Soviet espionage is traitorous; American espionage is patriotic. The mechanism works both ways: Soviet authorities view with indulgence the repressive actions of the KGB (Committee on State Security) against religious or political oppositionists, while the high rate of unemployment among blacks in the United States is regarded as proof of capitalist iniquity.

One consequence of the hostile stereotyping of the adversary is that, by dehumanizing the enemy, it relieves the inhibitions against immoral behavior. The hostile stereotype justifies any action, in the name of the pernicious notion that one must "fight fire with fire." In the French proverb, "each one takes on the visage of his adversary," and the process culminates in a Soviet-style anti-Sovietism.

Psychological Analysis of Soviet-American Problems

The preceding discussion of certain psychological processes is no more than illustrative, and in its brevity it treats inadequately even the few examples selected. But perhaps it will nevertheless serve to suggest some tools of psychological analysis that may be productively applied to a number of familiar problems in Soviet-American relations, including the following:

Deterrence. The idea of deterring the adversary from a nuclear attack, on which the present tenuous stability of the nuclear military competition rests, depends fundamentally on psychological assumptions that are rarely articulated or examined. What does it take to deter? How many cities would have to be destroyed and what percentage of industrial capacity impaired in order to set the threshold of deterrence? The answer, clearly, is not an abstraction. It is surely not independent of the particular values of the leadership or its political culture, nor is it independent of the circumstances in which the question might arise or the alternatives to attacking or not attacking as seen by the leadership in particular situations.

A special case with regard to the Soviet Union has been debated recently in the Western literature. Some have argued that because the Soviet Union suffered 20 million deaths in World War II, the Soviet leaders would accept very high casualties in the event of another war. Others maintain that the effect of these losses has made the Soviet leaders all the more cautious and their deterrence threshold therefore extremely low. A related question is whether the passing of the wartime military leaders would result in a less cautious attitude toward the risks of war. In either case, the answer would surely depend on the perception of the risks of not initiating war.

Influencing Soviet behavior. The question of how to influence Soviet behavior in desired directions, or how to negotiate effectively with the Soviet Union, also involves psychological assumptions that are rarely examined. Is it the case, as some maintain, that "the Russians only respect toughness" and that therefore only ultimatums or a show of force will evoke Soviet concessions or restraint? Or is it more likely that toughness, ultimatums, or a show of force will produce a corresponding bellicosity from the Soviet Union?

Paradoxically, either extreme — toughness or weakness — may have the effect of encouraging greater Soviet militancy, and the combination of firmness (which is different from toughness), clarity, and fairness is most likely to evoke corresponding qualities in Soviet negotiating behavior.

Assessing the military relationship. The military aspect of Soviet-American relations abounds in problems with significant psychological dimensions. Despite the complexity of modern military technology, often quantified down to the third decimal place, aggregate judgments concerning the military relationship necessarily involve critical assumptions about behavior that generally go unexamined. The state of the military balance involves comparisons of asymmetrical weapons arsenals, in which the disparities in the various indices used to measure the central strategic balance — numbers of launchers, numbers of warheads, accuracy, throw-weight, and the like — sometimes favor one side, sometimes the other. Certain people in both countries tend to emphasize the significance of those components of the military balance in which the other side has an advantage and therefore to proclaim a vulnerability that must be overcome by "catching up." That is one source of the dynamism for the continuing upward spiral of weapons acquisition. And even when it is granted that, given the scale of destructiveness of nuclear weapons, such disparities do not have usable military advantages, such advocates argue that the disparities have psychological and political importance because they affect the political behavior of the leadership on the other side — or of allied nations — and these proclaimed disadvantages tend to become self-fulfilling. Scenarios that rest on the putative advantages of disparities favoring one side or the other are rarely tested for plausibility. Any theoretical advantage, such as the "window of vulnerability," receives wide acceptance if it serves the purposes of the advocates of particular weapons systems, even though it rests on the assumption of total irrationality on the part of the adversary.

Given the preconceptions that prevail in each country concerning the other, it has often been assumed that the other country will develop its capabilities to the utmost; and this assumption has led us into a series of projected "gaps," which, though proved erroneous, have powered military programs and which in turn have stimulated new rounds of effort on the other side. The "missile gap," for example, drove the United States military programs into an almost vertical ascent in the fiscal year 1961 budget, even though it had been shown to be false at the time. The consequence was that Soviet military programs began an upward climb immediately afterwards.

It does not detract from the force of these projected fears that they sometimes have great volatility and may reverse themselves on occasion. The appearance of sputnik in 1957 suddenly transformed the prevailing stereotype of the Russians as mechanically incompetent ("their tractors rust in the fields for want of spare parts") to one of superhuman omnicompetence. Similarly, the stereotype of Chinese military and political capabilities shifted radically from threatening hostility to benign weakness in the course of the Vietnam War.

Assessing foreign policy. Projecting their fears and hostility, many Americans attribute to Soviet foreign policy near-perfect coordination, planning, coherence, and design, and correspondingly downgrade the element of political or bureaucratic interplay or the response to opportunities that present themselves in unplanned ways. Correspondingly, the Soviet Union, largely because of ideological preconceptions, tends to see in American behavior the workings of a unified power structure. It is difficult for those who have not had the experience of living in a pluralistic society to conjure up the complex interplay of multiple power structures. At the time of the issue concerning the "Soviet brigade in Cuba" in the summer and fall of 1979, it was difficult for the political leadership in Moscow to believe that the alarm raised in the United States had resulted from faulty interpretation of intelligence data rather than from a deliberate effort to apply the *coup de grace* to prospects for the ratification of SALT, which was the objective consequence of this artificial issue.

The prevalence of primitive and hostile stereotypes creates a predisposition to believe the worst of the other side rather than to hold uncertainties in suspension. This is currently illustrated by the readiness to make judgments in advance of the evidence on such issues as the possibility of Soviet involvement in the assassination attempt on the pope, the charges of Soviet use of bacteriological or chemical warfare, or the charges of Soviet violation of the threshold test ban on underground nuclear tests.

The lessons of history. Another area in the relationship that is often driven by repressed psychological predispositions is the evocation of lessons from history that serve unexpressed purposes. Such is the parallel often drawn between the Soviet regime and the Nazis. The lessons of Munich are drawn to argue that any conciliation must be equated with appeasement.

Conclusion

I have suggested, by illustrations drawn from psychological literature and from some dimensions of the Soviet-American relationship, an agenda for the study of psychological factors in that relationship. What is needed in the first instance is a greater awareness of the way in which psychological mechanisms affect our perceptions, our attitudes, and our responses to these problems. That awareness can free us to distinguish what is real from what is fancied in our perceptions of each other, and to move in some small measure toward at least a greater degree of objectivity and insight into the way the world looks from the other side.

To the extent that both sides can subject the "pictures in our heads" to the process of reality-testing and can raise to the conscious level the buried assumptions that shape our prevailing attitudes, we liberate ourselves from the self-destructive effects of displaced anxieties and hostilities and enable ourselves to respond more effectively to the real challenges of this competitive relationship.

I do not underestimate the difficulties of doing so. The human mind needs its stereotypes, to make more manageable the reception of complex data and stimuli, from such sources as each morning's newspaper. But we can seek continuously to refine our stereotypes and to make them more differentiated, so that they come closer to a reflection of reality. This will in turn make possible a mobilization of the intellect, helping us to act with greater rationality on the basis of a more objective understanding of the nature of the problems we face. It may be that only under great duress do human beings bring their intellects into play to give a sense of proportion to the urges and beliefs that arise from instinct and emotion. The present headlong course of events surely heightens that great duress.

NOTES

1. Calvin S. Hall and Gardner Lindzey, *Theories of Personality*, 3d ed. (New York: John Wiley & Sons, 1978), 188.

2. John E. Mack, M.D., "The Perception of US-Soviet Intentions and Other Psychological Dimensions of the Nuclear Arms Race," *American Journal of Orthopsychiatry* 52 (Oct. 1982): 596.

3. Charles A. Pinderhughes, M.D., "Differential Bonding: Toward a Psycho-physiological Theory of Stereotyping," *American Journal of Psychiatry* 136 (Jan. 1979): 1. See also "Paired Differential Bonding in Biological, Psychological, and Social Systems," *American Journal of Social Psychiatry* 2 (Summer 1982).

The Soviet Union and the Strategic Arms Race

ROBBIN F. LAIRD
DALE R. HERSPRING .

The Soviet strategic challenge can be characterized by answering four central questions. First, do Soviet leaders believe in the reality of mutual deterrence? Second, do they believe they could survive and win a strategic nuclear war? Third, do they accept strategic parity with the United States as a desirable, even inevitable, state of affairs? And, fourth, does the Soviet approach to arms control embody a concept of strategic parity? .

Attempts to characterize the Soviet strategic-arms effort have created much controversy in the West. Some argue that the USSR sees its strategic weapons primarily as a deterrent to an American attack, that it remains in the strategic-arms race to keep the United States from gaining a usable strategic superiority. From this point of view, the Soviets are interested primarily in strategic stability and parity, not in engaging in an unbridled arms race.

Others argue that the USSR strives for usable strategic arms superiority as a means of advancing its policy interests. The strategic-arms race is seen as the product of the Soviet desire for global dominance through strategic superiority. Indeed, it is thought that the Soviet Union seeks military superiority by winning the strategic-arms race.

These two opposing viewpoints have produced quite different responses to the four questions raised at the outset of this essay. Our view is the following:

First, the Soviet leaders have deployed strategic forces capable of inflicting assured destruction against American territory and have recognized the "objective reality" of the American ability to reciprocate. Second, the Soviet leaders, while not anticipating a meaningful "victory" in an all-out nuclear war, have developed a flexible military-force structure that would prevail in a conventional

For an elaboration of the central themes of this essay, see Robbin F. Laird and Dale R. Herspring, *The Soviet Union and Strategic Arms* (Boulder, Colo.: Westview Press, 1984). The views expressed in this essay are the authors' and do not reflect United States government policy.

war at the European theater level. They have developed the military capability for the exercise of a limited nuclear war as well. Third, the Soviet leaders have perceived strategic parity, rather than superiority, to be all that is necessary in the military competition with the United States. Fourth, the Soviets have acted on a concept of strategic parity in the arms-control process that has contradictory political and technological faces. Politically, the Soviet Union has insisted on an equality with the United States that seriously complicates American relations with and obligations to the Western alliance. Technologically, the Soviets have tried to use the arms-control process to limit American modernization programs in the 1980s while protecting their most significant modernization programs, especially their intercontinental ballistic missile (ICBM) forces. Despite such contradictions, arms-control agreements were forged in the 1970s. But will the political and technological contradictions of the strategic parity problem become so exacerbated in the 1980s and 1990s that the arms-control process of the 1970s becomes a historical relic, like the Washington Naval Treaty of 1921?

The answer to this question has three parts. First, how will the Soviet Union view the strategic environment of the 1980s and 1990s? Second, what are the likely Soviet strategic "responses" to this environment, and how will the United States view the subsequent strategic environment? Third, given the conflicting assessments of the evolving strategic environment, what are the prospects for arms-control agreements?

The Soviet View

Table 1 indicates the Soviet view of the strategic environment as the interaction between political and technological factors. A significant political dimension is the desire to maintain "equivalence" with American central or intercontinental systems. The major technological challenges to equivalence are the proposed American modernizations, namely, the MX ICBM, the Trident submarine-launched ballistic missiles (SLBMs), and the bomber/cruise missile combinations. Another political dimension is the desire to maintain assured-destruction capabilities vis-à-vis the United States. The major American technological threats to assured destruction are the new ballistic-missile defense systems and the development of new technologies, such as the stealth technologies, that will make it more difficult for the Soviet Union to destroy American systems. Still another political dimension is the desire to ensure "equal security" with the United States. From the Soviet standpoint, two technological problems are critical challenges to "equal security": (1) the United States capitalizing on geographical asymmetries by deploying ground-launched cruise missiles and Pershing IIs in Europe to gain strategic advantage; and (2) the West gaining strategic superiority through French and British nuclear modernizations developing outside the American-Soviet strategic balance. A final political dimension is the desire to deny the United States the possibility of attaining usable strategic

TABLE 1

The Strategic Environment in the 1980s and 1990s
(From the Soviet Perspective)

The Political Dimension of Strategic Parity	Western Strategic Programs (The "Technological Threat" to Strategic Parity)
1. Maintain equivalence with the United States	1. Qualitative transformation of United States forces (MX, Trident I and II, cruise missiles, and new manned bombers)
2. Maintain assured destruction capability	2. United States R and D Programs (Midgetman, stealth bomber and cruise missiles, strategic defense, and ASW systems)
3. Equal security a. Geographical assymetries b. Third country systems	3a. United States GLCMs and Pershing IIs 3b. French and British nuclear modernization
4. Deny American strategic superiority	4. Qualitative transformation of American forces together with French and British modernization programs.

superiority. The Soviet Union might well be wary of the qualitative transformation of American intercontinental- and intermediate-missile systems, together with the French and British modernizations, that could enable the United States to conduct a limited nuclear war from Europe that would wreak unacceptable damage on the Soviet homeland.

The qualitative transformation of American strategic forces will especially threaten the mainstay of Soviet strategic power — the ICBM. By 1988, the United States plans to deploy 100 MX missiles in fixed silos. Each MX will cary ten warheads of a new type — the W87 — with an explosive power of more than 300 kilotons. The W87 warhead will be carried by a new reentry vehicle, the Mk-21, which has a more accurate guidance system than the Mk-12A, which is currently deployed on more than 300 Minuteman IIIs. The 1,000 MX warheads could hypothetically destroy almost the entire core of the Soviet ICBM force, the 308 SS-18s and 310 SS-19s. By 1998 the United States plans to deploy twenty Trident class submarines, each with twenty-four missile tubes. The first eight will carry the Trident I missiles, but by 1998 all will carry the Trident II or D-5 missiles. The D-5, which will be capable of carrying from ten to fifteen warheads, will have the capability to attack all potential targets effectively from submarines. The Trident force carrying a minimum of 4,800 warheads when conjoined with the MX force could be theoretically capable of destroying the entire Soviet ICBM force in a first strike.

The United States also plans to deploy at least 4,348 air-launched cruise missiles (ALCMs) by 1990. According to the 1984 American military posture statement, "the extremely accurate ALCMs will be able to destroy the hardest Soviet targets."[1] The ALCMs will be supplemented by a force of 4,068 submarine-launched cruise missiles by 1988 (not all SLCMS will carry nuclear warheads).

In addition, the United States plans to deploy a force of 100 B1-B penetrating bombers by the late 1980s. From the Soviet perspective, the cruise missiles together with the bombers will significantly enhance United States second-strike capabilities.

In addition to already programmed force modernizations, the United States has generated a number of programs that could further reduce the efficacy of the Soviet Union's strategic forces. For example, the United States appears to be moving in the direction of supplementing its fixed-silo ICBMs with a smaller, more survivable Midgetman. In addition, the development of a stealth bomber would significantly increase the United States's ability to penetrate Soviet airspace. The United States also plans significant improvements in its strategic defense. The navy plans to build a new class of attack submarines in the 1990s that will be larger, faster, quieter, and more lethal than the world's best nuclear attack submarine—the Los Angeles class attack submarine. In addition, the United States has an active program in ballistic missile defense. The United States reportedly believes that "an active defense could protect some high-value strategic assets from ballistic missile attack."[2]

President Reagan, in a major speech in March 1983, underscored the United States's desire to develop an effective defense against ballistic missiles while reducing the threat of mutual assured destruction. The speech has been followed up by Pentagon studies on the feasibility of "high confidence" ballistic missile defense systems. By the late fall of 1983, key defense officials were reportedly encouraging the president to adopt an ambitious ballistic missile defense research and development program that would provide deployment options, possibly by the end of the decade or, at least, by the end of the century.

In addition to the challenges posed by improvements in American "central systems," the Soviet Union faces nuclear challenges in the European theater that seriously complicate its quest for "equal security." The United States will deploy nearly 600 hard-target capable missiles in the European theater. From the Soviet standpoint, these programs will enhance United States first-strike capabilities as well as provide for a much more diversified second-strike capability. France and Britain are also carrying out significant modernization programs. The two countries plan to have more than 1,000 strategic warheads by the mid-1990s. For Moscow, such programs challenge the credibility of the Soviet conventional-warfighting option or at a minimum, clearly complicate Soviet plans to exercise escalation dominance in a European war.

The Soviet Union might be confident that in the absence of widespread and effective American antiballistic missile (ABM) deployments, the United States will not be able to reestablish strategic superiority on the central-systems level. Moscow must be concerned, however, with the technological challenge posed by Washington's strategic-force modernization program. As John Steinbrunner noted:

Tacitly, the material pressure on the Soviet Union emerging from the Reagan administration is qualitative in character. The apparent intention is to develop a more sophisticated, more diverse U.S. strategic arsenal rather than a larger one and thereby to force major adjustments in the large Soviet deployments. The implied purpose is to force the Soviets to waste the heavy investment they so recently completed by making it technically obsolete. (The most compelling threat from the Soviet perspective is the Trident II ballistic missile, expected to give the U.S. submarine force the capability to attack hardened Soviet ICBM silos.)[3]

For the Soviet Union, the United States could most likely reestablish a semblance of strategic superiority by enhancing NATO strategic-nuclear capability in the European theater. The United States long-range theater nuclear forces (LRTNF) systems when conjoined with British and French strategic systems *even if numerically inferior* to Soviet systems targeted against Western Europe, would still potentially lead to American strategic superiority, from the Soviet standpoint. If Moscow hopes to fight a conventional war in Europe, the British and French independent nuclear forces represent serious threats. If either a conventional or a nuclear war is limited to the European theater, the discharge of United States LRTNF, British, and French nuclear systems could wreak substantial damage on the USSR itself. In fact, the damage could be so substantial that Moscow would have to terminate the war in order to preserve what remained of its state and society. Such termination would occur in this scenario without the use of American or Soviet central systems. American territory would remain intact. As a result, the Soviet Union might conclude that the greatest threat to the strategic balance involves changes in Western strategic capabilities in the European theater. Moscow might feel that derailing such changes by military deployments, arms-control measures, and various political actions is a central priority in the 1980s and 1990s.

Soviet Strategic Programs

The Soviets have a panoply of central strategic systems under development with which to define their "response" to United States strategic modernization efforts. To begin with, the Soviets are developing two new ICBMs. The SS-X-24, a large solid-fuel missile, was first successfully tested in December 1982. It is a medium-sized ICBM carrying ten warheads and is the replacement for the single-warhead SS-11.

The Soviets are also testing a follow-on to the SS-13, known as the PL-5. A relatively small, single warhead missile, it was probably designed to be deployed on a mobile launcher. Some Western sources claim that the PL-5 is actually a variant of the SS-16.

The Soviets also have an important SLBM modernization program in the form of the Typhoon class submarine. The Typhoon carries twenty SS-N-20 missiles and has "design features that would permit them to poke up through the polar sea ice to fire. Flight time to U.S. missile silos would be 15 minutes, or half the time it would take other Soviet warheads to reach U.S. targets."[4]

Moscow is also working to develop a new long-range strategic bomber—the

Blackjack A. This bomber will be used in multiple roles in delivering both gravity bombs and ALCMs to intercontinental range and is expected to be operational in the late 1980s. The Soviet ALCM program is closely associated with the Blackjack, as an official United States government source noted: "The Soviets are developing at least one long-range ALCM with a range of some 3,000 kilometers. Carried by the Backfire, the Blackjack, and possibly the Bear, it would provide the Soviets with greatly improved capabilities for low-level and standoff attack in both theater and intercontinental operations. ALCMs could be in the operational force by the mid-1980s."[5]

The Soviet Union also has several programs aimed at strengthening its strategic defenses. Its air defense is being enhanced by the deployment of new SAM systems (especially the SA-10) as well as the development of a new generation of look-down, shoot-down aircraft (SU-27, MIG-29, and MIG-31). Its antisubmarine warfare capabilities are being improved by the development of a new generation of nuclear attack submarines. The Soviet Union is also pursuing ballistic-missile defense systems. It has "continued to pursue extensive ABM research and development programs, including a rapidly deployable AMB system and improvements for the Moscow defenses."[6]

The Soviet Union could combine these programs in a number of alternative patterns to deal with its growing ICBM vulnerability and to protect its strategic assets for second strikes. One response could be to maintain fixed-site ICBMs but to protect them with ABM systems. A deployed ABM system has the advantage of undercutting the effectiveness of the French and British systems. It has the disadvantage, however, of stimulating an "analogous" United States response that might actually erode the effectiveness of Soviet strategic systems.

A second response could be to maintain the ICBM as the premier strike force but to go to mobility to enhance survivability. The fixed-base ICBMs could be used as the first strike force, with a mobile ICBM force as the reserve or second strike force. The development of a common intermediate-range/intercontinental missile (as in the SS-20/SS-16 pairing) would provide the Soviet Union with a much more flexible weapons mix.

A third response could be to develop a more balanced force or "triad" of ICBMs, SLBMs, and bombers. The SLBM could emerge as the first strike force as the Soviets develop hard-target-kill capability in their SLBMs. They could then be targeted on United States ICBMs, with Soviet SLCMs targeted against United States bomber bases. Soviet mobile ICBMs could then be used in a second strike role, with long-range bombers providing further countervalue coverage of United States territory.

It is more difficult for the Soviet Union to formulate an adequate response to its conception of the Eurostrategic threat posed by American nuclear weapons. The Soviet Union already has a full spectrum of nuclear weapons deployed in Europe. There is no readily apparent "analogous" response to American LRTNF that has not already been made. Of course, greater numbers of SS-20s, SS-21s, or SS-23s could be deployed in "response" to American deployments.

However, the Soviet Union has an even greater difficulty in defining an "analogous" response from the standpoint of a similar capability to use tactical or theater weapons to strike United States territory. One possibility might be the forward deployment of Soviet bombers carrying ALCMs to Cuba in order to threaten the United States. Another possibility might be the deployment of a new class of attack submarines armed with cruise missiles, which could pose a serious undersea threat to the United States. If the Soviets intend to use their SLCM in a land-attack role, these submarines could pose an especially significant threat to United States C³ systems and bomber bases. The closer a submarine can get to a land target, the less warning there would be of a cruise-missile attack. Soviet leaders will apparently focus on the forward deployment of SLCMs as their analogous response to the United States deployments in Europe.

Even more difficult to formulate would be a weapons system's response to the modernization of French and British strategic forces. The Soviets already have a broad array of conventional and nuclear options to deal with British and French systems. New systems, as opposed to augmenting the capabilities of existing systems, seem unnecessary. From the strategic standpoint, Moscow could implement a policy that would treat the use of British or French strategic weapons against Soviet territory as if they were American. From a political standpoint, however, the Soviet leaders will continue to follow a policy of trying to exacerbate diplomatic relations among the Western allies in peacetime in the hope that serious disunity would be evident in wartime. In a wartime setting such disunity would allow the Soviet Union the possibility of reaching separate war-termination agreements with each major Western power at the expense of the others.

The American View

The significant array of strategic programs that the Soviet Union has under development and its possibilities for alternative-deployment mixes create a challenging strategic environment for the United States (see table 2.). The *first* political dimension — to maintain equivalence with the Soviet Union — is threatened by the qualitative transformation of Soviet forces. United States C³ systems and bomber forces are especially threatened by Soviet SLBM and SLCM modernizations. In addition, the deployment of mobile ICBMs, if the United States is unable to respond for domestic reasons, might be especially challenging to United States targeting requirements. The *second* political dimension — to maintain assured destruction capability — is threatened by continued improvements in Soviet ABM and strategic air-defense systems, especially if the Soviets decide to deploy a significant number of advanced ABM systems. The United States's recent discovery of a probable ABM radar system in violation of the 1972 agreement raises such a prospect. The *third* political dimension requires the United States to maintain a credible extended deterrence capability, that is, to have suffi-

TABLE 2

The Strategic Environment in the 1980s and 1990s
(From the American Perspective)

The Political Dimension of Strategic Parity	Soviet Strategic Programs (The "Technological Threat" to Strategic Parity)
1. Maintain equivalence with the Soviet Union	1. Qualitative transformation of Soviet forces (SS-X-24, PL-5 Typhoon, Backfire-Blackjack/cruise missile combination)
2. Maintain assured-destruction capability	2. R and D in ABM and strategic air-defense systems
3. Maintain extended deterrence capability	3. SS-20, SS-21, SS-22, and SS-23 deployments and their follow-on systems.
4. Deny Soviet military superiority	4. Soviet conventional "superiority" in the Eurasian landmass combined with the qualitative transformation of Soviet nuclear forces

cient nuclear forces to protect Western European as well as American territory. The SS-20, SS-21, and SS-23 deployments are especially threatening to the credibility of extended deterrence. The *fourth* political dimension requires that the United States deny the Soviet Union the ability to attain military superiority. Especially threatening in this regard has been the Soviet effort to maintain conventional "superiority" in the Eurasian landmass while continuing to transform qualitatively their nuclear forces, both intercontinental and intermediate.

In light of the projected American and Soviet assessments of the evolving strategic environment, will there continue to be significant opportunities for superpower arms control agreements? From the structure of the two assessments, the greatest probability for agreements seems to lie in the first two dimensions, namely, trying to maintain equivalence and assured-destruction capabilities. Purely from a military planning perspective, it would seem useful to have agreements to provide parameters to guide the modernization or qualitative transformation process. For example, one Reagan administration official in describing the threat to the United States inherent in the Soviet shift to a mobile ICBM in the years ahead stated that "whether mobile weapons ever represent less of a threat than today's weapons depends upon the total number of warheads allowed on each side."[7] In other words, without controlling the number of deployed warheads, mobile ICBMs might increase, rather than decrease, the Soviet threat to the United States.

It will remain useful to bargain about what constitutes equivalence, especially with regard to intercontinental strategic systems. The assured-destruction dimension will be threatened by changing strategic defensive capabilities, ABM, antiair, and ASW. ABM systems remain the area of greatest possibility for limitation, even if the 1972 agreements are modified to permit more possibility for ICBM protection, thereby obviating the need to go to mobile ICBMs. But if there are no controls on the numbers of warheads, ABM systems might be rendered inefficacious.

The least likely area for agreement involves "resolving" the Intermediate Nuclear Forces (INF) problem in Europe. The United States wishes the Soviet Union to recognize, in effect, the Soviet threat to "extended deterrence" posed by Soviet INF systems. The Soviet Union in turn, wishes the United States to recognize the American and Western European threat to "equal security."

Thus the Soviet approach to arms control in the 1980s will probably embody several objectives. Although the contours of the American strategic modernization programs are increasingly clear, the Soviet Union will hope to control the number of deployed United States systems. For example, the United States Air Force appears to consider the plan to deploy 100 MXs as only a first step in a plan to deploy 200 of these missiles. The Soviet Union clearly wants to limit the number of MXs deployed, and an arms-control agreement would be useful in this regard. Moscow is also interested in protecting its strategic modernization program from technological obsolescence by controlling as much as possible the introduction of new technologically advanced systems in the United States inventory. But the experience of the 1970s should make the Soviet Union less than sanguine in this regard. Finally, the Soviet Union will try to gain Western acceptance of the equal security concept whereby Soviet nuclear capability would be weighed against United States, French, and British systems as a totality.

The arms-control approach of the Reagan administration has separated the problem of limiting intercontinental from intermediate systems. Although there have been sound political reasons to separate the two forums—strategic and intermediate—there will be significant technological pressure to merge them when the Soviet Union begins to deploy mobile ICBMs. It would be politically and militarily questionable for any American administration to leave uncounted mobile two-stage IRBMs while counting mobile three-stage ICBMs, for there would be obvious potential interchangeability between the two. In addition, "as a general rule, incorporating intermediate forces into the Strategic Arms Limitation Talks (START) would expand the scope of possible trade-offs."[8]

At the Strategic Arms Reduction Talks (START), the United States has made a number of proposals aimed at controlling the process of modernizing intermediate strategic systems. On 9 May 1982 President Reagan indicated that the United States sought a two-phase reduction in strategic arms. In the first phase, as shown in table 3, land- and sea-based ballistic missiles would be reduced to 850 on each side. Warheads for these missiles would be limited to 5,000, of which no more than 2,500 could be deployed on ICBMs. In the second phase, the United States would consider limits on other systems, including long-range bombers and cruise missiles.

The key rationale for the United States proposal was to halt and reverse the "destabilizing growth" in ballistic-missile warhead numbers. The United States has been especially concerned with the "heavy missiles," the SS-18s. The United

TABLE 3

Reagan Proposal for START, Phase I

	ICBM and SLBM				ICBM Warhead Component	
	Launchers		Warheads[1]			
	US	USSR	US	USSR	US	USSR
1982 levels (SALT count)[1]	1,572	2,367	7,920	8,395	2,152	6,170
Proposed ceiling	850	850	5,000	5,000	2,500	2,500
Reduction required	722	1,517	2,920	3,395	—	3,670

[1] Assuming maximum force loadings permitted under SALT II counting rules: actual warhead totals would be lower.

Source: *The Military Balance 1982–1983* (London: HSS, 1982).

States would prefer to follow a "deep cuts" approach to achieving equivalence in intercontinental systems. The United States position was modified, however, in June 1983. The new proposal allowed each side more land- and submarine-based missiles (somewhere between 850 and 1,450 launchers) but would continue to limit the number of warheads these launchers could carry to 5,000 on each side. The United States also continued to insist on a sublimit of 2,500 ICBM warheads.

In August 1983, the chief United States START negotiator, Edward Rowney, indicated that progress in the START negotiations had reached the point where a preliminary agreement with the Soviet Union on guidelines for reducing intercontinental strategic weapons was possible. Such guidelines would include counting warheads rather than missile launchers, setting an overall ceiling on the number of warheads on each side, and agreeing on equality in total missile throw-weight or lifting power.

But major difficulties remained. The Soviet Union proposed that all missile warheads and bomber-carried weapons by "aggregated" into a single total for nuclear weapons allowable for both sides. The United States, in contrast, proposed one limit for ballistic missile warheads – ICBM and SLBM – and another for bomber weapons. According to a Reagan administration official, "the talks so far have revealed a major Soviet concern about the approximately 3,000 air-launched cruise missiles with which the Reagan administration plans to equip U.S. bomber forces."[9]

In October 1983 the administration introduced a version of the "build-down" approach to arms control at the START. Three proposals were at the heart of this approach. First, two old ICBM warheads would be destroyed for every new fixed land-based missile warhead, such as those on the MX. Second, three old SLBM warheads would be replaced by two new SLBM warheads, such as the D-5. Third, mobile ICBMs, such as the Midgetman, would be on a one-for-one basis. According to Leslie Gelb, "this would penalize modernization of potential first-strike weapons and reward modernization in the direction of submarine-launched and mobile missiles."[10]

The Soviets have been less than enthusiastic about Washington's basic START proposals. Initially, they proposed that the SALT II parameters be accepted with one major change, namely, the banning of ALCMs. After the new United States proposals in June 1983, the Soviets showed some movements from this position. They no longer sought a complete ban on new United States systems, such as ALCMs. But the Soviets continued to reject any United States proposal that limited their ICBM force without limiting American cruise-missile and bomber programs. In addition, the Soviets have proposed that long-range nuclear weapons should be limited to about 1,100 multiple warhead missiles and bombers on each side but with no special limits on the SS-18 or SS-19 forces.

Raymond Garthoff commented on the reason for Moscow's rejection to date of the American START proposals:

> From the Soviet perspective, the revised proposals are fatally flawed. . . . The advertised flexibility does not extend to the key provisions that made the Administration's original negotiating proposal fundamentally unacceptable to Moscow. These crucial flaws are not affected by the flexibility on total ballistic-missile numbers and are in fact made worse by the American plan to deploy the MX.
>
> . . . The 2,500 warheads ceiling would mean a cut of more than half in the Soviet warheads on intercontinental missiles, while permitting an increase in comparable American warheads. The President did not go so far as to impose explicit limitations on missile throw-weight . . . but he kept severe indirect constraints on throw-weight that would require Moscow to reduce by two-thirds its biggest and best strategic missiles, the SS-18 and SS-19, while Washington could go ahead with plans to build up its MX and Trident II missiles.
>
> Worse still, from the Soviet standpoint, while the proposed agreement would alleviate the vulnerability of American land-based intercontinental missiles . . . it would greatly increase the vulnerability of comparable Soviet missiles — which are the most important component of Moscow's strategic force. There would be no equality of sacrifice and no "equal security."[11]

It should be noted, however, that Soviet unwillingness to recognize the legitimacy of American concerns over the vulnerability of United States ICBMs to Soviet attack is at the heart of the current American arms-modernization program. Although the United States is now seeking additional countersilo capabilities, it is doing so in reaction to Soviet force deployments. Because the Soviet Union has been unwilling to talk about the Minuteman vulnerability problem, the United States has concluded that its only recourse is likewise to threaten Soviet forces.

From an American standpoint, Soviet insistence throughout the arms-control negotiations of the 1970s and 1980s on protecting their strategic assets (especially the ICBM force) and on reducing the American technological advantage has been, at the very least, troubling. Thomas Wolfe has noted one of the core issues of the strategic arms talks: "Where to draw the line at which Soviet insistence upon safe margins of force levels would cease to represent legitimate compensation for technological and other asymmetries favoring the United States and would become a demand for unilateral advantage threatening to tip the strategic balance perceptibly in Soviet favor."[12] The United States is not about to let that happen.

The Soviets cast a shadow over the START process when they suspended their participation in those talks in December 1983. They did so in "response" to the initiation of United States deployments of GLCMs and Pershing-IIs in Europe. The Soviet delegation said it felt compelled "to re-examine all the issues" in view of the deployment of these new American systems. That deployment has created "a change in the overall strategic situation."[13]

Conclusion

The strategic arms race during the next decade promises to make a determination of what constitutes parity very difficult. The Soviet Union is apparently unable to derail (despite their best diplomatic efforts to do so) American, French, and British modernization programs. These Western programs coupled with what the Soviets deem to be their appropriate "responses" will threaten to undermine parity as it was established in the strategic arms agreements of the 1970s. But parity will continue to exist in the form of mutual assured destruction, especially if the United States and the USSR do not engage in widespread deployments of ballistic missiles defense systems.

It is not clear how—or if—superpower arms control talks will effectively curb technological competition or channel the Soviet and American modernization processes into some form of bargained equivalence. There is a real danger that technological competition will become so intense that the effort to define parity through arms-control agreements will collapse. An open-ended and dangerously unregulated arms race might well be unleashed.

Notes

1. *United States Military Posture, OJCS, Fiscal Year 1984* (Washington, D.C.: GPO, 1983), 39.

2. *Annual Report to Congress, Secretary of Defense, Fiscal Year 1984* (Washington, D.C.: GPO, 1983), 227.

3. John Steinbrunner, "Arms and the Art of Compromise," *The Brookings Review* (Summer 1983):8.

4. *Los Angeles Times*, 26 June 1983.

5. *Soviet Military Power* (Washington, D.C.: GPO, 1983), 26.

6. Ibid., 28.

7. *Washington Post*, 19 Aug. 1983.

8. *National Journal*, Oct. 1983, 2179.

9. *Baltimore Sun*, 9 Sept. 1983.

10. *New York Times*, 5 Oct. 1983.

11. *New York Times*, 12 June 1983; *Washington Post*, 27 June 1983; *Christian Science Monitor*, 23 June 1983.

12. Thomas Wolfe, *The SALT Experience* (Cambridge, Mass.: Ballinger, 1979), 156.

13. *New York Times*, 9 Dec. 1983.

Soviet Arms Trade with the Noncommunist Third World

ROBBIN F. LAIRD

The Soviet Union exports more arms than any other country. In 1980 the Soviets were responsible for 34 percent of the world's total arms exports, and their significance as an arms exporter to the Third World is even greater than such an aggregate figure indicates, especially with regard to the Arab Middle East. At least 70 percent of all Soviet arms sales to the non-communist developing countries in the 1970s went to the Arab Middle East. In 1980 the Soviet Union was the primary supplier for five of the seven major arms-importing states in the Third World (Syria, Libya, Iraq, India, and Vietnam).[1]

The degree to which the Soviet Union dominates Third World arms sales is best indicated by analyzing the major military equipment end-items shipped to the Third World. In the period from 1979 to 1982, the Soviets were the major supplier of tanks, self-propelled guns, artillery, supersonic combat aircraft, surface-to-air missiles, guided-missile boats, subsonic aircraft, and helicopters. The Western Europeans were the prime suppliers of noncombat aircraft, major- and minor-surface combatants, and submarines. The United States was the prime supplier only of armored personnel carriers and armored cars.[2] In other words, the only significant competitors with the Soviet Union in arms sales to the Third World have been the Western Europeans, especially the French.

Soviet arms sales are motivated by three key factors. First, the Soviet Union believes that the achievement of United States-Soviet strategic parity has resulted in an increase in the significance of conventional military power. In the 1970s, the Soviets emphasized conventional arms modernization, and arms sales are a critical component of this program.

Adapted with permission of the publisher from Robbin F. Laird, *Soviet Arms Trade with the Non-Communist Third World in the 1970s and 1980s* (Washington, D.C.: Wharton Econometric Forecasting Associates, 1983). The views expressed in this essay are the author's and do not necessarily represent those of the Center for Naval Analyses.

Second, the Soviet Union has developed a version of Henry Kissinger's "regional influentials" policy. It uses arms sales to develop ties with key powers in the Third World, regardless of a given country's social structure or its prospects for Soviet-style "socialist" revolution. Western economic power in the Third World is apparently too great for the Soviet Union to compete successfully on that basis. In contrast, the Soviet Union is in a much more favorable position to compete militarily. The economic aid and arms-sale data support such a conclusion. From 1976 through 1980, the value of Soviet arms sales was four times that of economic aid to developing countries.

Third, Soviet arms exports to developing countries are an increasingly important source of the hard currency needed to pay for Soviet imports from the West. In the 1970s, the Soviet Union shifted away from a policy of using arms primarily for geopolitical influence toward a policy that also provided economic benefits by requiring hard-currency payments for arms from virtually all of its customers. This policy evidently applied even to customers valued for political reasons, such as Ethiopia. Approximately 65 percent of Soviet arms sales to developing countries in the 1971–80 period were for hard currency. Indeed, arms sales represented 22 percent of the total export earnings from trade with non-socialist countries, second only to fuel exports, which reached 56 percent.

Another economic contribution of Soviet arms sales has been to lower the cost of the Soviet conventional arms-modernization program. By exporting, an economy of scale is created with a lower cost for end-unit items. Current front-line aircraft — Mig-23s and Mig-25s — are sold widely abroad. The new generation aircraft expected to be deployed in the late 1980s — Su-27s and Mig-29s — will probably be available for the export market as soon as they are deployed in the Warsaw Pact countries. In many ways, the only industrial export for the Soviet Union that is competitive with the West is military equipment.

But all is not auspicious for Soviet arms exports. A number of Soviet arms clients in the 1970s began to diversify their sources of supply, particularly for aircraft. For example, Iraq and India have purchased French aircraft because they want a weapons system with the advantages of Soviet equipment (e.g., simplicity of design) but with the superior Western performance characteristics. Many Soviet arms clients are dissatisfied with the service they receive from the Soviets as well.

In the end, the issue is the quality of Soviet military equipment, especially aerospace products. The Syrian debacle in 1982 did not help and has already had an impact of Soviet arms sales. India, for example, is rethinking the wisdom of purchasing the T-72 tank from the Soviets. In short, the Soviet Union now confronts a very tight and competitive arms market. It faces direct competition from Western European and Third World arms producers, while economic pressures impel it to increase either its market share or its profits. Nonetheless, it will be difficult for the Soviets to do so.

Strategic Deterrence and Soviet Arms Sales

The Soviet Union's attainment of strategic-nuclear parity with the United States in the 1970s had an important political impact for the Soviets, because it increased the significance of conventional power as an instrument of foreign policy.[3] Strategic-nuclear deterrence provides a more stable foundation for the Soviet Union's use of conventional power to further its interest than would be the case in conditions of strategic uncertainty. As Roman Kolkowicz observed: "The Soviets clearly understand that in the nuclear era, major powers need the security of a credible strategic-nuclear deterrent force before they can safely adopt limited-war doctrines and policies. The reason for this lies in the logic of deterrence and limited war. To remain limited, wars involving the major powers, whether directly or indirectly, need credible fallback reserves: a strategic (assured destruction) retaliatory threat that will both act to reduce escalatory pressures and provide boundaries. Espousal of limited war without such a credible retaliatory threat would leave the state open to manipulation and blackmail."[4]

From the Soviet point of view, "imperialism" has been "forced" by strategic-nuclear deterrence to exercise its military power in various forms of conventional "armed violence." The most frequent target has been the Third World, where "imperialism" recognizes the existence of the most vigorous and open conflict between capitalism and socialism as world historical forces. As the authors of an authoritative Soviet study of armed conflict in the Third World put it: "Adapting to changes in the world balance of power and encountering such a factor as the unified military might of the socialist nations, the aggressive forces of imperialism are directing their "local" attacks against individual socialist countries, the revolutionary movement of the proletariat, the national liberation movement, and against developing countries in which progressive regimes have been established. They understand full well that the outcome of the struggle between socialism and capitalism depends in large measure on how the world revolutionary process develops, what path will be taken by peoples which become liberated from the colonial yoke."[5]

The Soviet Union vigorously countered "imperialist" aggressions, precisely to make it clear that it will use military power to achieve its political goals. As Colonel D. Volkogonov commented on Soviet aid to Vietnam in its "struggle" against the United States, "the activities of the Soviet Union and other socialist countries in furnishing assistance to the Vietnamese people in their just struggle and the promoting of successful peace negotiations have revealed to the entire world both our firmness and our sincere desire to solve vexing problems through political means."[6]

The Soviet use of its power-projection forces has reflected an acute sense of the political dimensions of the use of military power in the Third World. Above all, the use of Cuban surrogates in a number of Soviet military interventions reflects a distinct Soviet preference to avoid direct conflict with the United

States. By avoiding direct conflict with the United States, the Soviet Union clearly hopes to isolate Third World military action from questions of general United States-Soviet military confrontation.

Stephen Kaplan, in his work on Soviet armed forces as a political instrument, has emphasized the centrality of political considerations in the framing of Soviet military policy toward the Third World: "In general, Soviet leaders were adept at legitimizing their use of force, timed their introduction of military means well, showed good sense in the types of forces called on, and did not gloat over successes. The Kremlin preferred a naval presence, covert tactical air assistance, logistical support, and the use of Cuban combat formations over the open deployment of Soviet military units in Third World nations. Moscow knew that it was better to create new political facts rather than risk issuing ultimatums."[7]

The centrality of conventional arms in the violence of Third World political development means that military assistance has become a critical tool in the exercise of Soviet influence. Colonel E. Rybkin has underscored this development as follows: "Oppressed and dependent nations waging wars of liberation were no longer alone in the struggle against colonizers. They receive moral, political, economic, and, where possible and necessary, military assistance from countries of socialism."[8]

Soviet analysts have increasingly concluded that the military forces in the Third World are the critical elites in shaping the development in those countries. Thus, Soviet military assistance is designed to exercise influence over the political orientations of Third World development by shaping the commitments of Third World military elites. As Charles Peterson has noted, "it is certain from the evidence of Soviet writings that the relative importance of military cooperation as an instrument of policy has grown in the measure that Third World military elites have become a leading focus of Soviet attention."[9]

The growing significance that the Soviets have attached to military assistance as an instrument of influence reinforces the importance of further developing Soviet power projection forces. Andrew J. Pierre in his study of the politics of arms sales has described the interrelationship between Soviet military assistance and power projection forces in the following manner: "During the 1970s the Soviet Union greatly improved its capacity to transport arms over long distances by developing long-range cargo aircraft and by expanding its maritime capabilities. In the previous decade Moscow's ability to aid Lumumba in the Congolese civil war was limited. No such logistical problems hampered the impressive capability of the Soviet Union to bring Cubans to Angola and Ethiopia or to support them with sea and airlift operations, ferrying thousands of tons of arms and military supplies."[10]

In short, a condition of strategic-nuclear parity between the superpowers has not reduced the significance of military power to the Soviet Union. Rather, strategic-nuclear deterrence has increased the significance of the effort to create usable military power — nonnuclear military power. Arms sales have played a key part in strengthening Soviet conventional military power. As Anthony

Cordsman noted, "while the linkages involved are often politically complex, there is a clear relation between the expansion of Soviet forces and the expansion of Soviet arms sales."[11] Soviet arms sales to the Third World have been a key dimension of the Soviet conventional arms modernization process in the 1970s and 1980s.

The Role of Arms Sales in Soviet Third World Policy

Increasingly throughout Brezhnev's rule, the Soviets came to view noncommunist Third World states as significant global actors in their own right. Whereas in the 1950s and 1960s Soviet interest in the noncommunist Third World was generated primarily by competition with the United States, increasingly the Soviet Union began to perceive the advantages in improving ties for economic and military reasons outside of the superpower framework. Ideologically, the Soviets placed greater emphasis on the legitimacy of developing relationships with Third World states, regardless of their social structure, as long as those relationships provided political, economic, or military benefits to the Soviet Union. It became not only possible but also desirable to expand the network of "mutually beneficial" economic and military ties with noncommunist Third World states.

The expansion of military arms sales has been perceived as an especially appropriate means for developing such ties. This is due in part to the perceived significance of military elites to the management of Third World states. Because Soviet analysts have concluded that Third World military elites play a vital role in shaping political development, a major thrust of the Soviet approach to the noncommunist Third World has been to generate military arms sales and to make significant military assistance efforts. Military arms sales and assistance also reinforce the need to develop Soviet forces for military power projection. Especially significant in this regard is the further development of the capability to transport arms over long distances with the deployment of a new type of long-range cargo aircraft and by the expansion of military and civilian maritime capabilities. In other terms, the Soviets have developed a version of Kissinger's "regional influentials" policy. The Soviets use political, economic, and military means to develop ties with key powers in the Third World, regardless of a given country's social structure or its prospects for Soviet-style "socialist" revolution. Rather, ties are to be developed in order to enhance Soviet economic and military capabilities.

Nonetheless, the Soviet Union has not always accepted the concept of the legitimacy of developing a congruence of interests with the noncommunist Third World. Rather, the Soviet goal historically has been to transform the Third World in the Soviet image. It was only in response to the very mixed results of Soviet Third World involvement in the early post-Stalin period that the Soviets began to lower their expectations or, alternatively, to develop more realistic expectations of the prospects for social transformation in the Third World.[12] The evolution of those expectations went through the following phases:

Phase One, 1946–53: The Late Stalin Period. The "National Liberation Movements" in this period were characterized by an effort to remove the formal vestiges of colonialism. While championing the decolonization effort in forums such as the United Nations, the Soviets devoted virtually no economic or military resources to the development of its relations with the Third World. In particular, Soviet military-aid programs in the postwar Stalinist period were mainly limited to China and to North Korea. No military aid was given to any noncommunist Third World state.

Phase Two, 1954–57: The Early Post-Stalin Period. In the immediate post-Stalin period, Soviet leaders expressed interest in the revolutionary potential of the Third World. Khrushchev was an especially visible advocate in this period of extending support to the new regimes in the Third World in order to promote the global process of transformation to "communism." For example, he viewed the 1955 Bandung Conference as an indication of the trend toward Soviet-style socialism in Africa and Asia. This conference was followed by a much publicized trip by Khrushchev and Bulganin to the Near East in late 1955. Concurrently, Soviet arms began appearing in the Middle East (primarily through Eastern European channels, especially Czechoslovakia). It was in this period that Khrushchev developed his "zone of peace" concept. In contrast to the Stalinist concept of the "two camps," Khrushchev put forth an image of the Soviet Union as the ally of all "nonaligned" states. It was argued that there was a virtually automatic commonality of interests between the Soviet Union and the Third World in advancing the cause of "socialism."

This phase included the real beginning of the development of economic and military ties with noncommunist Third World states. Egypt was the first major arms recipient. The initial shipment of arms to Egypt included several Mig-15 fighters, IL-28 jet bombers, T-34 tanks, and several naval vessels. This sale was followed by others in early 1956 to Syria and Afghanistan.

Soviet arms sales were made possible by Western — especially American — unwillingness to supply arms on a favorable basis to key "nonaligned" states in the Third World. For example, Indonesia sought arms in the mid-1950s to strengthen its ability to crush domestic rebellion and to seize control of Western Guinea from the Dutch. When the United States refused to sell arms to them, the Indonesians turned to the Soviets.

A key dimension of the Soviet ability to enter new arms markets in this period was the speed with which the Soviets could deliver equipment. The speed of delivery was facilitated by the stockpiles of surplus equipment made available by the Soviet arms modernization program of the late 1950s.

Phase Three, 1958–64: The Khrushchev Period. During this period, the Soviet Union assumed that socialism would spread throughout the Third World. This would be accomplished by the efforts of "progressive" forces within the

Third World itself, which would supposedly seek to ally themselves with the Soviet Union against the common "imperialist" enemy. The Soviets would only have to provide limited economic support that would include the transfer of arms.

In the first part of the period (1958–60), the Soviet Union was able to enter the Iraqi and Indian markets. Iraq turned to the Soviet Union for arms following the overthrow of the pro-Western monarchy in 1958 by General Kassem. The Soviets entered the Indian market primarily because they were able to meet Indian requirements at a lower cost than the United States and were more flexible in allowing barter terms as well. Initial sales were small, however, being limited to the transfer of transport aircraft and helicopters. Other arms sales in this period were made to Algeria, Guinea, Ghana, and Mali.

The largest recipients of arms in the period from the mid-1950s to 1960 were Egypt and Indonesia. Each received more than $500 million in arms, and together they accounted for more than half of Soviet arms sales. Roughly a third of the sales went to Syria, Iraq, and Afghanistan, each of which received more than $200 million in arms.

Soviet arms sales intensified in the early 1960s. During the period 1961–64, Soviet arms sales rose in value about 20 percent over the preceding six years. Military sales to India increased significantly in 1962, largely by making good the losses created in fighting with China. Among the most significant Soviet arms agreements with India was the creation for the first time of a coproduction arrangement outside of the Warsaw Pact. The Soviets agreed to build two aircraft plants in India to produce the airframes and engines for the Mig-21 fighters. Arms sales were also dominated by an upsurge of shipments to Egypt and Indonesia in the 1961–64 period. Egypt, Indonesia, and India accounted for more than 70 percent of the total. Egypt was the largest recipient of arms with more than $700 million in arms sales. Indonesia and India received more than $500 million each in arms from the Soviet Union in this period.

Sales in this period brought relatively low profits. The Soviet Union provided arms to Indonesia and Egypt on exceptionally favorable terms. The sales to India were more profitable but were still priced below the general arms-transfer market. But it must be remembered that the Soviets were selling older equipment from preexisting stockpiles, and the actual terms of Soviet "military assistance" were often much less generous than appeared to be the case. Rarely did the Soviet Union offer military grants rather than commercial sales. This was in contrast to the American practice at the time of extending large military grants-in-aid to Third World states. Soviet credits for arms purchases usually carried 2 to 3 percent interest, repayable over five, seven, ten, or twelve years. In addition, the provision of arms in exchange for commodities was much less generous than it appeared. Even though Soviet prices were reasonable, massive arms deals could require a significant mortgaging of the commodities production of a given Third World state to the Soviet Union. Clearly, however, economic motivations were secondary to political goals in this period.

Phase Four, 1965–69: The Early Brezhnev Years. In this period the Soviet Union experienced a number of setbacks in the Third World as radical governments allied to the Soviet Union were overthrown by military coups, notably in Algeria and Indonesia. In part, because of such setbacks, the Soviets began to recognize the existence of serious obstacles to the growth of "socialism" in the Third World. Earlier hopes of telescoping the Third World's transition to socialism into a relatively brief period was replaced by a more pessimistic assessment. It was now thought that the revolutionary process in the Third World would require "an entire historical epoch." The role of the military in shaping the indigeneous processes of change was given greater significance, although its role was not necessarily considered to be a progressive one. But the military elites seemed a natural target for the exercise of Soviet influence by means of the conduct of Soviet arms trade.

Recognizing the need to influence military elites, the Soviet Union was nonetheless more pessimistic about the prospects for development in the Third World. As one Soviet analyst noted, "the lesson of military upheavals in several states of Asia and Africa is that the army can play a progressive role in the national-liberation movement, but it can also easily turn into a tool of reactionary forces."[13] The experience with Egypt in the early 1970s would cause the Soviet Union further to examine the interests served by its arms trade.

In the early Brezhnev period, India became the largest recipient of Soviet arms, with sales of more than $400 million. Egypt was second, with sales of more than $300 million, while Iraq and Syria each accounted for more than $200 million in sales. Together, Egypt, Syria, and Iraq constituted more than one-half of all Soviet arms sales in the period.

A major Soviet effort in this period was to resupply Egyptian and Syrian forces after the 1967 war. More than 80 percent of Egypt's losses of military equipment were replaced. In addition, the number of Soviet advisers and technicans increased from 500 to 3,000 by the end of 1967. But the support given to Egypt and Syria clearly represented an exercise in the use of arms to achieve direct military and political advantage rather than the use of Soviet arms for economic profit.

Phase Five, 1969–75: The Middle Brezhnev Years. Soviet perspectives in this period underscored that "serious obstacles of an objective and sometimes subjective nature" stood in the way of the transition to socialism even in "countries of socialist orientation" and that some of these countries were regressing either by "turning aside from a progressive course or by slowing their advance."[14] The more realistic assessment of Third World developments was conjoined with the increased salience of the military dimension, including a more economically advantageous arms-transfer policy, to the successful exercise of Soviet influence in the Third World.

The debacle in Egypt was a major stimulus to the development of Soviet Third World policy in this period. The expulsion of Soviet military personnel in mid-1972 serves as a traumatic reminder of the reversibility of military ties, because the Soviet expulsion by Sadat came despite massive arms transfers and unprecedented Soviet participation in the active defense of Egyptian air space in 1970.

The period was also characterized by the increased significance of arms sales to petrodollar countries in the Middle East. Iraq and Libya became increasingly significant recipients of Soviet arms, each receiving more than $2 billion in arms. Syria became the leading recipient of Soviet arms, with Egypt close behind. Both received more than $2.5 billion in arms, stimulated largely by the resupply efforts associated with the 1973 war.

Phase Six, 1975–82: The Late Brezhnev Period. In this period, the Soviet Union became increasingly pessimistic — or, alternatively, more realistic — in regarding the need to place relations with the noncommunist Third World on a sounder economic and military basis. The Soviets began to recognize that their opponent in the Third World was not only the United States but also the process of indigenous change in the Third World. Opposition by indigenous Third World forces to the exercise of Soviet influence has been a disappointment to the Soviet Union. Historically, it has regarded Third World hostility to Western influence as an acceptance of the Soviet Union and a rejection of the Western powers. The Soviets began to realize that most indigenous Third World forces want independence from both East and West. Specifically, the purchase of Soviet arms has frequently reflected the desire to become independent from the West but not a desire to be under Soviet military tutelage. In the mid-1970s the Soviet Union found itself under increasing market pressure by petrodollar countries able to choose alternative suppliers, such as Iraq and Algeria. These countries favored a mixed arms procurement policy as a means of seeking greater national independence.

In this period several Soviet analysts explicitly underscored that there is no automatic commonality of interests binding the Third World to Soviet foreign-policy interests. Consequently, the Soviets needed to follow a flexible approach that would take into account such factors as the degree of independence a given country had from the world capitalist system. Some Soviet analysts began to emphasize that the critical line of demarcation in the noncommunist Third World was between dependent capitalist regimes and independent capitalist regimes. It was in the Soviet interest to develop ties with independent capitalist regimes, including the sale of arms, even if such ties would not lead to the ultimate triumph of "socialism."[15]

Table 1 indicates that for the period 1975–79 new arms-sales commitments totaled more than $30 billion, more than double that of the previous five-year period (these figures include not just Soviet arms sales but arms sales by Eastern Europe as well).

During the late 1970s hard-currency sales of arms to petrodollar countries in Africa and the Middle East began to replace the earlier Soviet practice of providing arms at attractive discounts or terms of payments. With the end of the Soviet-Egyptian arms relationship in 1975, the Soviets focused their arms shipments on Iraq, Libya, and Algeria. Iraq became the largest Third World recipient

TABLE 1

Soviet-Bloc Military-Aid Commitments, 1975–79
($US billions)

Year	USSR	Eastern Europe	Total
1975	3.3	0.64	3.94
1976	5.5	0.34	5.84
1977	8.7	0.47	9.17
1978	2.5	0.55	3.05
1979	8.4	0.25	8.65
Total	28.4	2.25	30.65

Source: Central Intelligence Agency, *Communist Aid Activities in Non-communist Less Developed Countries, 1979 and 1954–79* (October 1980).

of Soviet arms. Syria also received large quantities of arms, but, in contrast with Iraq, Libya, and Algeria, Syria made no substantial hard-currency payments for Soviet arms.

Arms sales played a much greater role in overall Soviet hard-currency earnings in the mid-to-late 1970s. Given the importance of hard-currency purchases in Soviet industrial trade with the West, arms sales to the Third World became in effect a major industrial export supporting East-West technology transfer. In terms of manufacturing exports, arms sales became a major end-item for trade in this period.

Phase Seven, 1982–Present. It is difficult to identify the content of the Andropov and Chernenko policies toward arms sales with the noncommunist developing countries. There are, however, a number of clearly identifiable factors that will affect the formation of policy. First, the decline in world oil prices will have an immediate impact on the ability of the Soviet arms clients to pay in hard currency. Second, the economic stringencies of the 1980s will increasingly pressure the Soviets to place arms trade on an economically sound footing. Third, the rising cost of the new generation of Soviet military equipment, especially aircraft, creates an additional incentive to export in order to reduce the unit cost of key end-items, such as the new Su-27 and Mig-29 fighters. Fourth, the defeat of Syria by Israel in the June 1982 war is having continuing repercussions on the Soviet arms sales markets. The Soviets have clearly tried to blame Syria for the Syrian defeat at the hands of Israeli forces. But a number of Soviet arms clients have expressed concern over the performance of Soviet equipment, and, at a minimum, Soviet arms clients will increasingly wish to receive the top-of-the-line Soviet military equipment when at all possible.

In short, the Soviets face a challenging arms-sales market in the 1980s. At the same time, they hope to place their arms sales on an increasingly sound economic basis in order to support their own military modernization efforts as well as to support their more general foreign policy efforts.

The Basic Structure of Soviet Arms Trade with
Noncommunist Developing Countries

More than 70 percent of Soviet arms sales to the noncommunist developing countries in the 1970s and 1980s have been made with the Arab Middle East. When arms transfers to India are added to the total, more than 80 percent of Soviet arms sales are accounted for. A major change in the 1970s involved a shift to Syria as the major recipient of Soviet arms in the Arab world. In the decade from 1965 to 1975, Egypt was the single most significant recipient of Soviet arms in the Middle East. With the breakdown of Soviet-Egyptian relations in the mid-1970s, Syria became the primary geopolitical actor in the region for whom the Soviets were willing to provide a significant arms transfer that was partially subsidized.

Arab orders for Soviet arms increased dramatically in the 1970s. Soviet arms sales to the region were five times as great in 1974–79 as in the period 1967–73. In the 1970s, Iraq, Libya, and Algeria became the key hard-currency customers for Soviet arms. The value of exports increased in part due to the sale of more expensive late-model equipment, which sometimes predated exports to Soviet Warsaw Pact allies.

The Soviets have sold a broad array of weaponry to the Third World in the past few years. Some sense of the scope of Soviet arms exports can be provided by figures contained in table 2, from the Pentagon's most recent version of this report, *Soviet Military Power*. The table does not differentiate between communist and noncommunist developing countries receiving Soviet equipment, but it does provide an understanding of the geographical focus as well as of the major categories of equipment shipped. Overwhelmingly, Soviet arms exports in the 1977–82 period went to the Middle East, North Africa and South Asia.

TABLE 2

Major Soviet Equipment Delivered to the Third World, 1977–1982

	Total	Near East and South Asia	Sub-Saharan Africa	Latin America	East Asia and Pacific
Tanks/self-propelled guns	7,065	5,205	1,140	80	640
Light armor	8,660	6,500	1,590	175	395
Artillery (100-mm and over)	9,590	5,115	3,510	420	545
Major surface combatants	32	19	5	1	7
Minor surface combatants	126	10	45	27	44
Missile patrol boats	53	33	4	11	8
Submarines	6	3	–	3	–
Supersonic combat aircraft	2,235	1,635	220	130	250
Subsonic combat aircraft	290	150	80	5	55
Helicopters	910	620	125	35	130
Other military aircraft	345	100	70	65	110
Surface-to-air missiles	11,680	9,495	1,575	435	175

This same Pentagon report estimated the value of Soviet military sales agreements to all Third World states at $47.5 billion, of which $29.1 billion went to the Middle East, North Africa, and South Asia. Again, these figures do not isolate sales to noncommunist developing countries.

In the period 1975–82, the Soviet Union was the major supplier to the Third World of tanks and self-propelled guns, artillery, supersonic combat aircraft, surface-to-air missiles, and guided-missile boats. The major Western European suppliers led in deliveries of major and minor naval surface combatants, submarines, and helicopters. In contrast, the United States led only in deliveries of light armored vehicles and subsonic combat and other aircraft.

The single most successful export has been of Soviet tanks. The Soviet Union has shipped three generations of tanks to the Third World since the 1960s — the T-54/55 MBT in the 1960s and T-62 and T-72 MBTs throughout the 1970s and into the 1980s. In the opinion of many Western experts, the Soviet tank force may be the finest in the world. The evolution of Soviet tank designs has given the Soviet tanks much compatibility among components of the various generations. This provides a significant pool of war reserves.

The large pool of Soviet tanks (more than 50,000 in the Soviet Union alone) and of Soviet client states purchasing tanks provides the opportunity for the Soviets to have large production runs of tanks, thereby significantly reducing the unit cost. In addition, the purchase of significant numbers of Soviet tanks creates a sunk cost for the client state, which in turn creates a key incentive to continue purchasing the evolutionary Soviet tank that is designed for compatibility over time. No Western competitor can compete with the Soviets in the sale of tanks, neither in the length of production runs nor in compatibility of generations (with the exception of the compatibility of German tanks over time).

A second major category of military equipment widely sold by the Soviets in the 1970s and 1980s has been ground-air defense systems, notably surface-to-air missile (SAM) systems. The cutting edge of Soviet sales in this category has been to politically valued clients under attack from adversaries. In 1970–71 Egypt was the first noncommunist state to receive the SA-3 low-level SAM system and the mobile ZSU-23-4 radar-controlled antiaircraft gun. In the early 1980s, Syria was the first state outside of the Soviet Union to receive the SA-5s and the first noncommunist state to receive the SA-8s.

The most significant category of sales from the standpoint of hard currency earnings, however, has been military aircraft. Since the 1960s, the Soviet Union has exported three generations of aircraft to the noncommunist Third World. In the 1960s, it exported the first generation Mig-17s and Mig-19s. In the early-to-mid 1970s, it sold second-generation aircraft, most notably the Mig-21. In the mid-to-late 1970s and early 1980s the Soviet Union exported Mig-23s, Mig-25s, and Su-20s.

Soviet aircraft development has been nearly a generation behind American aircraft, and Soviet exports reflect this gap. For example, the Israelis recently destroyed Syrian aircraft with a fourth-generation aircraft that the Soviets only hope to deploy in significant numbers in the late 1980s. The Soviets lag in the development of aircraft generations with respect to Western European producers as well. As a result of the lag in Soviet aircraft development, Western producers are in a much more favorable position to compete with the Soviets than in the case of armored equipment, especially with regard to tanks.

Major Trends in Soviet Arms Sales

A number of key trends in the practice and structure of Soviet arms sales characterized the 1970s and 1980s.[16] One of the most significant trends has been the shifting of Soviet arms sales from a strictly or mainly political basis to an economic basis as well. Many Soviet arms sales are politically motivated, especially with regard to the communist Third World, notably Cuba and Vietnam. But Soviet arms sales with the noncommunist Third World have increasingly been made to states more capable of paying for Soviet arms.

Even in the case of Syria, for example, there is an economic basis to Soviet policy. With their expulsion from Egypt, the Soviets placed greater reliance on their ties with Syria to maintain their hand in the military confrontation with Israel. But the Soviets have not done so in the absence of an economic motivation. A large portion of Syrian arms imports from the Soviet Union in 1982 was paid for in hard-currency cash. Since Syria is a relatively poor country with no significant oil income, its arms imports were apparently paid for by its Arab neighbors, with Saudi Arabia and Kuwait contributing most of the funds. Thus, at least indirectly, Saudi Arabia and Kuwait probably became the largest buyers of Soviet military hardware in 1982.

The importance of Soviet arms exports to developing countries in the overall Soviet hard-currency balance of trade and payments has risen dramatically over the last decade. During 1971–73, when arms sales to Egypt accounted for a major portion of total Soviet arms sales to developing countries, the percentage of arms sold for hard currency was probably below 40 percent. But after 1973, when Libya and Iraq became increasingly important buyers, the share of hard-currency sales probably exceeded 75 percent. Estimates prepared by Wharton Econometric Forecasting Associates (WEFA) indicate that during 1971–80 approximately two-thirds of Soviet arms sales to developing countries – or $21.1 billion – were for hard currency.

According to estimates prepared by WEFA, of all commodities of significant importance in Soviet exports to nonsocialist countries, arms were the most dynamic item. Their share of the Soviet export earnings in developing countries increased from 55 percent in 1981 to almost 62 percent in 1982. As for their contribution to total Soviet export earnings in nonsocialist countries (excluding gold), the share of arms increased from 19 percent to almost 22 percent, second only to the share of fuels, which reached 56 percent. Soviet exports of arms to developing countries cannot be viewed only as an instrument of Soviet foreign policy and global military strategy, but are of increasing importance as a source of hard currency and as a means of paying for Soviet imports.

Although outright grants of arms have become much rarer, generous terms still prevail when the Soviet Union wants to keep its hand in the East-West trade competition. For example, the terms of the $1.6 billion sale to India are extremely generous. Repayment is spread over seventeen years at an annual interest charge of 2.5 percent.

The Soviet Union has been able to deliver weapons systems much more quickly than its competitors for arms sales. Soviet arms are extremely attractive to countries in quick need of weapons, because they can be delivered rapidly from stock, something which Western arms suppliers have found difficult or even impossible to match. In addition, the arms offered for sale have been increasingly sophisticated. Recently, the Soviet Union has sold much of its front-line equipment to the Third World states. Especially important in this regard has been the sale of heavy tanks, aircrafts, and multitube artillery.

The increased cost of each successive generation of Soviet aircraft, in particular, has placed pressure on the Soviets to lower costs through the use of exports. By exporting, an economy of scale is created with a lower cost for end-unit items. Current front-line aircraft — Mig-23s and Mig-25s — are sold widely abroad. The new generation of look-down, shoot-down aircraft that is expected to be deployed in the late 1980s — Su-27 and Mig-29s — will probably be available for the export market at the same time as they are deployed within the Warsaw Pact countries.

In addition to the advantages of scale economies, the Soviet Union has been pressured to sell its front-line aircraft to key client states if they wish to remain in the market. The Soviets are in keen competition with the French Mirage 2000 in many of their chief target areas in the noncommunist Third World. Also, the United States sells to many of the states that rival Soviet client states. Soviet clients will pressure the Soviet Union to provide a counter to the United States F-16, which the Soviets apparently believe to be the Mig-29.

There has also been increasing pressure from Soviet client states regarding the quality of service provided by the Soviet Union in maintaining equipment, especially in the case of aircraft maintenance, including engine overhauls. A number of Soviet arms clients have pressured the Soviet Union to build aircraft or at least engine-overhaul facilities in their countries to provide for timely and efficient servicing of their weapons system. Both Peru and Iraq wish to follow the Indian example of having engine-repair facilities on their own soil, rather than having to send aircraft engines to the Soviet Union for repair.

The problem of service has especially intensified with the growing sophistication of military hardware. The more sophisticated the equipment sold, the more pronounced the importance of the continuing relationship between arms supplier and arms user. The value of an average contract between the Soviet Union and one of its arms clients is usually 60 percent for the cost of the weapon, 33 percent for support, and 7 percent for infrastructure. By contrast, the value of an average contract with the United States is 35 percent for weapons, 35 percent for support, and 30 percent for infrastructure. A Soviet arms client therefore relies on its supplier more than United States customers for such things as training support, construction, and technical assistance, which comes under the infrastructure category.

As the sophistication of military equipment increases, so do the demands to provide technical training and support to the indigenous personnel using the more advanced equipment. The influx of large quantities of modern, complex military equipment into less-developed countries has demanded a level of military skills that are lacking in the recipient states. This lack of skilled military manpower is underscored especially by the speed with which military equipment has been delivered and by the necessity for rapid assimilation. The manpower base in the recipient countries has been unable, in most cases, to supply enough men capable of being trained to command, operate, and maintain much of the more sophisticated Soviet equipment within the necessary time. Hence an important dimension of the Soviet arms sales effort has been to provide training at Soviet military installations for Third World military personnel or to dispatch large numbers of Soviet military technicians to the Third World.

The training dimension of arms transfer may affect the future of Soviet arms sales. On the one hand, the sale of military equipment requiring the creation of increased ties with Third World military elites poses the possibility for expanding Soviet influence with these elites. The Soviets obviously favor such a development. But on the other hand, the use of military advisers to expand Soviet influence inhibits many Third World states from buying Soviet arms. The expansion of Soviet global military presence poses a threat to many Third World states, and these states do not want to import Soviet influence with Soviet arms.

An additional pressure being placed by Soviet Third World arms clients is to establish coproduction facilities in the recipient country. Coproduction facilities reduce the end-item cost to the recipient country and allow the indigenous manpower base to attain higher skill levels. Coproduction provides the potential for greater independence of the Third World state with the creation of a learning curve for the skilled domestic base.

The only case to date of coproduction arrangements has been India, which has been producing Mig-21s since the 1960s. The Soviet Union offered to coproduce Mig-23s as part of the unsuccessful effort to block the 1978 sale of the Anglo-French Jaguar to India. Evidently as part of the 1980 arms agreement, the Soviet Union and India will coproduce Mig-25s. India was also authorized to produce T-72 tanks as part of the 1980 agreement. Reportedly, Iraq has been particularly adamant in establishing coproduction arrangements with the Soviet Union in order to supplement the practice of direct arms-transfer.

Since the early 1970s, the Soviet Union has made a sustained effort to enter new arms markets. A major element of its effort to expand sales to the non-communist Third World has been an attempt to use the extensive Soviet experience in barter or compensation trade to advantage. Particularly with the capital shortages in the Third World and with the decline in hard-currency available to Third World oil producers in the 1980s, the Soviets hope to play on the desire of Third World states to provide more stable "nonmonetary" exchanges to expand Soviet sales. For example, the Argentinian-Soviet grain arrangements reportedly include an agreement to spend a significant amount of Argentinian earnings in the Soviet market, a provision clearly pointing to the Soviet hope that Argentina will use its Soviet account to purchase Soviet arms. However, the anticommunist Argentinian military has thus far resisted such a purchase.

The Soviets have also faced increasing competition from the suppliers of Soviet-produced or Soviet-copied equipment in the communist countries and the Third World. Such competition simply limits the potential political leverage that the Soviets can obtain from arms sales. It is possible that increased competition from non-Soviet producers or suppliers of Soviet equipment could paradoxically increase the scope of Soviet sales if Third World states could be certain of blocking the Soviets from exercising undue influence from the sale of their arms.

Competition is provided by non-Soviet producers or suppliers of Soviet equipment. Egyptian arms exports consist almost entirely of Soviet equipment. China has continued to produce copies of Soviet equipment and is entering traditional Soviet markets by providing an alternative source of supply, as in Iraq. In 1980, the Soviets embargoed arms shipments to Iraq because of the Iran-Iraq war, but Iraq obtained spare parts and replacement equipment from Yugoslavia, Romania, and Poland.

The Soviets are also facing increasing competition from Western European, arms producers in their traditional arms markets. France especially has aggressively sought to displace the Soviets from key countries in the Middle East, especially in aerospace products, by marketing the Mirage 2000 to Soviet disadvantage in several Third World states. Similarly, Britain has been offering armored products and naval systems in markets that the Soviets have been attempting to enter. West Germany has been selling naval systems and other equipment to several Third World states that do not wish to place themselves under United States domination but also do not wish to purchase Soviet arms.

In the Soviet-Western European competition for arms markets in the Third World, the Western Europeans have a number of advantages over the Soviets. The Western Europeans provide far better service and, in general, a better quality product. They also have a limited global projection capability, which in turn limits the military influence that can be obtained from arms sales.

The Soviet Union also faced competition from Third World arms producers. The Brazilian armaments and aerospace industries provide a limited supply of armored vehicles and artillery rockets to other Third World states, such as Iraq, which in the past would have purchased them from the Soviet Union.

An additional source of competition has come from arms producers willing to upgrade Soviet equipment. For example, Britain has offered to reengine Soviet tanks for Egypt. Israel is offering an upgrading package for Soviet tanks as well. Several Western European producers have expressed a willingness to provide enhanced avionics packages to countries possessing Soviet aircraft.

In short, the Soviet Union will confront a very tight and competitive arms market in the late 1980s. It faces direct competition from Western European and

Third World arms producers, competition that both complements and contests Soviet dominance over the Soviet-produced arms market. The Soviet Union is also indirectly pressured by American arms sales. As the United States exports products like the F-16, the Soviet Union must provide its highest quality weapons at favorable prices. Moreover, there is pressure on the Soviet Union to use countertrade or barter trade effectively in maintaining its market share. These competitive market conditions come precisely as economic pressure on the Soviet Union compels it to increase either its market share or its profits. It will, nonetheless, be difficult to do so. Furthermore, the Soviet Union has little hope of sustaining the level of hard-currency imports from the West unless it maintains or increases its arms sales. With the net decline in oil prices, the role of arms sales in providing the hard currency for the Soviet Union's balance of payment with noncommunist countries is being enhanced. The Soviet Union will thus seek to sell as many arms to the developing world with as much profit as possible.

The Soviet Union, however, does have several advantages in the competition with Western European arms producers. It can produce and deliver armaments faster, and it can undersell the Western Europeans. The size of the Soviet stockpile provides the option of massive arms transfers when a given client-state is embroiled in military conflict. Also, the size of the Soviet economy allows more flexibility in conducting the sort of barter trade that many Third World countries might well be impelled to engage in throughout the decade ahead.

NOTES

1. *World Military Expenditures and Arms Transfers, 1971–1980* (Washington, D.C.: Arms Control and Disarmament Agency, 1983).

2. Richard Grimmett, *Trends in Conventional Arms Transfers to the Third World by Major Supplier, 1975–1982* (Washington, D.C.: Congressional Research Service, 1983).

3. See Robbin F. Laird and Dale R. Herspring, *The Soviets and Strategic Arms* (Boulder, Colorado: Westview Press, 1984), chap. 1.

4. Roman Kolkowicz, "United States and Soviet Approaches to Military Strategy," *Orbis* 2 (Summer 1981): 322–23.

5. I. E. Sharova, ed., *Lokal'nye voiny: Istoriia i sovremennost'* (Moscow: Voenizdat, 1981), 5–6.

6. D. Volkogonov, "Peaceful Coexistence — An Alternative for War," *Kommunist* 19 (October 1973) (translated in Joint Publications Research Service, 60454, 5 Nov. 1973): 38.

7. Stephen S. Kaplan, *Diplomacy of Power* (Washington, D.C.: Brookings Institution, 1981), 668.

8. E. Rybkin, "The 25th CPSU Congress and Wars of Liberation of the Contemporary Era," *Voenno-istoricheskii zhurnal* 11 (Nov. 1983); trans. in JPRS, 072543, 2 Jan. 1979), 42.

9. Charles C. Peterson, *Third World Military Elites in Soviet Perspective* (Alexandria, Va.: Center for Naval Analyses, 1979), 37.

10. Andrew J. Pierre, *The Global Politics of Arms Sales* (Princeton: Princeton University Press, 1982), 77.

11. Anthony H. Cordesman, "The Soviet Arms Trade: Patterns for the 1980s," *Armed Forces Journal International* (June 1983): 97.

12. This section draws on material presented in Steven T. Hosmer and Thomas W. Wolfe, *Soviet Policy and Practice toward Third World Conflicts* (Lexington, Mass.: Lexington Books, 1983).

13. A. Iskenderov, "Armiia, politika i narod," *Izvestiia*, 17 Jan. 1967.

14. O. Orestov, "Independent Africa in the Making," *International Affairs*, no. 11 (Nov. 1975), 75.

15. See especially, K. N. Brutents *Osvobodivshiesia strany v 70-e gody* (Moscow: Politizdat, 1979).

16. This section draws on material presented in various issues of *Aviation Week and Space Technology* as well as in the annual reports on arms sales of the Stockholm International Peace Research Institute.

The Stalinist Legacy in Soviet Foreign Policy

CHARLES GATI

The central arguments of this essay are that Stalin's foreign policy was less aggressive and revolutionary than is commonly assumed; that his successors' foreign policy has been more aggressive and revolutionary than is commonly assumed; and that there has therefore been more continuity in the conduct of Soviet foreign policy than is commonly assumed. All of these arguments run counter to widely held Western views.

Since Stalin's death in 1953, many Western students of Soviet foreign policy have emphasized "change" rather than "continuity" in the international orientation of the Soviet Union — change for the better, evolution toward moderation and restraint. They seem to have concluded that Soviet foreign policy — responding both to a new external environment and to different internal circumstances — has successfully shed its Stalinist past. They believe that the Soviet Union, having substantially reduced its revolutionary commitments, has become an essentially status-quo power — steady and ambitious but not reckless, at times assertive but not adventurist, and invariably pragmatic. Rather than an aggressive revolutionary power, the Soviet Union is thus seen as primarily, if not exclusively, interested in protecting its own security and achievements in an atmosphere of relative international stability.

Is such a general appraisal of post-Stalin Soviet foreign policy — and the cautious optimism it has produced in the West — really warranted? Did de-Stalinization in foreign policy accompany Soviet domestic de-Stalinization?

I think not. The year 1953 was not a watershed in Soviet foreign policy. A comparison of post-Stalin Soviet foreign-policy patterns with Stalinist behavior from 1928 to 1953 reveals far more continuity than change. As a basic approach

This is a slightly revised and updated version of a chapter originally published in *The Soviet Union since Stalin*, ed. Stephen F. Cohen, Alexander Rabinowitch, and Robert Sharlet (Bloomington: Indiana University Press, 1980), 279–301.

to the outside world, Stalin's conduct of foreign policy was calculating and circumspect, and his historic mix of expansion-and-accommodation, or revolutionary assertiveness-and-peaceful coexistence, which served the Soviet state so well for so long, has remained deeply ingrained in the Soviet political mind. On balance, Stalin cannot be said to have placed more emphasis on revolution making than his successors have on upholding or maintaining the status quo. Essentially cautious and opportunistic, the Soviet leaders since Lenin have displayed revolutionary assertiveness when and where it seemed safe to do so, while favoring the status quo and peaceful coexistence when and where it seemed necessary or useful to do so. All of them, and perhaps especially Stalin, consistently refused to risk the security of the Soviet Union for distant, revolutionary goals. After all, as early as the mid-1920s Stalin had already advocated a largely inward-looking posture for the emerging Soviet state — "socialism in one country" — against Trotsky's more radical, outward-looking alternative of "permanent revolution."

It is true, of course, that the scope of Soviet foreign policy has changed. Stalin did not develop a coherent policy toward the colonial areas of Asia and Africa, for example, while his successors have certainly done so toward what is now called the Third World. It is also true that some of the issues on the Soviet agenda are new — such as the current preoccupation with and the management of nuclear weapons systems. And it is true that it remained for Stalin's successors to cope with such problems as the rise of new communist party-states and to define the meaning of "socialist internationalism" and "international relations of a new type." Yet, important as some of these changes in the scope, issues, and problems of Soviet foreign policy may seem, they are not so far-reaching as to assume that Stalin himself would not have made them. Indeed, if Stalin could now survey the achievements, strategies, and methods of Soviet foreign policy since 1953, he would likely endorse its general thrust and congratulate his successors on their skillful adaptation of his approach to new international circumstances.

Furthermore, even if one were inclined to dismiss as political rhetoric Khrushchev's remark that so far as foreign policy toward the West was concerned he and his colleagues did regard themselves as Stalinists, the fact remains that Stalin's foreign policy has never been subjected to extensive criticism in the Soviet Union — not even during the height of the domestic de-Stalinization campaign in the mid-1950s. In fact, Stalin was criticized for only two foreign-policy faults: the country's military unpreparedness on the eve of World War II and his unduly harsh, and ultimately counterproductive, treatment of Yugoslavia in 1948 and 1949 (and, by implication, the rest of Eastern Europe). He was not accused of excessive aggressiveness or adventurism, nor did his successors ever promise to de-Stalinize Soviet foreign policy and indeed place it on new foundations.

The reason for the apparent gap between the promise and early pursuit of domestic de-Stalinization, on the one hand, and the lack of de-Stalinization in foreign policy, on the other, is self-evident. While his successors believed that Stalin's domestic policies—particularly the intimidation and terror aimed against the Soviet elite—began to threaten the cause of socialism within the Soviet Union, his foreign-policy record spoke well of his skills in promoting Soviet security and the cause of socialism abroad. After all, when Stalin became *primer inter pares* in 1928, the Soviet Union was weak and vulnerable, an essentially second-rate power; yet by 1953, it was recognized as one of the two superpowers. His successors, having inherited a tested and successful approach to the outside world, had no reason either to criticize or to change the basic orientation of Stalin's foreign policy.

Stalin's Foreign Policy Revisited

The emphasis in Western studies on "change" rather than "continuity" in Soviet foreign policy since 1953 stems in part from an undue emphasis on Stalin's foreign policies from the end of World War II to the Korean War. Admittedly, this was an era of expansion and unprecedented aggressiveness in Soviet foreign relations, beginning with the Soviet domination of Eastern Europe, the Berlin crisis of 1948–49, and the unnecessary and avoidable conflict with Yugoslavia — all coupled with intransigent statements and undiplomatic posturing. While some of these policies were indicated by the geopolitical opportunity that World War II had created, Stalin probably did push too hard during the early years of the cold war. His aggressiveness provided the glue for Western unity against the Soviet Union—as expressed by the Truman Doctrine, the establishment of NATO in 1949, and even the consideration of such radical countermeasures as the use of atomic weapons against Moscow during the Berlin confrontation (recommended by Churchill but quickly rejected by both the British and United States governments). To the extent that Stalin's postwar policies led to the mobilization of the West and the containment of further Soviet advances, therefore, these policies were not only unduly assertive but—from the perspective of long-term Soviet interests—probably counterproductive.

Aggressive Soviet behavior in the early years of the cold war, however, was only one aspect of the Stalinist pattern in foreign policy. During Stalin's reign, a pragmatic Soviet Union first sought to ally itself with Nazi Germany and then formed a grand coalition with such bastions of imperialism as England and the United States. Communists fought along with noncommunists in the Spanish Civil War. In the early 1930s, the Soviet Union concluded a number of treaties and cooperative agreements with such bourgeois states as France, Poland, and Czechoslovakia. In 1935 the Seventh Congress of the Communist International, reversing the Comintern's 1928 Sixth Congress, issued an analysis that justified the broad, flexible, coalition-seeking approach—the "Popular Front" strategy — adopted by Communist parties everywhere. And to accommodate the Soviet Union's immediate foreign-policy needs, Stalin repeatedly modified certain features of Marxist-Leninist ideology pertaining to international relations.

Stalin's thinking in nonideological, power-political terms — meaning that he recognized both the uses and the limitations of Soviet power — was even demonstrated during the expansionary postwar era. A reluctant supporter of uncertain revolutionary causes abroad, Stalin denied extensive assistance not only to his comrades in the French Communist party but also to Mao's revolutionary forces in the Chinese civil war. He maintained relations with Mao's enemy, the Kuomintang's Chiang Kai-shek, as long as the outcome of the civil war was in doubt. Even in Eastern Europe, in the fall of 1945, when Stalin thought that he might need Western cooperation, he dramatically reversed previous decisions and as a gesture of goodwill ordered competitive elections in Bulgaria and then agreed to free elections in Hungary. Moreover, while purging Jews in the Soviet Union, he supported the Zionist cause for the establishment of a Jewish state in Palestine — no doubt calculating that such a state would weaken the British in the Middle East. And, finally, around 1950 Stalin gave new emphasis to the old concept of "peaceful coexistence" and subsequently initiated the coalitionary "peace campaign" of the early 1950s.

Although this brief summary cannot do justice to the complexities of Stalin's foreign policy, it does suggest that Stalin was a rather cautious guardian of the Soviet Union's international interests. During his last years, as Adam Ulam noted, his policies "created an air of tension which, apart from being a source of danger to Russia, was largely unnecessary."[1] Moreover, the language he used to assess international developments and explain Soviet goals abroad contained more ideological referents than can be found in his successors' pronouncements. But Stalin's actual policies invariably reflected his sensitivity to the international balance of forces. As a result, he made all the necessary compromises in order to gain time and strength.

Has anything important really changed since Stalin's time? Surely both the internal and external environments of Soviet foreign policy have changed. Neither the Soviet domestic scene nor the world at large is the same as it was in the 1940s and 1950s. Very much at issue, however, is the influence of these internal and external environments have had on the conduct of Soviet foreign policy.

Internal Influences on Soviet Foreign Policy

The first and by far the most important change in the internal environment of Soviet foreign policy has been the substantially increased relative power of the Soviet Union since Stalin's reign. Although its economy remains uneven and technologically inferior to that of the West, the diverse and steadily growing military capability of the post-Stalin Soviet Union attests to its new status in world politics.

If Stalin's foreign policy had in part stemmed from a sense of weakness and insecurity, what policy change would follow enhanced Soviet domestic strength? To answer this question, one should assume that the Soviet leaders believe some or most of their self-congratulatory messages about the successes of the Soviet state. But has the new Soviet leaders' confidence about internal strength helped them overcome their often-noted historic sense of insecurity vis-à-vis the outside world, especially the West? Has their self-confidence about domestic strength led them to pursue a more accommodating foreign policy?

Alternatively, one may suppose that, despite their remarkable achievements, the post-Stalin leaders still lack sufficient confidence in the viability of the Soviet domestic order. Perhaps they measure their accomplishments against more ambitious ultimate objectives or against the power of the United States and thus find these accomplishments lacking. Their self-congratulatory messages may be no more than the official optimism and wishful thinking characteristic of political discourse everywhere. In that case, the Soviet leaders' apparent lack of self-confidence about the internal health of the Soviet Union should reinforce their historic sense of inferiority vis-à-vis the outside world, especially the West. Such lack of self-confidence about domestic strength could prompt them to compensate for perceived weakness at home by pursuing an assertive or even aggressive foreign policy.

In his analysis of the interwar period — an era of considerable Soviet weakness — Alexander Dallin concluded that "perceived weakness need not always produce a conciliatory mood in Moscow; nor does the willingness to seek a détente or compromise need to stem from weakness alone."[2] Similarly, in his analysis of the post-Stalin years — an era of increasing Soviet strength — Morton Schwartz presented two contrary interpretations as equally plausible. In one passage, he said: "Convinced of their superiority — a conviction strengthened by their vast military power — the Kremlin leaders may be anxious to flex their new muscles. Thus, in the years ahead they may probe for ways to expand Soviet influence around the world." In another passage, however, Schwartz concluded: "A secure Soviet leadership has already become a somewhat more relaxed Soviet leadership."[3]

Unable to reach a firm conclusion about causality, no Western analyst has been able to offer conclusive evidence about the validity of any of the following hypotheses:

1. Domestic weakness leads to foreign-policy accommodation.
2. Domestic weakness leads to foreign-policy assertiveness.
3. Domestic strength leads to foreign-policy accommodation.
4. Domestic strength leads to foreign-policy assertiveness.

The validation of any of these hypotheses would have considerable implications for Western policy. It would indicate whether the West should try to encourage a strong and confident Soviet Union or whether it should try to keep Moscow weak and uncertain of its relative power position. But without such a validation, any advice about "keeping" the Soviet Union weak or strong must be prudent and qualified. No one knows how much the Soviet Union's newly acquired domestic strength will influence its foreign policy. But common sense argues against a Western policy that would seek an internally strong and confident

Soviet Union, because it would entail excessive risks for Western security in exchange for tempering, presumably, Moscow's "nervous aggressiveness."

The second frequently discussed change in the post-Stalin domestic order has been the apparent decline of ideological rigidity. The reason given for a more pragmatic and flexible Soviet approach to the outside world is that the new leaders did not experience the early, prerevolutionary days and that their mindset was thus formed during the years of socialist construction. As party bureaucrats, managers, soldiers, and engineers, they have devoted their lives to practical tasks, not to the making of revolution. While they have certainly participated in political intrigues, most of them did not take part in prerevolutionary conspiracies.

Moreover, the new Soviet leaders have repeatedly modified Stalin's ideology of international affairs. Wars were once said to be inevitable; now they are not. Revolutions were once said to be inevitable; now there can be a peaceful transition to socialism. The international class struggle used to be the major dogma of foreign policy; now it receives less public emphasis than peaceful coexistence. Autarky was to exclude devious foreign influences; now it is the international division of labor and even interdependence that pave the road to socialism and communism. Automation used to show capitalist inhumanity; now computers (often imported) are the new signposts of the scientific-technological revolution. At Lenin's grave, Stalin pledged to uphold the sacred and unshakable unity of the international communist movement; now his successors have yet to find an ideologically adequate explanation for Soviet military contingency plans against China.

Yet it remains doubtful whether Stalin's successors have been less influenced by ideological precepts than Stalin was supposed to have been. After all, ideological innovation and foreign-policy flexibility, not doctrinal rigidity, were Stalin's traits, and his successors have only outperformed him in ideological gymnastics. But even if one were to assume otherwise, does the professed decline of ideological rigidity amount to flexibility? Does more flexibility necessarily translate into an accommodating or moderate foreign policy? It may well be, instead, that neither of these hypotheses is valid:

1. Rigid ideological environment leads to foreign-policy assertiveness.
2. Decline of ideological zeal leads to foreign-policy accommodation.

Without denying the steady erosion of faith since Lenin's days and the far-reaching, though only long-term, implications of this process for the future of Soviet political culture, what should be emphasized, therefore, is that the necessity of legitimizing every twist and turn in foreign policy by ideological incantation is hardly a novel phenomenon in Soviet history. Stalin offered an eloquent ideological rationale for the "hard" line adopted in 1928, as he did for the "soft" line in 1935. His successors presented an ideological explanation for their 1968 military intervention in Czechoslovakia (the "Brezhnev Doctrine") and for their more recent détente policies toward the West ("peaceful coexistence").

Stalin saw no way to avoid confrontations between the forces of socialism and imperialism. In 1953 and 1954, however, Malenkov revised Stalin's assessment, stating that because of the destructive quality of atomic weapons and the increasing might of the Soviet Union, an all-out war with imperialism was no longer inevitable. That was good news, of course, but one must note that (1) Stalin's belief in the inevitability of war did not propel him to begin such wars (as he always sought to enhance Soviet power and influence gradually, indeed incrementally); and that (2) his successors have not denounced "small" or "just" wars: the so-called wars of national liberation (e.g., Cuba, Vietnam, and Cambodia) and military intervention in their sphere (e.g., Hungary and Czechoslovakia). In the final analysis, Malenkov's revision of Stalin's dogma merely signifies the acceptance of, and the concurrent ideological rationalization for, what Stalin had practiced. The same can be said about other changes in the "ideological environment" of Soviet foreign policy since Stalin's time. For example, *Pravda* still holds that "there are essentially no neutrals in the struggle between the two world systems."[4] And according to the authoritative Soviet *Diplomatic Dictionary*, peaceful coexistence "is a specific form of class struggle between socialism and capitalism."

The third change in the domestic environment of Soviet foreign policy since Stalin has been identified as the broadening of the decision-making process, including the rise of elite factions and competing interests. Foreign-policy alternatives are debated more openly among a wider circle of advisers and decision makers. Resource allocation between military and nonmilitary uses, for example, is a particularly lively issue. Concurrently, the Soviet view of international life has become more sophisticated, with specialists now covering all conceivable aspects of foreign-policy analysis and international-relations theory from the classical balance of power to simulation and beyond.

The controversial issue here is less the existence of "conflicting domestic pressures" and factional political struggle (which had been particularly evident during the three succession crises of 1953–57, 1964–68, and the early 1980s) than their consequence for foreign policy. Political deals and compromises in the Kremlin need not lead to an accommodating foreign policy, because the deal could also produce "relaxation" at home and "vigilance" abroad. In other words, the mere existence of divergent interests, needs, views, perceptions, and approaches cannot be said to ensure any consistent pattern in Soviet foreign policy — conciliatory, centrist, or belligerent. A compromise among competing interest groups does not require a foreign policy of restraint.

Nor can one necessarily expect moderation from a divided post-Stalin foreign-policy elite, even if it is better informed and more sophisticated. After all, more expertise does not necessarily mean more caution.

Since we do not know how incoming foreign-policy information is processed, the parameters of the policy debates, and, in particular, the political benefits or penalties derived from the transmittal of "bad news" and the offering of new ideas, it is difficult to judge the validity of any of the following hypotheses:

1. Narrow (Stalinist) decision making leads to foreign-policy assertiveness.
2. Broadening of the decision-making process leads to foreign-policy accommodation.
3. Limited knowledge of international life leads to foreign-policy assertiveness.
4. Expanding knowledge of international life leads to foreign-policy accommodation.

External Influences on Soviet Foreign Policy

The apparent lack of causality between domestic inputs and foreign policy makes it particularly apposite to explore the external environment of Soviet conduct. Can that environment be the source of change in Soviet foreign policy?

To begin with, the members of the international community engage in activities that have a bearing on the Soviet Union. States engage in generally self-serving activities, though not necessarily contrary to the interests of the Soviet Union. Under all circumstances, however, given the military might, economic power, political influence, and the global reach of the Soviet Union — in short, its preeminent position in the international system — most states have reason to seek to alter some aspect of Soviet foreign policy. In turn, since the Soviet Union does not operate in a political, military, or economic vacuum, it has to respond to at least some of these attempts to influence its behavior.

The primary external demands on the Soviet Union are (1) for foreign policy "moderation" (i.e., demands on Moscow to help maintain the status quo by refraining from war and intervention) and (2) for "assistance" (i.e., demands to help change the status quo by extending political support and economic as well as military aid). Since these two broad categories of demands are mutually exclusive, the Soviet Union — taking into account domestic needs, pressures, and preferences as well — must evaluate and respond to such contradictory external demands, trying to satisfy as many of its more important or more powerful foreign audiences and constituencies as possible. Simply stated, the Soviet Union is linked to too many external causes, issues, and audiences whose demands on and expectations of the Soviet Union greatly differ. Moscow can satisfy some of these demands and expectations some of the time; it cannot satisfy all of them all of the time.

Since Stalin's reign, the international environment has dramatically changed. The world communist movement has disintegrated. The communist bloc that Stalin built after World War II has all but ceased to act as a united entity. Almost one hundred new and, in many cases, radical states have emerged. Those rich in resources have come to present a major challenge to the Western industrialized world. Interdependence is a new economic fact of international life. The "leading role" of the United States in the Atlantic alliance has eroded. The "liberation" of Eastern Europe is no longer on the Western agenda. Finally, the extraordinarily rapid modernization of weapons systems, spearheaded by the United States, has led to fundamental revisions in the concepts and strategies of warfare.

Some of the changes in the international system, such as the development of new weapons, require Moscow to exercise caution and accommodation; others, such as the rise of new states, may mean opportunities for the expansion of Soviet influence. It seems that the Soviet Union can respond to external influences calling for moderation in two ways. First, it can respond tactically — an essentially limited adjustment to external demands. This response is the well-known "one step backward," a temporary concession whose primary purpose is to gain time. This type of response originated with Lenin, and it has long been recognized as part of the repertoire of Soviet diplomacy.

The other kind of reaction, as William Zimmerman has suggested, is far more complex and seldom recognized. It can begin, perhaps, as a tactical adjustment to international reality; but over time — if properly stimulated and reinforced — it would transform itself into a learned response. Learning from the benefits of experience and subjected to carefully orchestrated external stimuli, the Soviet Union would thus become capable of genuine and lasting attitude-modification and "structural adaptation."[5] If the Soviet Union has the capability to produce such a response, as Zimmerman argued, the implications would be far-reaching indeed. It would signal a major opportunity — and responsibility — for the outside world to influence the Soviet foreign-policy elite and to contribute to lasting change. The United States, for example, could act and speak in such a way as to reinforce the position of "moderates" in the Kremlin; it could attempt to show, by words and deeds, the benefits of détente and cooperation for both sides.

Unfortunately, there is reason to be skeptical about the possibility of achieving a "lasting adaptation" in Soviet foreign policy as a consequence of external influences. For one thing, there is the practical problem of policy coordination by the outside world. Neither now nor in the future can Western leaders know the parameters of internal debates on foreign policy in the Kremlin. But, assuming that they could make a good guess at the choices discussed, can the outside world then coordinate its policies in such a way as to bring about the desired result? Even though the United States is the most closely watched and surely the most important single external input, it is not the only one; and even if it could develop a set of finely tuned policies aimed at properly "educating" and influencing the Kremlin, the foreign policies of other nations would cancel out or at least mitigate the impact of the United States's efforts.

Even more fundamental is the problem of conceiving the appropriate mix of external inputs. It is not at all clear whether the outside world should be or should appear to be weak or strong, reassuring or threatening, in order to generate "moderation" in Soviet foreign policy. Soviet strategic superiority, for example, could help the Soviet leaders overcome their historic sense of inferiority vis-à-vis the West — a possibly valid but rather risky assumption — and thus produce a more accommodating Soviet foreign policy. Alternatively, the United States could aim at strategic superiority, following the long-held belief that it can influence the Soviet Union only from a position of strength. But if that approach only reinforces a sense of inferiority in the Soviet leadership, the concessions will likely be only tactical or short lived.

Accordingly, unless the West has some reasonably accurate assessment of the impact of external "strength" versus external "weakness" on the Soviet foreign-policy debates—in other words, unless it knows what combination of external incentives and prohibitions may pave the way to a lasting tendency toward foreign-policy moderation—it cannot be confident about the international environment producing such moderation in Moscow. This is not to deny the import of what the non-Soviet world does or is, or how it goes about conducting its relations with the Soviet Union; it is only to suggest that external environmental influences entering into the calculations of the Soviet leadership will generate no enduring change in Soviet conduct. Finally, it is not a set of often conflicting demands, conditions, or policy inputs that make for change; only the balance of perceived needs will do so: the Soviet leaders themselves must decide that external developments demand policy reassessment.

The Balance of Perceived Needs: Key to "Change"?

So far, this essay has focused on the logic of assigning change to Soviet foreign policy on the basis of analyzing the internal and external environments of Soviet conduct. Yet, fascinating as it is to speculate about changing influences on Soviet behavior, the ultimate criterion for a judgment has to be the record—the output—of Soviet foreign policy itself.

Six "new departures" stand out in the history of Soviet foreign policy:

1. The Soviet Union discarded the early ideal of "revolutionary diplomacy" almost immediately after its establishment in 1917. Accepting the practice of what it had once regarded as "bourgeois" diplomatic intercourse with the outside world, the Soviet leaders promptly decided to enter into regular negotiations with other states and generally observe diplomatic protocol. Mainly because Lenin wanted to make peace with Germany and thus to cement his shaky regime at home, he did not hesitate to tell Trotsky that the very survival of the Soviet state required the adoption of "old" diplomatic practices.

2. The Communist International's "exclusionary" strategy of the 1920s — better known as the "United Front from below" — was replaced in the early 1930s by the "inclusionary," or Popular Front strategy. Sanctioned at the Soviet-dominated Seventh Comintern Congress in 1935, the new approach encouraged all Communist parties to cooperate with the noncommunist left in order to form a united front against the rise of fascism. Inherent in this fundamental shift was the danger of reducing the once-sacred "leading role" and ideological purity of Communist parties. Yet Stalin accepted the potential danger of ideological ero-

sion by socialists, social democrats, and others, because he assumed that only a broader left coalition could ensure the security of the Soviet Union and defeat the greater danger — Nazi Germany and its allies.

3. Compared with the cautious, quasi-isolationist posture in the interwar period, Stalin initiated an expansionary phase in Soviet foreign policy after World War II. With the establishment of pro-Soviet regimes in Eastern Europe, "socialism in one country" gave way to "socialism in one region," because the prewar revolutionary rhetoric could now be translated into policy. As noted earlier, the change was due to the opportunity created by World War II and the lack of countervailing power in the international system.

4. Around 1950–51, the confrontationist strategy of the postwar years was replaced by the peace campaign in Europe and the sudden opening to the Third World. Unable to break the European impasse and unwilling to risk a military showdown with the United States, Stalin — and subsequently his successors — shelved the rigid "two-camp" doctrine of 1946–47, resuscitated the "peaceful coexistence" line, and shifted to a rather low-tension policy toward the outside world. Clearly, the Berlin crisis and the Korean War demonstrated that the confrontationist strategy had failed to advance Soviet interests and should therefore be modified. For years to come, the Soviet Union was to look beyond the old world for new gains, relying less on the military than on the economic instrument of foreign policy.

5. Since the mid-1950s, Stalin's successors have come to accept, however grudgingly, a degree of experimentation in Eastern Europe. Khrushchev's overture to Tito in 1955 marked the beginning of greater Soviet tolerance toward national traditions and characteristics in Eastern Europe. Despite subsequent interventions aimed at curtailing far-reaching liberalization in the region, Stalin's insistence on strict uniformity was altered — no doubt because it had created chronic and dangerous instability.

6. The Soviet Union, having learned during the Cuban missile crisis that its inferior military posture vis-à-vis the United States had been a major political handicap, initiated a massive program of military investments in the 1960s to catch up with, and possibly surpass, the United States in the arms race. An estimated 12 to 15 percent of the Soviet GNP has since been devoted to military procurements, presumably in order to avoid the kind of humiliation that Moscow suffered in 1962.

These are among the more important new departures — some accommodating, some assertive in character — in the history of Soviet foreign policy. They suggest three conclusions.

First, in each case the Soviet leaders embarked on a new course either when the previous policy had failed or when a new opportunity for the expansion had presented itself. Irrespective of whether the new course was initiated under Stalin or his successors, it was usually the Soviet leaders' perception of policy failure that prompted the adoption of new approaches and solutions. In 1955,

Khrushchev used the issue of Tito's rehabilitation as part of his political struggle against those who, like Molotov and Malenkov, had been implicated in the early anti-Tito campaign under Stalin. On the whole, however, the perceived needs of the Soviet state rather than political infighting can be said to have produced new departures in Soviet conduct.

Second, the record of Soviet foreign policy indicates tactical adjustments rather than lasting adaptations. While it may be premature to make a definitive judgment about the most recent period, it is quite clear that, as Zbigniew Brzezinski and others have noted, Soviet policy toward the outside world has been characterized by a cyclical pattern—"by alternating offensive and defensive phases."[6] On the same point, Henry Kissinger said: "Peace offensives, of course, are not new in Soviet history. Peaceful coexistence has been avowed since the advent of Communism in Russia. It was stressed particularly between 1934-1939; between 1941-1946; at the time of the Geneva Summit Conference of 1955; again on the occasion of Khrushchev's visit to the United States in 1959; and following the Cuban Missile Crisis in 1962. . . . On each occasion the period of relaxation ended when an opportunity for expanding Communism presented itself."[7] Given the cyclical pattern of the past, it would require excessive optimism, if not naïveté, to emphasize aspects of lasting change in Soviet foreign policy since Stalin.

Third, the records of both Stalin and his successors suggest neither a rigid "master plan" for global conquest nor a conservative policy aimed at the maintenance of the status quo. If there has been a basic pattern in Soviet foreign policy since Lenin, it is characterized by the persistent, though cautious, pursuit of opportunities abroad—"persistent" because the overall objective of advancing Soviet influence has not changed and "cautious" because the Soviet leaders have sought to promote Soviet influence so gradually as to make strong and concerted Western countermeasures unjustifiable.

Post-Stalin Soviet foreign policy reflects a curious paradox. While the internal and external environments in which it operates are different now, the Soviet leaders—under conflicting pressures, impulses, and demands for both change and continuity—have nonetheless continued to rely on the old, historic mix of assertiveness-and-accommodation. Stalin's heirs must assume that this mix has been successful, and hence they perceive no need even for the kind of change that de-Stalinization has signified in the domestic realm.

Notes

1. Adam B. Ulam, *Expansion and Coexistence* (New York: Praeger, 1968), 543.

2. Alexander Dallin, "Soviet Foreign Policy and Domestic Politics: A Framework for Analysis," in *The Conduct of Soviet Foreign Policy*, 2d ed., ed. Erik P. Hoffmann and Frederick J. Fleron (Hawthorne, N.Y.: Aldine, 1980), 41-42.

3. Morton Schwartz, *The Foreign Policy of the USSR: Domestic Factors* (Encino & Belmont, Calif.: Dickenson, 1975), 89–91.

4. 30 April 1969.

5. William Zimmerman, "Choices in the Postwar World: Containment and the Soviet Union," in *Caging the Bear: Containment and the Cold War*, ed. Charles Gati (Indianapolis: Bobbs-Merrill, 1974), 85–108.

6. Zbigniew Brzezinski, "The Competitive Relationship," in *ibid.*, 157–99.

7. Henry A. Kissinger, *The Troubled Partnership: A Reappraisal of the Atlantic Alliance* (Garden City: Doubleday, 1966), 189–90.

Soviet Politics in the 1980s

ERIK P. HOFFMANN

This volume has analyzed how the Soviet Union's domestic and foreign policies are influencing and in turn being influenced by the changing socioeconomic and scientific-technological conditions in the USSR and abroad. But how will the Soviet political system influence such policies and conditions in the remainder of the decade? Specifically, how will the Soviet policy-making process — the perspectives of Communist party leaders, the policies on how to make policy, and the relations among the major bureaucracies, between the bureaucracies and the citizenry, and among the citizenry — affect the Soviet leadership's responses to present-day challenges?

Since these questions have only been touched on in the preceding essays, this conclusion will examine the enduring characteristics of the Soviet polity, the evolving Soviet views on political-administrative, socioeconomic, and scientific-technological developments, and the policy implications of institutional stability and ideological adaptation in the USSR. Although the Soviet political system changed significantly in the transition from Stalin to Khrushchev and changed moderately from Khrushchev to Brezhnev, it is unlikely to change much in the 1980s. Notwithstanding a new generation of Soviet leaders' imminent rise to power, adjustments in national policy making will probably be only incremental. But these adjustments, together with traditional practices and with innovations firmly established in the Brezhnev years, will shape Soviet internal and external policies. Soviet policy-making procedures are a powerful though not an insurmountable obstacle to new policies.

Fundamental Characteristics of the Soviet Political System

A Western analyst affirmed that China has experienced "almost unprecedented dynamism" since the death of Mao Zedong. "Virtually every institution in the country — from the agricultural communes to the literary establishment, from the universities to the party, from industrial management to ideology — has undergone thorough reexamination and extensive change. The China of the 1970s has been transformed almost beyond recognition."[1]

Recent Soviet experience has been quite different. To be sure, the Soviet political system was transformed from an authoritarian one-party system under V. I. Lenin to a personal dictatorship under J. V. Stalin and back to an authoritarian one-party system under N. S. Khrushchev, L. I. Brezhnev, Yu. V. Andropov, and K. U. Chernenko. But many of the political-administrative foundations and virtually all of the socioeconomic foundations of the current Soviet polity were laid or reinforced during the collectivization of the countryside and the centralization of economic planning and management in the 1930s. These structures survived the Nazi invasion of World War II, the demise of Stalin, and the subsequent declining increase of economic growth, productivity, and capital investment. Other durable basic characteristics of the Soviet political system — all of them initiated by Lenin — include: the proscription of factions in the party; the proscription of associational interest groups; restrictions on freedom of expression; a judiciary that is subject to party domination in political cases; a security police with few limitations on its power; and patronage practices (nomenklatura) enabling party leaders to appoint officials in all of the major bureaucracies and mass organizations.[2]

Probably the most important development in Soviet policy making since Stalin has been the revitalization of the public and private debate over many domestic policies and selected political-administrative procedures. In 1956 Khrushchev denounced Stalin's personal dictatorship and consequently had to defend himself against domestic and foreign critics from the communist "left" and "right." Brezhnev ignored Khrushchev's utopian party program, rejected his impetuous leadership style, and was much more circumspect in criticizing Stalin's legacy. Andropov and (to a lesser extent) Chernenko have deplored the lethargy of Brezhnev's waning years, but they have impugned the functioning and performance rather than the structures and purposes of the present-day system, especially in the economic sphere. Hence, the politics of principles and the politics of details have become increasingly blurred. Although disagreements about ends are deemed illegitimate and disagreements about means legitimate, Khrushchev's successors have paid closer attention to ends-means relationships and have solicited constructive criticism of policies and policy implemenation from various quarters.

Soon after becoming general secretary, for example, Brezhnev launched an open discussion about the economic activities of the party and the responsibilities of particular types of officials; Andropov encouraged economists and managers to propose diverse remedies for the ailing economy; and Chernenko precipitated a heated exchange among educators, production executives, and citizens that was followed by a reorganization of the nation's schools and a reemphasis on vocational training. To be sure, the party leadership initiates and terminates debates, restricts them largely to the printed media, often limits them to specialists, and forbids criticism of the fundamental characteristics of the Soviet polity. But Brezhnev, Andropov, and Chernenko have emphasized the complexity, interconnections, and dynamism of socioeconomic and scientific-technological developments, as well as the concomitant needs to tolerate ambiguities, to obtain more policy relevant information, and to find partial solutions to ongoing problems. The linkages among and the solutions to contemporary challenges are not presumed to be already known.[3]

Lenin's, Stalin's, and (to a lesser extent) Khrushchev's view that "conscious" political leaders know how to eradicate the "spontaneity" of the masses and of impersonal forces has undergone substantial revision. Lenin and Stalin knew their priorities and how to accomplish them; Khrushchev knew his priorities but did not know how to accomplish them; and Brezhnev knew with certainty only that oligarchical policy making was essential to the formulation of feasible policies. Brezhnev, unlike his predecessors, was not a single-minded visionary with delusions of omniscience and omnipotence. While professing a deep understanding of the "laws" of historical progress, Brezhnev's "collective leadership" broadened and deepened elite participation in the shaping and implementation of policies. Hence, Brezhnev reduced the party leader's aura of infallibility, openly acknowledged the intractibility of socioeconomic problems, and enlisted expert advice about the nature of these problems and the most efficient methods of resolving them. These trends were forcefully accelerated by Andropov and are continuing, intentionally or unintentionally, under Chernenko. Not surprisingly, both ends and means have been frequently in dispute.

At least three distinct political orientations surfaced in the last years of Stalin's rule and have competed with one another ever since. "Conservatives," "centrists," and "reformers" have advocated different substantive policies and policy-making procedures. For example, conservatives favor an economy founded on self-sufficiency, autocratic centralism, command planning, and military and heavy industrial priorities. Reformers favor selective interdependencies with capitalist countries; authoritarian centralism that encourages specialized elites to participate in policy making and administration; optimal planning that responds to market forces; and the application of science-based high technology in both military and civilian industries.[4] All three orientations conceptualize East-West relations as a dynamic mix of conflict and cooperation. But conservatives emphasize East-West conflict and West-West cooperation; reformers emphasize East-West cooperation and West-West conflict; and the entire party leadership emphasizes the competitive aspects of international politics. Although Soviet conservatives acknowledge that nuclear weapons have decisively altered the nature of warfare, they stress that cooperation with the United States is impossible in both the strategic and the conventional spheres and that the USSR must be capable of surviving a full-scale nuclear war. In contrast, Soviet reformers stress that the spiraling East-West strategic arms race is highly interactive and that the USSR's national security is enhanced by selective military and economic cooperation with the United States. All party leaders view conventional military forces as a means of projecting power abroad, but centrists and especially reformers contend that conventional forces are most effective if strategic competition is limited by formal treaties and if tensions that could lead to a nuclear war are diminished.[5]

From 1953 to 1957 the leading conservative was V. M. Molotov; the leading reformer was G. M. Malenkov; and the leading centrist was Khrushchev. Molotov and Malenkov were removed from the Presidium in 1957 after failing to oust Khrushchev, but lesser conservatives and reformers remained in power. Combining autocratic policy-making proclivities with erratic organizational practices, Khrushchev became a reformer on many substantive issues and, for all of these reasons, was eventually deposed by his Presidium colleagues – his administration's legitimacy dissipated and its effectiveness seriously undermined.

From 1964 to 1982 the leading conservative was M. A. Suslov; the leading reformer was A. N. Kosygin; and the leading centrist was Brezhnev. Taking mainstream positions on virtually all procedural and substantive issues, Brezhnev died in office – his administration's considerable legitimacy beginning to erode and its effectiveness diminishing.

From 1982 to 1984 the conservative and reformist orientations persisted but without dominant spokespersons (Suslov and Kosygin had died); and the leading centrist was Andropov, the former KGB head who had bested another centrist, Chernenko, a Brezhnev protégé closely identified with the stability and inertia of recent years. Despite a debilitating illness and opposition at the highest levels of the party and state, Andropov replaced many key national and regional cadres. He launched a series of reforms intended to curb corruption, waste, and indolence throughout the bureaucracies and society and to enhance cooperation among the existing political, economic, and social institutions and the population. Andropov died in office – his administration's legitimacy and effectiveness rising steadily.

Since Andropov's death in February 1984, the leading conservative has been G. V. Romanov; the leading reformer, M. S. Gorbachev; and the leading centrist, Chernenko. Having a mediocre formal education, little experience in fields other than ideological work, and no previous experience directing an organization, Chernenko is the least distinguished and influential general secretary in Soviet history. He symbolizes the tenacity of the generation of party officials who came to power under Stalin after the blood purges of 1936–38. (Chernenko, a septuagenarian, is a decade older than Romanov and two decades older than Gorbachev.) Chernenko also symbolizes the declining authority of the central party apparatus vis-à-vis the regional party apparatus and the key institutions of the Soviet state. (Gorbachev and Romanov have only recently been transferred to Moscow from regional party posts and appointed to the Politburo, and all of the chief state bureaucracies have been represented in the Politburo since 1973.) Given Chernenko's advanced age and precarious health, his administration is almost certain to be brief. Its legitimacy and effectiveness are already declining, and Chernenko's power is likely to dissipate even more rapidly if he does not implement Andropov's modest reforms. To date, Chernenko has shown little inclination or ability to alter existing personnel, prerogatives, and practices, and he has stolidly taken centrist positions on procedural and substantive issues. He recently reinstated the ninety-four-year-old Molotov into the party, a symbolic tribute to conservatism and possibly an augury of things to come.

In short, conflict over power and policy is fundamental to Soviet politics, and centrists have consistently prevailed since Stalin's death in 1953. Bureaucratic motives and methods have become more and more ingrained, and vested interests in existing policies have increased considerably, primarily because of the routinization of policy making under Brezhnev. However, the political-administrative "superstructure" and especially its socioeconomic and scientific-technological "base" are not immutable. Soviet commentators are cognizant of these facts but differ with Westerners about the most likely and desirable changes in the near future.

Let us now examine official Soviet thinking more closely. First under Khrushchev but chiefly under Brezhnev, new perspectives emerged that shaped as well as legitimized important initiatives, such as the Twenty-fourth Party Congress program of 1971. Since then Soviet leaders and analysts have emphasized the complexity, interconnections, contradictions, uncertainty, and dynamism of domestic and international politics, and some have cautiously suggested that power relationships and managerial procedures should be modified accordingly. To be sure, there has been considerably more talk about innovation than innovation itself, with much ritualistic discussion of familiar themes and many authoritative pronouncements that are quite general or deliberately vague. But the party leadership's claim to rule on the basis of a special knowledge of historical forces has been gradually deemphasized or discredited. Thus, the ideological foundations have been laid for major policy and policy-making changes, if and when future Soviet Politburos should choose or be impelled to make them.

"Socialist Democracy" and "Democratic Centralism"

Identifying the main challenges confronting the Soviet polity, G. Kh. Shakhnazarov, a Central Committee department official and president of the Soviet Association of Political Sciences, has affirmed that "the number one task is to further democracy — to secure broader participation of people in decision making, broader equality, and broader rights and freedoms of individuals. Task number two is to improve the state machinery and to optimize the administrative process."[6] To accomplish these goals, Soviet spokespersons contend that a society needs a single political party that is highly respected by all classes and strata and that possesses the authority to induce or compel all organizations to serve the public interest. Tsarist Russian and Soviet traditions have always rejected the Western idea that power, if concentrated, will be abused. The contemporary official Soviet view may be summarized as follows: in a capitalist nation, under a government that furthers only the material well-being of the upper and middle classes, organizational power corrupts and mass political activities are a sham; in the Soviet Union, under a one-party system that furthers the material and sociopsychological well-being of all citizens, organizational power and public participation in administration must be enhanced.

According to the USSR Constitution, the party is "the leading and guiding force of Soviet society, the nucleus of its political system and of its state and public organizations."[7] The party's chief responsibilities are to elicit information and efforts from all organizations and social groups in order to formulate just and realistic policies and to monitor their implementation and effects. As the Soviet Union becomes more structurally differentiated and its people better educated, the integrating, coordinating, and regulating functions of the party become more important. In a developed socialist society, top party bodies are to transform into viable policy alternatives the diverse interests of the proletariat, peasantry, and intelligentsia and their subgroups. According to Shakhnazarov, the "nonantagonistic contradictions" generated by competing strata in the USSR "may on occasion become extremely sharp unless prompt and sensible steps are taken to resolve them."[8] The party's self-imposed responsibility is to consider the needs and opinions of different organizations and strata, to adjudicate conflicts and claims for scarce resources, and to motivate bureaucrats and citizens to carry out programs that promote the welfare of all. Briefly stated, party leaders are to identify the common good, harmonize interests, shape national policy, supervise its implementation, and improve policy making and administration.

The government institutions—especially the councils of ministers, soviets, army, and secret police—are the other major sources of societal guidance in the USSR. Party officials affirm that the government must expand its involvement in economic and social development. State power is viewed as a creative and active force stimulating the economy. Ministerial cadres are exhorted to eliminate the many barriers to scientific-technological innovations and to apply new technologies and management methods to production. Also, the standing committees of the Supreme Soviet and local soviets and (to a lesser extent) the trade unions, Communist Youth League, and other public organizations are to play a greater role in assessing the economic, social, ideological, and cultural consequences of national policies and in drafting laws in selected fields. More and more government officials are to participate at various stages and levels of policy making, and more and more citizens are to participate in policy implementation.

Contemporary Soviet theorists equate democratization with the expansion of state activities and affirm that "the withering away of the state and the emergence of communist public self-administration" are goals that can be achieved only in the "distant future."[9] Contending that "essential formal changes" in the present-day Soviet polity are unnecessary, leading ideologists view the USSR as a "dynamically developing society" whose party, state, and mass organizations can and must "perfect" their structures and operations. In a word, Soviet institutions are to be "modernized," thereby accelerating the democratization of the political system.

Soviet leaders and analysts reiterate that democratic centralism is the cardinal organizational principle of party and state management, and they stress that both democracy and centralism must be enhanced during the contemporary "scientific-technological revolution" (STR). The post-Khrushchev collective leaderships have tried to delegate greater responsibility to the major bureaucracies and at the same time have guarded against the possible dissipation of the national party organs' power to initiate policies. Brezhnev, Andropov, and Chernenko have also facilitated the upward and downward flow of information within the bureaucracies and society, while trying to preserve the Politburo's and Secretariat's capability to choose among policy alternatives supported by major institutional coalitions and social strata. Today's party leaders recognize that matters of secondary or merely local importance continue to clog the central policy-making mechanisms and that such matters could be decided at lower levels more effectively and efficiently and on the basis of more timely and pertinent socioeconomic and scientific-technological information. But leading Soviet officials must weigh this potential benefit against the distinct possibility that national power will be further dispersed into weakly connected and self-serving departmental and local units. Especially since the late 1970s, bureaucratic and parochial interests have reduced the oligarchs' capability to implement domestic programs. General secretaries after Stalin have been frustrated by this trend but, with the fleeting exception of Andropov, have been unable to reverse it.

More and more Soviet spokespersons are addressing the key issue — namely, the need to increase elite and mass participation in the assessment and adjustment of decisions *after* they have been made, while curbing fissiparous tendencies in the growing party and state bureaucracies. Soviet officials must be circumspect, because the party rules still proscribe discussion of political-administrative questions once a decision has been taken. The authority to alter decisions gravitated long ago to the highest levels of the party. But the theory of democratic centralism ignores the ongoing nature of decision making and the need for continuous feedback to help reevaluate goals and, if necessary, to revise them.

Present-day Soviet theorists stress that the nature of centralism and democracy, not merely the "balance" between them, are evolving. V. G. Afanas'ev, a Central Committee member and editor in chief of *Pravda*, declared: "In order to *strengthen* centralized and planned management, it is necessary to *redistribute* certain functions from top to bottom and from the center to the localities, over an increasingly wide circle of organizations and people."[10] Soviet commentators contend that deconcentrating decision-making power and encouraging initiatives from below (especially from the industrial and production associations) are essential to "scientific management." That is, they recognize that the problem-solving capabilities of the central party organs can be *increased* by the delegation of selected responsibilities to administrative and territorial subunits.

Soviet analysts have linked the concept of democratic centralism with the democratization of a maturing socialist society. Shakhnazarov has maintained that democratic centralism is the core principle of the party, state, and "entire socialist political system" and is a "decision-making mechanism" only in a "narrow sense."[11] R. I. Kosolapov, a Central Committee member and editor in chief of the party's major theoretical journal, *Kommunist*, affirmed that "the most effective correlation of democracy and centralism in the life of a socialist society takes shape gradually and is continuously corrected by practice, with *democracy always gaining additional ground*."[12] A jurist, M. I. Piskotin, has suggested that one must distinguish between two groups of problems concerning democratic centralism: "The first consists of questions connected with guaranteeing the democratic nature of centralized leadership. . . . The second group consists of problems of combining centralization and decentralization. . . . In an intermediate position between these two groups lie questions concerning concentration or deconcentration, the distribution of decision-making responsibilities, and the degree of centralized leadership at various levels, including all-union, union-republic, and republic organs of state management."[13]

The first group of problems is not well developed in Soviet theory, but Shakhnazarov, Kosolapov, Piskotin, and others do address them. Shakhnazarov poses an important question: Can democratic principles be violated in a developed socialist society? His answer is "no," and it rests heavily on the assumption that "a strong and highly authoritarian central power may be wholly democratic." Hence, the democratic nature of the state depends "chiefly on its planned character, on whether the central and local bodies of power are in the hands of the people and exercise the people's will and interests, and on whether the mass of people participate in the work of these bodies and keep them under their control."[14]

Shakhnazarov argues that social, administrative, and legal controls ensure the democratic functioning of central institutions under mature socialism. Among the USSR's "antidotes" to bureaucratism and elitism are the abolition of privately owned land and corporations; the restrictions on transferring personal wealth to one's heirs; the illegality of using money as a means of acquiring political power; and the constitutional provision (Article 49) enabling citizens to submit proposals to state and public organizations and to "criticize shortcomings," as well as obligating such organizations promptly to reply to grass-roots proposals and to correct any shortcomings uncovered without "persecution for criticism." Also, Soviet citizens have the right to judicial review of "complaints against the actions of officials" and to "compensation for damages caused by illegal actions of state and public organizations" (Article 58). Are party organizations subject to such constraints, in theory if not in practice? Significantly but ambiguously, the USSR Constitution (Articles 6 and 100) and analysts such as Shakhnazarov note that the party is both a public organization and the "nucleus" of all other public and state organizations.[15]

Soviet theorists argue or imply that leadership rests on authority, not on coercion, and that greater elite participation in the politics of principles and greater public participation in the politics of details are important sources of legitimacy and effectiveness. Too much centralism will stifle the creativity of specialists and lead to arbitrary rule. Too much democracy will spur individualism, even anarchy, and seriously weaken the party-state's governing capabilities. Final decision-making power must remain concentrated in top political bodies in order to preserve the fundamental characteristics of the Soviet polity. But bureaucracies, collectives, and individuals must take more and more initiatives "*in accordance with the goals of communist construction . . . and for the purpose of strengthening and developing the socialist system*" (Articles 47 and 50 of the USSR Constitution — emphasis added).

The second group of problems that Piskotin identifies is receiving increasing attention from Soviet commentators and is the source of considerable disagreement. Afanas'ev has asserted that the "optimal combination" of democracy and centralism "depends in the final analysis on the level of production, on the state of social relations, and on the specific historical circumstances." Taking a highly differentiated approach to democratic centralism, Afanas'ev affirms that management organs must continuously adapt their decisions *and* decision-making procedures to changing contextual conditions. But Soviet observers disagree about the specific spheres to be centralized or decentralized, and some of these differences are significant. For example, Afanas'ev contends that "decision making . . . demands centralization"; Shakhnazarov identifies decision making as one of the most promising areas for "worker participation in management."[16] Piskotin minimizes the importance of precisely delineating administrative rights and responsibilities; Afanas'ev emphasizes its importance.[17] B. Z. Mil'ner, an organization theorist, calls for the centralization of research and development and of "the application of scientific and technical achievements"; Piskotin observes that "one can hardly expect centralized measures to introduce scientific and technological achievements into practice unless production collectives are really interested in utilizing them."[18]

Diverse views about centralization and decentralization are a by-product of the Brezhnev, Andropov, and Chernenko Politburos' desire for scientific-technological and socioeconomic progress, on the one hand, and political stability, on the other. One could argue that institutional change *or* continuity is especially important in the era of the STR, and Soviet analysts have advanced both of these competing arguments. Because party leaders have not endorsed a uniform theory of the STR and because many economic and social problems have worsened since the mid-1970s, Soviet disputes about the policy and policy-making implications of scientific-technological and socioeconomic developments are not surprising.

What *is* surprising are the occasional Soviet assertions about the harmful consequences that will ensue if political-administrative changes are obstructed or delayed. Words and phrases such as *inertia, policy mistakes, philistine, toady,* and *abuse of power* appeared in the party press during the second half of the Brezhnev administration, and these criticisms were leveled (indirectly but unmistakably) at *contemporary* national policies, policy making, and individual policy makers (including, on rare occasions, Brezhnev himself).[19] Also, ominous hypothetical situations were discussed or noted by analysts such as A. P. Butenko, a department head of the USSR Academy of Sciences of the World Socialist System. *If* a ruling party neglects the interests of the working people, it will lose their "trust" and "enormously weaken" its political power. *If* a party makes "gross mistakes" in its policies, "extremely dangerous consequences" will ensue, "no matter what historical stage of socialist construction is involved." *If* a socialist party and state fail to give adequate consideration to the interests, moods, and opinions of the masses, and *if* these factors are "ignored" or minimized, "the danger that the society's political organization might break away from the broad laboring masses arises." Butenko identifies as "crisis situations" the years 1968–69 in Czechoslovakia and 1970 and 1980–81 in Poland. But Butenko makes it clear that, without the appropriate kind of leadership for a particular phase of development, "political crises" can occur in *any* socialist society and in *any* developmental phase.[20]

In other words, Soviet theorists affirm that the effectiveness and legitimacy of party leadership depend on the feasibility of its policies and the consultative nature of its policy-making procedures, especially on the extent to which both respond to the objective requirements of the STR and the changing needs of the masses. These needs, it is presumed, are best served by a one-party system. Butenko would criticize the middle-class intellectuals of the Prague Spring and the working-class Solidarity trade union movement as well as the reformist Czech and Polish party leaders—all of whose activities are thought to have jeopardized the predominant role of the indigenous party and Soviet control over it. Lacking in both Czechoslovakia and Poland were "scientifically substantiated" policies combining traditional Soviet values and structures with the STR, new management methods enhancing but regulating elite and mass participation in public administration, and ideological ties binding all organizations and citizens and restraining radical elements.

Leading Soviet officials are not anticipating political unrest of the kinds that have periodically jarred Eastern Europe since Stalin's death. However, Butenko is even more apprehensive than Shakhnazarov about the "nonantagonistic contradictions" of socialist democracy and calls emphatically for innovative leadership and institutional adaptation. Also, Butenko would probably criticize the deterministic implications of Kosolapov's view that democracy "always" gains ground over centralism and would stress instead that the laboring masses must increasingly participate in making *"final decisions on vitally important issues."*[21] Butenko declared in 1981: "If obsolete forms of leadership and management of public affairs are not eliminated in time, the situation would become all the more intolerable in view of not only socioeconomic but also political development. . . . Power implemented through the political organization must be power not only for all laborers but also through the laborers themselves."[22]

The Outlook for Policy Changes

Although Soviet leaders acknowledge that various political, economic, and social problems are intensifying, it is highly unlikely that any major reforms will occur during the Chernenko administration or in the initial years of the following administration. Some Soviet officials and commentators have advocated economic reforms that would give greater play to market forces. But decentralizing economic planning and management would also require decentralizing the political system. Because the bureaucratic elites benefit so much from the present system, no coalition is likely to jeopardize its privileges by supporting reforms other than piecemeal responses to pressing problems. Further, because economic performance improved under Andropov, his campaigns against corruption, waste, and sloth will probably be reinvigorated by Chernenko's immediate successor, especially if work incentives decline precipitously and consumer dissatisfaction festers. Such efforts to revitalize rather than restructure the polity and economy will most likely be given the chance to succeed before more comprehensive and potentially destabilizing reforms are launched.[23]

Western observers correctly stress the Soviet Union's economic and social problems. Economically, the Soviet nation faces declining increases in growth, productivity, and capital investment and mounting labor, housing, and food shortages. Socially, it must confront declining health care and male life expectancy and mounting alcoholism, environmental pollution, ethnic assertiveness, and preoccupation with private rather than civic goals.[24] Party leaders — reformers more so than conservatives — are troubled by most of these problems. For example, on several occasions after 1978, Brezhnev stated that inadequate food supplies were a significant "political" issue, implying that consumer discontent was undermining the stability of the regime. But one must distinguish between elite and mass discontent, because the Soviet bureaucratic elites thrived under Brezhnev and, after a brief scare under Andropov, are thriving under Chernenko. Thus, political debates in the Soviet Union focus on policy priorities and administrative practices, rather than on policy making and institutional relationships.

Chernenko has been much less willing and able than Andropov to reduce the perquisites of party cadres or the corruption in the political system and society. Chernenko probably believes that, because so many interrelated domestic and international problems are worsening, the authoritarian essence of socialist democracy and democratic centralism must be strengthened while encouraging specialist and grass-roots initiatives to speed the implementation of national programs. To be sure, Chernenko has written books and articles calling for a freer exchange of ideas within and among party, state, and economic bodies, an increased use of modern technology in administration and production, and an enhanced responsiveness of the major bureaucracies, mass organizations, and citizenry to one another's concerns. But Chernenko's ideological predispositions — especially regarding "trust in cadres," political participation, and the STR — are pragmatic and accommodating rather than utopian and disruptive, and hence he will probably continue to restore, reinforce, and readjust Brezhnev's political-administrative preferences. Chernenko is the consummate *apparatchik* and, like Brezhnev especially, is a centrist among his Politburo colleagues.

Even if Chernenko were a well-disguised radical or ultraconservative, it is important to recall that in the post-Stalin period (1) all general secretaries have been less powerful than their predecessors, and none has been able to select more than a handful of his fellow Politburo and Secretariat members; (2) the power of these central party organs vis-à-vis the sprawling party and state agencies has been eroding—specifically, the articulation of scattered interests in the major bureaucracies and mass organizations has outstripped the capacity of the national, regional, and local party committees to aggregate these interests, to make authoritative choices among policy alternatives, and to mobilize support for policy implementation; and (3) the party-state has exercised less and less control over demographic forces in Soviet society, which has become more and more permeated by scientific-technological, socioeconomic, and (to a lesser extent) political influences from abroad. This modest diffusion or dissipation of power, together with the other key elements of Soviet policy making discussed earlier and in the introductory essay, considerably increases the chances that moderate programmatic and organizational changes will be undertaken if the gap between policy outcomes and popular aspirations continues to widen. A new generation of party leaders will recast current policy-making procedures into either a reformist or conservative mold only if a number of present policies dramatically fail.

The Soviet political system is indeed becoming outmoded in the rapidly changing global scientific-technological and socioeconomic environments. But, with the obvious exception of the ominous and intensifying strategic arms race, none of the Soviet Union's internal and external difficulties are so serious or are perceived to be so serious (by present and prospective Soviet leaders) that far-reaching or hasty changes in substantive policies, let alone in policy making, are likely in the immediate future. The consensual policy-making process bequeathed by Brezhnev will probably change incrementally in the 1980s and will continue to exert a centrist, rather than a reformist or conservative, influence on domestic and foreign policies. External influences—chiefly the West's scientific and technological advances, the international economy, the politics of Eastern Europe, and the foreign policy of the United States—will have some effect on the content of Soviet policies but little effect on the procedures by which they are formulated.[25]

Some Westerners have concluded that the disintegration of détente is ushering in "a new cold war."[26] But we need only to observe the altered geopolitical situation to realize that the East-West confrontation of the late 1940s cannot be repeated in the 1980s. Postwar Soviet and American foreign policies rested on one overwhelmingly important factor: the superiority of American strategic arms. The Soviet Union, however, achieved nuclear parity in the early 1970s. Further, conventional military power and economic power are becoming more significant means of exercising global influence. Hence, the Soviet-American rivalry is being shaped in the context of an increasingly multipolar and interdependent world and of unprecedented scientific-technological and socioeconomic changes. Although the United States and other Western nations must be prepared to counter Soviet military power, they must remember from the Vietnam War especially that sophisticated weaponry is not enough to defeat or deter adversaries and to engender confidence in allies or in the countries that stand outside the East-West conflict. The United States is a superpower economically and militarily, whereas the Soviet Union is a superpower only militarily. Because the West also possesses abundant political, scientific-technological, cultural, and spiritual capabilities and potentials, it can eschew hegemonic aspirations and allay anxieties of the kind that gave rise to the Soviet occupation of Afghanistan and to the suppression of the Solidarity movement in Poland.

Given the critical importance of East-West relations and the proliferation of regional, global, and outer-space problems and opportunities, the United States must continuously reassess Soviet perspectives, pursuits, and performance. The Soviet Union presents a formidable military challenge — but less formidable economic and ideological challenges — to the United States and other Western nations. It is imperative that we better understand these challenges if we are to compete and cooperate effectively and judiciously with the Soviet Union in the future.

NOTES

1. Harry Harding, "The Transformation of China," *Brookings Review* 2 (Spring 1984): 3.

2. See the editor's introductory essay and the essay by John N. Hazard in this volume. See also Hazard's *The Soviet System of Government*, 5th ed. (Chicago: University of Chicago Press, 1980), 228–43.

3. See the essay by Ellen Mickiewicz in this volume.

4. See the essays by Henry S. Rowen, Joseph S. Berliner, and Loren R. Graham in this volume.

5. See the essays by Zbigniew Brzezinski, Seweryn Bialer, Marshall D. Shulman, Robbin F. Laird and Dale R. Herspring, and Charles Gati in this volume. See also Erik P. Hoffmann and Robbin F. Laird, *The Politics of Economic Modernization in the Soviet Union* (Ithaca, N.Y.: Cornell University Press, 1982); and idem, *"The Scientific-Technological Revolution" and Soviet Foreign Policy* (Elmsford, N.Y.: Pergamon Press, 1982).

6. G. Kh. Shakhnazarov, *Sotsialisticheskaia sud'ba chelovechestva* (Moscow: Politizdat, 1978), 179–80; trans., *The Destiny of the World: The Socialist Shape of Things to Come* (Moscow: Progress, 1979), 136.

7. Robert Sharlet, ed., *The New Soviet Constitution of 1977: Analysis and Text* (Brunswick, Ohio: King's Court Communications, 1978), 78.

8. G. Kh. Shakhnazarov, *Sotsialisticheskaia demokratiia*, 2d ed. (Moscow: Politizdat, 1974), 68; trans., *Socialist Democracy: Aspects of Theory* (Moscow: Progress, 1974), 43–44.

9. Shakhnazarov, *Sotsialisticheskaia sud'ba chelovechestva*, 209–13; trans. 157–60.

10. V. G. Afanas'ev, "Nauchnoe upravlenie obshchestvom i demokraticheskii tsentralizm," in *Sovetskaia demokratiia v period razvitogo sotsializma* (Moscow: Mysl', 1976), 152 (emphasis added); trans., *Soviet Democracy in the Period of Developed Socialism* (Moscow: Progress, 1979), 145.

11. G. Kh. Shakhnazarov, *Fiasko futurologii: Kriticheskii ocherk nemarksistskikh teorii obshchestvennogo razvitiia* (Moscow: Politizdat, 1979), 258; trans., *Futurology Fiasco: A Critical Study of Non-Marxist Concepts of How Society Works* (Moscow: Progress, 1982), 166.

12. R. I. Kosolapov, *Sotsializm: K voprosam teorii* 2d ed. (Moscow: Mysl', 1979), 462 (emphasis

added); trans., *Socialism: Questions of Theory* (Moscow: Progress, 1979), 409.

13. M. I. Piskotin, "Demokraticheskii tsentralizm: Problemy sochetaniia tsentralizatsii i detsentralizatsii," *Sovetskoe gosudarstvo i pravo* 5 (May 1981): 40.

14. Shakhnazarov, *Fiasko futurologii*, 258–65 (emphasis added); trans., 166–71. The quoted statement is by N. Iribadiakov, a Bulgarian philosopher whom Shakhnazarov cites with praise.

15. Ibid., 265–71; trans., 171–75.

16. Afanas'ev, in *Sovetskaia demokratiia v period razvitogo sotsializma*, 145, 148–49; trans., 140, 143–44. Shakhnazarov, in ibid., 166; trans., 158.

17. M. I. Piskotin, in *Problemy obshchei teorii sotsialisticheskogo gosudarstvennogo upravleniia*, ed. M. I. Piskotin (Moscow: Nauka, 1981), 213. Afanas'ev, in *Sovetskaia demokratiia v period razvitogo sotsializma*, 147; trans., 142.

18. B. Z. Mil'ner, "Organization of the Management of Production," *Social Sciences* (Moscow) 7, no. 3 (1976): 53; M. I. Piskotin, "Centralism and Democratic Principles," *Social Sciences* (Moscow) 13, no. 4 (1982): 63.

19. See, e.g., A. Vodolazskii, "Vysshii printsip partiinogo rukovodstva," *Kommunist* 12 (1979): 38 ff.

20. See, e.g., A. P. Butenko, *Politicheskaia organizatsiia obshchestva pri sotsializme* (Moscow: Mysl', 1981): 95–96, 169, 193, 203 ff.

21. Ibid., 183 (emphasis added).

22. Ibid., 189–90.

23. See Timothy J. Colton's essay in this volume. For a brief but comprehensive analysis of contemporary Soviet politics and society, with emphasis on the prospects for reform, see Colton's *The Dilemma of Reform in the Soviet Union* (New York: Council on Foreign Relations, 1984).

24. See the essays by Henry W. Morton, Murray Feshbach, Gail W. Lapidus, and Robert Sharlet in this volume.

25. For a variety of Western views on these questions, see Erik P. Hoffmann and Robbin F. Laird, eds., *The Soviet Polity in the Modern Era* (Hawthorne, N.Y.: Aldine Publishing Co., 1984); Erik P. Hoffmann and Frederic J. Fleron, Jr., eds., *The Conduct of Soviet Foreign Policy*, 2d ed. (Hawthorne, N.Y.: Aldine Publishing Co., 1980); and Robert F. Byrnes, ed., *After Brezhnev: Sources of Soviet Conduct in the 1980s* (Bloomington: Indiana University Press, 1983).

26. The following paragraphs are adapted from a speech by Robbin F. Laird and Erik P. Hoffmann for delivery by a presidential candidate.

Index